Commitment in Dialogue

SUNY series in Logic and Language
John T. Kearns, editor

Commitment in Dialogue

Basic Concepts of Interpersonal Reasoning

Douglas N. Walton and Erik C. W. Krabbe

STATE UNIVERSITY OF NEW YORK PRESS

Production by Ruth Fisher
Marketing by Bernadette LaManna

Published by State University of New York Press, Albany

© 1995 State University of New York Press

For information, address the State University of New York Press,
State University Plaza, Albany, NY 12246

Library of Congress Cataloging-in-Publication Data

Walton, Douglas N.
    Commitment in dialogue : basic concepts of interpersonal reasoning
/ Douglas N. Walton and Erik C.W. Krabbe.
        p.   cm. — (SUNY series in logic and language)
    Includes bibliographical references and index.
    ISBN 0-7914-2585-1 (alk. paper). — ISBN 0-7914-2586-X (pbk. :
alk. paper)
        1. Reasoning. 2. Logic. 3. Persuasion (Rhetoric) I. Krabbe, E.
C. W. (Erik C. W.), 1943– . II. Title. III. Series.
BC177.W323   1995
160—dc20   94-37799
                                                               CIP

10   9   8   7   6   5   4   3   2   1

To Karen and Tineke,
with Love

Contents

Preface

Although the authors had corresponded and were acquainted with each other's work, it was not before the First International Conference on Argumentation in Amsterdam in June 1986 that we had a chance to actually get together and work out the motivating idea for this book as a joint project. Both of us had already written on various aspects of argumentation in dialogue, and we perceived a need to follow up these efforts by some sort of analysis of the concept of commitment, which we felt was the most basic concept in using structures of dialogue to model argumentation. The goal of our joint project, which resulted in this book, was to provide conceptual tools for the theory of argumentation, primarily to flesh out the concept of commitment.

Our decision to work together has proved very fortunate, we believe, because it brought together two different traditions and perspectives that had not previously been integrated. Erik Krabbe's contributions to the field of argumentation have come from a background in Lorenzen-style formal dialogue logic, a branch of logic that originated in Germany, most of whose writings are not accessible in English. Douglas Walton is a researcher on informal fallacies who has made contributions to the development of Hamblin-style formal dialogues in the field of logic. In this book an extensive case study of a discussion in medical ethics is used to show how these two types of formal structures of dialogue are related. One—a rigorous Lorenzen type of dialogue—is embedded in the other—a more permissive Hamblin type of dialogue.

Since both of the authors were brought up in a "formalistic" tradition of logic and analytical philosophy, we had to take special care to make this book as widely accessible as possible to workers in other fields, especially the field of speech communication. We attempted to achieve this by keeping technical refinements to a minimum and by using plenty of examples of arguments used in everyday conversations to test out and illustrate our contentions. Our methods are inherently formal, but, nevertheless, it was very important for us that they also be useful for those pursuing the empirical study of discourse analysis and allied disciplines.

Although primarily meant as a scholarly contribution to be used by researchers in the areas of informal logic, argumentation theory, and critical thinking, the book can be assigned as reading material for advanced and intermediate courses in these fields. We also aimed at a nonspecialist readership. The plentiful and, we hope, interesting case studies, along with the nontechnical general descriptions of systems of dialogue rules, are designed to make the book accessible for readers with little or no prior background in the field of logic.

The collaborative research which resulted in this work was made possible by the Netherlands Institute for Advanced Study in the Humanities and Social Sciences (NIAS). Through the award of fellowships by NIAS to both authors in 1987, we got the opportunity to work together for a five-month period of intensive research in Wassenaar, Holland, free of our usual teaching and administrative duties. We gratefully remember the very special, congenial, and stimulating ambience, in which it was a privilege to work, as well as the technical assistance provided by members of the NIAS staff.

Doug Walton would also like to acknowledge two additional funding sources which helped to support his part in this project: a Killam Research Fellowship from the Killam Foundation of the Canada Council and a Research Grant from the Social Sciences and Humanities Research Council of Canada.

Erik Krabbe would like to acknowledge support from Utrecht University, specifically from the Department of Philosophy and from the logic section of that department. Without a leave of absence from the university and the willingness of colleagues to take over classes and other duties it would not have been feasible for him to join Walton at NIAS.

Further facilities were provided by NIAS, when Doug Walton was a fellow again in 1989 and 1990. The final series of dialogues, where the authors managed to work out the more technical parts of chapter 4, took place during the Summer Institute in Argumentation at McMaster Uni-

versity, Hamilton, Ontario, in June 1991. We are grateful to the organiz-
ing staff of the Summer Institute for providing us with opportunities to
conduct research, especially to David Hitchcock and Hans Hansen for
arranging for us to use the facilities in the Department of Philosophy.
Thus were were able to work together to achieve a first finished draft of
the manuscript at McMaster.

We had the opportunity to test our ideas before several audiences:
a conference on speech communication organized by the Vereniging
Interfacultair Overleg Taalbeheersing (VIOT) at the University of
Amsterdam in December 1987; a NIAS audience in July 1988; the Third
International Symposium on Informal Logic at the University of Windsor,
Ontario, in June 1989; the colloquium Rhétorique et Argumentation, at
the Université Libre de Bruxelles, sponsored by the Centre Européen
pour L'Etude de l'Argumentation, in January 1990; a NIAS Symposium
on Fallacy Theory in Wassenaar in May 1990; the Second ISSA International Conference on Argumentation at the University of Amsterdam in
June 1990; and the Summer Institute in Argumentation, already mentioned, at McMaster University in June 1991. Our thanks to the participants for their many useful critical comments and questions.

We are especially grateful to Rita Campbell for processing the text
and figures of the manuscript through many drafts.

Groningen, the Netherlands

Douglas N. Walton, Department of Philosophy
University of Winnipeg

Erik C. W. Krabbe, Department of Philosophy
Groningen University

Introduction

The method of argument evaluation put forward in Hamblin's pioneering book *Fallacies* (1970) used formal dialogues as contexts in which arguments could be evaluated. Commitment was the fundamental concept in a Hamblin dialogue, but Hamblin did not develop the idea very far. *Commitment in Dialogue* refines and develops Hamblin's idea of commitment as the central concept in models of dialogue used to evaluate arguments. Beginning with a philosophical analysis of the concept of commitment, the book goes on to study several distinct types of dialogue that can function as normative models to aid in the evaluation of argumentation in everyday conversations.

This book starts out with a philosophical analysis of the concept of commitment to a course of action and of the concept of propositional commitment in critical dialogue as a special case of commitment to a course of action. Systematic surveys of the verbal and nonverbal ways in which commitments may be incurred or lost are provided. Several types of relation between commitments are scrutinized. For instance, one commitment may imply another or be prior to it or may actually or potentially clash with it (the problem of inconsistency). Another important relation is that of specification: a global commitment to a cause may, under certain circumstances, lead to commitments to very specific actions.

1

Next, the book turns to a study of dialogue types. Traditionally, theory of argumentation has been concerned with persuasion dialogue, or critical discussion, and, indeed, our primary concern is with this type of dialogue as well. But there are different subtypes of persuasion dialogue, with associated types of commitment, and, moreover, there are other main types of dialogue that we found important in a study of commitment. Hamblin was aware that there were different kinds of dialogue, but to take this further, we realized we had to study the goals and rules of several especially important types of dialogue surrounding persuasion dialogue, including the quarrel, deliberation, negotiation, inquiry, and information-seeking types of dialogue. In our framework, a good argument is one that contributes to a goal of the type of dialogue in which that argument was put forward. Evaluating an argumentative move as good or bad, correct or fallacious, requires the asking of a key question: What type of dialogue were the participants supposed to be engaged in? For example, an argument that appeals to the respondent's insecurity by expressing a threat (traditionally called the *argumentum ad baculum*, or "argument to the stick or club") could be nonfallacious if it has occurred in a negotiation dialogue, but fallacious where it has occurred in a persuasion dialogue.

In our book we put forward a new approach to several of the traditional fallacies by showing how these fallacies are associated with shifts from one type of dialogue to another. In some cases, a shift can be licit or good in the sense that a dialogue of one type is functionally embedded in one of another type and actually improves the quality of the latter dialogue. In other cases, however, the shift, being illicit, conceals a fallacy, an error or tricky deception in the argument. Such an argument may appear correct in relation to the new type of dialogue yet actually be incorrect because it is inappropriate and obstructive in relation to the original type of dialogue the participants were supposed to be engaged in before the shift. For example, an *ad baculum* argument that appeals to a covert threat may be highly inappropriate in a persuasion dialogue, but if there has been a shift to negotiation dialogue, the veiled threat may not seem nearly so evidently out of place and may not be spotted as a fallacious move.

Lorenzen's Dialogue Logic

Traditionally, the study of argument belongs to logic. The idea that argument has something to do with dialogue, and therefore with obligations and commitments in dialogue, is as old as logic itself. Indeed, among the very first books on logical theory we find Aristotle's *Topics* and *De Sophisticis Elenchis*, texts that presuppose the existence of certain forms of regulated dialogue and that try to give us instructions for efficient behavior in a context of dialogue. The medieval treatises on obligations and the Obligation Game (from the thirteenth century onward), which most likely took their origin from these works by Aristotle, provide us with another illustration of the intimate connections between logic, dialogue, argument, and commitment. However, by the twentieth century "formal logic" had become very heavily, virtually exclusively, dominated by deduction-theoretic and semantic concerns. The pragmatic idea of systematically studying the context of dialogue in which an argument is used had ceased to be an acknowledged part of the serious pursuit of the discipline of logic.

In 1958 Paul Lorenzen presented a paper, *Logik und Agon*, in which he reinaugurated a dialogical, or dialectical, branch of formal logic.[1] He keenly pointed out how far logic had strayed from its agonistic roots; but what is more, he saw this situation as one to be amended:

> Vergleicht man mit diesem agonalen Ursprung der Logik die modernen Auffassungen, nach denen die Logik das System der Regeln ist, die angewendet auf beliebige wahre Sätze immer zu weiteren wahren Sätzen führen, so sieht man nur zu deutlich, daß aus dem griechischen Agon ein frommes Solospiel geworden ist. Als Partner des ursprünglichen Zwei-Personen-Spiels kommt höchstens noch Gott in Frage, säkularisiert "die Natur," als Besitzer aller wahren Sätze. Ihm steht der einzelne Mensch gegenüber— evtl. der Einzelne als Vertreter der Menschheit—und weiht sich dem Geduldspiel, aus Sätzen, die er glaubt von Gott schon erhalten zu haben (oder ihm schon entrissen zu haben), weitere Sätze nach den logischen Regeln zu gewinnen.[2]

(*Translation:* If one compares this agonistic origin of logic with modern conceptions, according to which logic is the system of rules that, whenever they are applied to some arbitrary true sentences, will lead one to further truths, then it will be but too obvious that the Greek agon has come to be a dull game of solitaire. In the original two person game only God, secularized: "Nature," who is in possession of all true sentences, would still qualify as an opponent. Facing Him there is the human individual—or perhaps the individual as a representative of humanity— devoted to the game of patience: starting from sentences that were, so he believes, obtained from God before, or snatched away from Him, and following rules of logic, he is to gain more and more sentences.)

Dialogue logic is an attempt to revert to the original idea of a two-person game. Whereas other branches of formal logic are concerned with semantic rules, or with rules of inference, dialogue logic focuses on rules of dialogue. A system of rules of dialogue defines a two-person game in which one party (the Proponent) is to defend a proposition (the thesis) *vis-à-vis* another party (the Opponent). The tournaments of the game are called dialogues. Together, the rules also provide a definition of the meaning-in-use of the logical constants (such as *and, or, for all, for some*) that figure in the dialogues. Indeed, from the beginning dialogue logic was concerned with rules that stipulate possibilities of attack and defense in terms of the logical forms of the sentences that are attacked or defended.

The degree of rigor displayed by the formulation of Lorenzen-type dialogue games made these games suitable subjects for mathematical study: they could be analyzed as games in the sense of mathematical game theory. Consequently, one may speak of the Proponent's having (or lacking) a winning strategy for a certain initial position. This gives us a dialectical concept of logical consequence: A Proponent's thesis *follows logically* from the Opponent's concessions if and only if there is a winning strategy available for the Proponent. Thus each system of dialogue rules (or dialectical system) defines its own concept of logical consequence (its concept of validity, its "logic").

However, from the point of view of argumentation, what is most interesting about dialectical systems is perhaps not that they yield new "logics," but rather their focus upon a conflict of avowed opinions as an initial situation, and upon the resolution of such conflicts by verbal means.[3]

Lorenzen's turn toward a dialogical, or dialectical, concept of logic, although a major innovation at the time, did not produce any major intellectual stir among philosophers and logicians. This lack of enthusiasm may be explained by several circumstances. First, most publications by Lorenzen and his followers were (and still are) accessible only in German.[4] Second, dialogue logic, in its first phases, was tied to rather special intellectual concerns and interests. Originally, it was supposed to provide a criterion of constructivity and thus to be of service to the philosophy of mathematics. Then it became part of a program for the development of normative foundations for the use of language (Orthosprache), that was worked out within the so-called Erlangen school of German constructivism. Though these were interesting applications in their own right, they made it more difficult to realize the wider significance of the dialectical conception of formal logic. Third, the most important circumstance may have been the uncongenial intellectual climate of the period. Things seem better now that a number of other dialogical, dialectical, or game-theoretical approaches have seen the light.[5]

Hamblin's Dialectical Systems

In order to study fallacies and other errors of reasoning, Hamblin, who was not aware of Lorenzen's dialogue logic, proposed extending the bounds of formal logic "to include features of dialectical contexts within which arguments are put forward."[6] To accomplish this end, Hamblin introduced the concept of a *dialectical system*, a rule-governed structure of organized conversation where two parties (in the simplest case) speak in turn, by asking questions and giving replies (perhaps including other kinds of locutions) in an orderly way, taking into account, at any particular turn, what occurred previously in the dialogue. Hamblin's idea was that such dialectical systems could be used to model contexts of dialogue in which argumentation takes place in everyday conversations of various kinds. Such systems, he argued, could even be constructed as artificial, formal models that could be useful in helping us to justify critical judgments that an argument in a real case is fallacious or nonfallacious.

This was a revolutionary idea, since the pragmatic conception of systematically studying the context of dialogue in which an argument is used had long ceased to be an acknowledged part of the serious pursuit of the discipline of logic.

Dialectic, as Hamblin conceived it, has nothing to do with dialectic of a Fichtean or Marxist kind, characterized by the triad (thesis, antithesis, synthesis). Dialectic, as Hamblin (and we) use the word, is the study of dialogue, more specifically, of dialectical systems. It comprises two branches: *descriptive dialectic*, which studies the rules and conventions operative in actual discussions of various types (such as parliamentary debates, lawsuits, committee meetings), and *formal dialectic*, which sets up "simple systems of precise but not necessarily realistic rules" and studies the dialogues that conform to these rules.[7] According to Hamblin: "Neither approach is of any importance on its own; for descriptions of actual cases must aim to bring out formalizable features, and formal systems must aim to throw light on actual, describable phenomena."[8]

Hamblin's conception of dialectic includes, but is much broader than, Lorenzen's formal dialogue logic:

> Dialectic, whether descriptive or formal, is a more general study than Logic; in the sense that Logic can be conceived as a set of dialectical conventions. It is an ideal of certain kinds of discussion that the rules of Logic should be observed by all participants, and that certain logical goals should be part of the general goal.

> The concept of a dialectical system is, at first, quite general and
> there are many systems that are of no interest whatsoever to the
> logician. For example, we can imagine a dialogue consisting of
> interchange of statements about the weather.[9]

This generality and potential multiplicity of Hamblin's idea of a
dialectical system was an important advantage. But it also seemed to
leave the idea a little vague. And, indeed, Hamblin did not himself try to
classify or identify the types of main goals that the most important types
of systems should have. He constructed some systems to illustrate the
basic idea, and left it at that. Even so, the ideas he put forward showed
an amazing grasp of how the fundamental concepts in such systems
should work, given the novelty of his proposal from a point of view of
the state of the art of logic in 1970.

The most important and fundamental idea in a Hamblin dialectical system was called the *commitment store*. According to Hamblin, a
participant in a certain type of dialogue might be "obliged to indicate
agreement or disagreement with a preceeding remark of the other speaker"
and hence build up a "store of statements" that represent his commitments in the dialogue. Furthermore, he might be "obliged to maintain
consistency," with this set of statements. For this purpose, a set of statements representing the previous commitments of each speaker is needed.[10]
Of course, in real-life arguments, we often fail to keep a transcript of a
discussion, and hence people often disagree on what they are committed
to. You may often hear arguments about what was said or what it implied: "Yes, George, you remember when you said that!" "I never did!"
"Yes, you did so," and so on. Hamblin thought of dialectical systems
with a commitment store as ideal models of how arguers would behave
(rationally) in their arguments if they kept a record of the previous parts
of their exchange.

Hamblin stressed that a participant's commitment is not necessarily a belief and that the "purpose of postulating a commitment-store is
not psychological."[11] In practice, we often don't know what an arguer's
commitments really are. The commitment store is a kind of idealization
representing how we might argue rationally if we carefully made a record
of our commitments in dialogue—say by listing them on a sheet of
paper—so that when doubts or questions arose about them, we could
consult the sheet of paper, and either that statement in question would
be on it or not. Clearly such a device would be helpful in judging the
worth of some arguments, and the problem of not being able to fairly
and clearly decide whether something is or is not a commitment of an
arguer often arises in connection with trying to evaluate arguments as
fallacious or not.

Dialogues as Contexts of Argumentation and Commitment

In this book, it has not been our aim to give a complete or comprehensive account of all the different types of dialogue or informal fallacies. Rather our aim is to give a theoretical basis that will be useful to those studying fallacies, and other problems and phenomena of argumentation (cf. section 5.1). Our basic assumption is that the critical discussion (what we call persuasion dialogue) is the most fundamental context of dialogue needed as a normative structure in which fallacies and other errors of reasoning can be analyzed and evaluated. But another finding, one that came to be more and more borne out by our study, was that there are several other key types of dialogue clustering around persuasion dialogue that are also very important in understanding fallacy (section 3.1). What we found, again and again, is that a fallacy tends to be associated with a shift or transition from one of these contexts to another. Very often, for example, a fallacy occurs because there has been an illicit or concealed shift from persuasion dialogue to some other type of dialogue like a negotiation or a quarrel. Without taking such a shift into account, it is impossible to understand or appreciate in a useful way how the fallacious argument functioned as a coverup for an error of reasoning, or as technique of artful deception, used by one participant in the original dialogue to unfairly or unreasonably get the best of the other (sections 3.3 and 3.4).

Like Hamblin, our aim was to help in the study of fallacies by providing an underlying theoretical basis for this field to go ahead. Although we aimed to advance beyond Hamblin, we were under no illusion that we could analyze all the fallacies or all the types of dialogue that are important in such analyses. By fixing on commitment, the core concept in Hamblin's framework, we wanted to push his work along a little further. But how to do this? Commitment seems such a despairingly vague idea, and the types of dialogue seem so multiple. Where could one start?

We began with some "ordinary language philosophy," looking at how the term *commitment* is used in everyday argumentation and speech (chapter 1). We were aided here by the use of the case-study method, which enabled us to focus on certain key problems in a concrete way. Through this, we came to think of commitment as a practical idea, one that has to do with imperatives directing an agent to a course of action in a particular situation. Curiously enough, Hamblin once again came to our aid here, and we found his "action-state semantics," especially his concept of a "partial strategy," from his book *Imperatives*, the key to the solution.[12]

Using Hamblin's technical apparatus, we were able, in chapters 1 and 2, to expound a general analysis of what commitment to a course of action is (section 1.1); of the various ways in which such commitments are incurred (section 2.1) and lost (section 2.2), by speech acts or otherwise; and of what it means to live up to, or to renege on, one's commitment. Propositional commitments, such as those of which Hamblin's commitment stores were supposed to keep track, constitute just a special case of commitment to a course of action and can be studied from the same angle (section 1.2).

Thus, typically, propositional commitments are incurred by the execution of certain types of speech acts in dialogue. But, just as with action commitment, this is not the only way to incur a propositional commitment. Also, several relations between (and problems about) commitments in general find their counterparts among relations between (and problems about) propositional commitments (section 2.3). For example, the relation of priority of one commitment over another and the associated problem of clashing commitments find their counterparts in the relation of priority between different kinds of obligation in dialogue and the problems connected with inconsistency (section 2.4).

Having once achieved what we thought was a fairly good analytical grasp of the concept of commitment, we then turned to tying this idea to practical problems encountered in the modeling of argumentation in everyday discourse by applying it to an extended case (section 3.2). This case, although it was written (invented) by the authors themselves, is a natural enough case of a segment of persuasion dialogue, involving several key features of argumentation related to problems of commitment modeling, that it could provide plenty of material for further analysis. And so it turned out. It was difficult to grasp what was really going on in the argumentation in this dialogue, in relation to incurring and retracting commitments at the various stages, but in the end we think we were able to construct profiles, or sketches of models, that are useful in analyzing and evaluating the argumentation.

The theme common to all the different types of dialogue, the factor that defines them as distinctive normative contexts of argumentation, is revealed in the book to be the concept of "commitment." How is commitment incurred, and how (if at all) can it be retracted? Each type of dialogue has its own distinctive rules and goals, its permitted types of move, and its conventions for managing the commitments incurred by the participants as a result of the moves they make. Each type of dialogue exhibits a normative model, an enveloping structure that can aid us in evaluating the argumentative and other moves contained in it.

Although each type of dialogue has its own characteristics, the way these characteristics need to be defined presents features and problems that are common to all the types of dialogue. Each type of dialogue has a goal, an initial situation, and certain useful means of moving from the initial situation toward the goal. But central to understanding how each type of dialogue functions as a normative context of argumentation is the problem of how commitment is handled in that type of dialogue. A dialogue is enabled to move forward because the participants are willing to take on commitments in a collaborative way, giving the other party some room for working toward her goal.

For example, in persuasion dialogue, the goal is to resolve a conflict of opinion, and in order to accomplish this goal successfully, each participant needs to be able to work with premises that are commitments of the other party.

In any type of dialogue there must be some reason or encouragement for the participants to incur commitments. Yet, at the same time, the possibility of retraction of commitment exists. Even though, in some types of dialogue, the general strategy is to try to minimize the need for retraction by working from premises that are established as "solid evidence," in other types of dialogue, there is a need for participants to be able to make retractions.

So a central feature defining any type of dialogue in which argumentation occurs is how commitment is to be managed. There must be rules for incurring commitments and rules that define when retractions are to be allowed. But retractions can be tricky. Whether it should be possible or not, in a given case, often seems to depend on a variety of factors in the context of dialogue.

The Problem of Retraction

One of the most fundamental (almost intractable) problems concerning commitment is the question of retraction. Suppose an arguer has asserted a particular proposition A at some point in a dialogue, and is clearly committed to it, but then retracts it at a later point, saying, "No commitment A." Should she be allowed to retract it or not? It was a problem with the main dialectical system proposed by Hamblin that there was no way of stopping a participant who has adopted a tactic of quickly replying "No commitment" at the first sign of any trouble. Is there some way of making commitments "sticky" or "binding" enough to prevent such an escape from commitment, while still allowing enough freedom to make sensible retractions possible?

In order for argumentation to have enough of a platform of stability and consistency to make sense or be reasonable as a dialogue unfolds, it is necessary that an arguer's commitments be fixed in place. If someone keeps denying propositions he just asserted, or keeps hedging and evading commitment whenever it appears, his argument may be open to challenge, since you can never get anywhere with this arguer. Arguing with him becomes pointless.

On the other hand, if someone who is supposed to be engaged in reasonable argumentation never retracts any of his prior commitments, no matter how overwhelming are the good arguments against them, then that is a problem too. Such an arguer has retreated into concrete fortifications, and reasoning with him, no matter how convincing your arguments are, won't do any good. Things are stuck.

New Features Used to Solve the Problem

The solution to the problem lies in some sort of middle way that moderates retractions in a flexible yet firm manner that is appropriate to the context of dialogue and the line of argument at any given point in the unfolding of a dialogue.

Our solution to this problem starts off by accepting Hamblin's idea of keeping a running tally of an arguer's expressed commitments in a commitment store. Rules for a dialogue determine which statements go into or out of this commitment store, according to the type of locution (speech act) made by a speaker at any particular point of a dialogue. But our solution goes beyond Hamblin's basic idea by adding a number of new features.

One feature is that commitment will depend on the type of dialogue involved. But even beyond that, retractibility will depend on how rigorous or permissive the dialogue is supposed to be. In most instances of critical discussion of an issue in everyday conversation, the dialogue is quite loose and forgiving in nature. If somebody wants to change his mind, that is not a problem, unless perhaps the retraction conflicts with his fundamental convictions or basic position expressed earlier in the argument. However, in other contexts, an argument can become much more "hard-nosed" and "legalistic"—participants will define their terms very carefully and insist on strict consistency. In this type of "tightened up" case, retraction will be much more difficult, perhaps even impossible without losing the argument altogether. Our analysis will take both of these types of context into account, and even study rules for the shift or transition from one type of dialogue to the other. We use a Lorenzen-type dialectical system to model the rigorous, tightened up parts and a Hamblin-type system to model the surrounding more permissive dialogue. Thus dialogues from the Lorenzen tradition are embedded in those from the Hamblin tradition (sections 4.5 and 5.1).

Another feature is that in our way of modeling argumentation, there will be argument diagrams associated with subsequences of the sequence of locutions in a dialogue. We model dialogue as a sequence of connected moves or locutions (speech acts) that you can keep track of as a tableau or list of exchanges by the participants. Attached to this tableau are commitment sets (or stores) for each participant. In addition, for key subsequences in the tableau, there is an attached argument diagram that keeps track of all the premises and conclusions in a participant's line of argumentation during that subsequence. This argument diagram will be a familiar-looking diagram (graph) of a set of premises and conclusions, joined together in "linked," and (possibly) other kinds of structures. The three components—the tableau, the commitment sets, and the argument diagram—give a complete picture of the sequence of argumentation in its context of dialogue (once this context is identified, and the rules for it given). The possibilities and consequences of retraction can then be defined by reference to these three components (section 4.3.3).

Another feature is that in addition to commitments that have been explicitly incurred through speech acts like assertions of a proposition, we also allow for hidden or veiled commitments—the so-called dark-side commitments—to play a role in some types of dialogue. These represent a participant's deeper or more fundamental commitments that she brings to the dialogue. These commitments are generally not known to the participants during the course of a dialogue, although they can come to be known as a result of the kind of questioning and challenging that takes place during the dialogue. These dark-side commitments have a significant inhibiting effect on retraction, because a participant can be challenged if he tries to retract his own dark-side commitment (sections 4.1 and 5.3).

The key to our solution to the problem of retraction in the permissive type of dialogue is the way the system PPD_0 (permissive persuasion dialogue) is constructed in section 4.3.4. In this type of dialogue, a participant is generally free to retract commitments she has previously incurred. But there are exceptions. If the proposition in question is a conclusion of an argument she has put forward during the dialogue, then she will have to retract certain crucial premises of that argument as well. This penalty makes retraction, in such a case, more difficult. Another exception is the kind of case where the proposition to be retracted coincides with a dark-side commitment of that participant. Here too, certain features of the system make retraction nonstraightforward.

A final innovation of the book is that it provides a framework for giving a clear and precise analysis of three key types of commitment in persuasion dialogue. Assertions are analyzed as commitments that a participant in a dialogue is obliged to defend if challenged. They have a burden of proof. Concessions are commitments that a participant agrees to take on for the sake of expediting the argument yet without being obliged to defend these in the dialogue. What we call "dark-side" or "veiled" commitments are propositions that are central to an arguer's underlying position, even if he (or the other party) is not aware of them as explicit commitments he has made. Retractions are handled differently for each of these three types (section 5.4).

In writing this book we hope to advance the foundations of argumentation theory as a new and emerging discipline, especially in three respects. First, the book gives a systematic treatment of normative models of dialogue as guidelines for evaluating argumentation critically. Second, it gives a novel perspective on fallacies as shifts in context. Third, it gives a treatment of commitment that is not psychological but pragmatic and critical. Each of the three key types of commitment is specifically related to kinds of actions in critical dialogue that are permissible according to the appropriate normative model.

1   The Anatomy of Commitment

It is not our goal to try to give a generally valid and universal definition covering every shade of meaning of the term *commitment* in natural language. For one thing, the word *commitment* and the corresponding verb *commit* are used in many different senses, and there is no reason to suspect that there is a common core meaning in all of them. The heterogeneous nature of some of these varieties of usage may be indicated by the following list of sentences:

1. a. The people committed all power to one man.
   b. The court committed the criminal to prison.
   c. The philosopher committed her thoughts to paper.
   d. She committed her writings to the flames.
   e. He committed a fallacy.
   f. This resolution commits the party to support the housing project.
   g. He avoided committing himself on controversial issues.
   h. She is committed to the same ideals as we are.
   i. Our ancestors were committed to certain odd scientific beliefs.

Of these *a* through *e* show what senses of "committing" do not concern us. Example *f* is a case of commitment to action (supporting the housing project), a subject we shall deal with in section 1.1. Examples *g*, *h*, and *i* are cases of propositional commitment. As we hope to show in section 1.2, propositional commitment is a special case of commitment to action. One dictionary gives the following sense for the verb *commit* such as it is used in *f* through *i*:

2. to oblige or bind to take some moral or intellectual position or course of action[1]

As a corresponding sense for the noun *commitment*, we may quote:

3. the state of being obligated or bound (as by intellectual conviction or emotional ties)[2]

These are lexical definitions we can start with, since they give roughly the senses we want. In this chapter we shall have more to say, both on the nature of commitment bonds and on the question of the objects of commitment, that is, the things or entities one is committed to. We shall not, as a result, need to abandon the definitions cited above, but we hope to give them a more precise meaning.

From now on we can put aside all the other senses listed by the dictionaries. Thus, for instance, we shall not expound on the sense of commitment displayed by example *e*, though of course we feel free to use the expression *committing a fallacy*, when discussing dialogue theory. But before leaving these other senses altogether, we should mention one of them that deserves to be looked into, since it is related to commitment in our sense and since it is a key concept of existentialist philosophy:

4. a decisive moral choice that involves a person in a definite course of action.[3]

We shall discuss commitment to a course of action presently, and we would be glad to add these words to definition (3) (they are already there in definition (2)!). On the other hand, making a decisive moral choice seems to be just one way of *incurring* a commitment (in our sense), hence it shall be listed among other such ways in section 2.1, but we shall not go into the underlying views on morality and freedom. Note that the words *involves . . . in* in (4) come close to *commits . . . to* in our sense. But what (4) especially brings out that is notable is the idea of commitment as a distinctively personal engagement which, in its deepest form, comes from the individual's heart or inner conscience. My commitments are deeply and fundamentally *mine*, in an important sense, as opposed to anyone else's. The root notion is that one's commitments are personal—that is, indexed to a distinct person, or individual—and they may even be, in some cases, private and only partially accessible to others.

Commitment is not to be confused with intention (to follow a course of action) or with involvement (in a course of action). One may make a promise without having an intention to keep the promise. Nevertheless, one is committed to following up on the promise. Involvement is a matter of degree, but having a commitment is a yes or no affair.[4] One is either committed to a course of action or one is not. The concept of obligation comes closer to that of commitment, but seems to be narrower. In such cases as commitment to philosophy or volleyball it would seem odd to speak of obligations. One's legal and moral obligations constitute commitments, but there are many other types of commitment.

1.1 Action Commitment

Our primary interest is with propositional commitment, but since commitment to a course of action, or "action commitment," seems in some ways more fundamental, we shall discuss that first. We shall call statements to the effect that someone is committed to a course of action (*simple*) *action-commitment statements*. In order to have a standard formulation for these, we could use the schema

    5. X is committed to A-ing

However, we shall prefer a less formal parlance:

    6. X is bound to A,

where 6 is to be understood as equivalent to 5 and not to be taken to express a physical necessity (as in: the tower is bound to topple over) or an assurance (as in: the audience is bound to laugh).[5] Examples:

    7. a. John is bound to take out the garbage.
       b. Mary is bound to have her car fixed.
       c. The court is bound to hear out the witness.
       d. Mary's father is bound to let Mary go to school.
       e. The government is bound to refrain from interfering with the real estate market.

As may be clear from the examples, the substituents for the variable "X" in 6 are singular terms for *persons* or *collectives*. Here by the word *collectives* we understand well-structured institutions or organizations that can act, take responsibilities, and so on.[6] Examples are governments, corporations, states, clubs, unions. But, generally, a mob, an audience, a school class, a gang, or a family would not qualify as a collective. We shall call a person or collective that is committed to a course of action the *subject* (*of that commitment*).

The substituent for the variable "A" in 6 is to indicate what we shall call the "*object (of commitment)*," that is, the course of action to which the subject is committed. By a happy accident of English grammar the variable "*A*" in 6 is replaceable by an imperative asking for exactly that course of action to which the subject is committed. Thus we may profit from the logic of imperatives in our analysis of action commitment. In fact, we shall apply Hamblin's *action-state semantics.*[7]

For each simple action-commitment statement 6, there is an *associated imperative* addressed to the subject of the commitment:

    8. a. *A* (addressed to *X*)!
        b. *X*, *A*!

(Notation 8b is available only when "*X*" is replaced by a proper name).

For example, these are the imperatives associated with the commitment statements in 7:

    9. a. John, take out the garbage!
        b. Mary, have your car fixed!
        c. Hear out the witness (addressed to the court)!
        d. Let Mary go to school (addressed to Mary's father)!
        e. Refrain from interfering with the real estate market (addressed to the government)!

Notice that sometimes one has to change an anaphoric pronoun, as when going from 7b to 9b. A statement like

    10. Everyone is bound to fight the enemy,

is not a *simple* action-commitment statement (since "everyone" is not a singular term). We may dub it a *complex* one. Its associated imperative is:

    11. Everyone, fight the enemy!

which is not the simplest type of imperative either. According to Hamblin's *addressee-action-reduction principle* an imperative has a clear meaning if and only if "the various addressees are each, under every conceivable circumstance, in effective receipt of injunctions in respect of their individual actions."[8] It is our contention that living up to a commitment is the same as satisfying the associated imperative. So, if 11 enjoins everyone, separately, to fight the enemy, this is what everyone, separately, should do in order to live up to the various commitments described in the complex action-commitment statement 10.

Puzzling commitment statements have equally puzzling associated imperatives. For instance

    12. a. 1. Someone is bound to open the door.[9]
            2. Someone, open the door!
        b. 1. Mary is bound to have the car fixed, if John takes out the garbage.[10]
            2. Mary, have the car fixed, if John takes out the garbage!

c. 1. Any citizen who sees a burglary is bound to report it to the police.
2. Report it to the police (addressed to any citizen who sees a burglary)![11]

This is not the place to discuss such puzzles, but it may be clear from these examples that advances in the analysis of imperatives will soon yield more insight into the meaning of puzzling commitment statements.[12]

We shall now have a closer look at the nature of the objects of commitment. To know what a subject is committed to is to know what the subject should do (or not do) to live up to this commitment, that is, to satisfy the associated imperative. According to Hamblin, with each imperative i there is associated a set of possible worlds W_i "within any one of which it would count as having been carried out." It is "the set of worlds in which i is satisfied *extensionally*," that is, where John takes out the garbage, Mary has her car fixed, and so on,[13] but, as Hamblin argues, extensional satisfaction is not enough for *full* or *wholehearted satisfaction*, and perhaps it is not even required:

> No imperative counts as wholeheartedly satisfied if it is possible to say of it *He wouldn't have done it if it hadn't been for so-and-so, or It only came about by accident, or It would have come about anyway, what he did was irrelevant to it (or impeded it)*. Conversely, even when extensional satisfaction is lacking, we sometimes want to say *Yes, but it wasn't his fault*, or *He did everything he could*. Full or wholehearted satisfaction perhaps includes extensional, but what it adds is sometimes seen as the more important component.[14]

Wholehearted satisfaction of an imperative i (given at the time t) is defined by Hamblin in terms of an addressee's *partial strategies*. Basically, to act, as from time t, conforming to an imperative i (and hence, we may say, conforming to a commitment statement that has i as its associated imperative) consists in the adoption of (and the following of) a so-called *partial i-strategy* at each time t' ($t' > t$).[15]

A *partial i-strategy* starting at t assigns, for each $t' > t$, to each *possible history of the world up to t'*, $j_{t'}$, a set of *deeds* (i.e., elementary or atomic actions). Think of this set as that from which the addressee of i should select one deed at time t', in order to follow the strategy, provided he thinks the history of the world up till then to be $j_{t'}$. The assigned set of deeds, D, should conform to the following two conditions: (1) if at t' (given $j_{t'}$) there are still deeds conforming to strategies for the addressee that will lead to the extensional satisfaction of i, D is to contain deeds conforming to one such strategy only; (2) if there are no such deeds, but there are deeds available for the addressee that do not obstruct the extensional satisfaction of i, D is to contain deeds of the latter type only.

In this connection, one might ask how many alternative histories of the world there are and how many choices an addressee has to make. But this question is not the metaphysical problem it seems to be. Rather, it is a matter of the required depth of analysis in the particular context of a given case. In a particular case, the number of alternative histories and the number of choices to be made by an addressee may be quite small. Time may be discrete, and the moments of time may be days or even periods of a year.

When can we legitimately say that someone adopted a particular strategy? As soon as you can answer all relevant questions of the type: if this or that had happened (some relevant change in circumstances), from what set of deeds would he have picked one; that is, what could he have done and what not (supposing that he had not changed his plans in the meantime)?

To wholeheartedly satisfy an imperative i is not just to adopt and follow one particular *partial i-strategy* at time t. For the addressee could change its strategies several times and yet be said to wholeheartedly satisfy i. Thus, in order to *wholeheartedly satisfy* an imperative i (up to time t'') the addressee should at each time t' such that $t'' \geqslant t' \geqslant t$: (1) adopt a strategy that is *as far as he or she knows*, a *partial i-strategy* $q_{t'}$, that starts at t'; (2) make an estimate of the history of the world (including deeds by other agents) up to time t' (let this history, according to the addressee, be $j_{t'}$); (3) do one of the deeds from the set that $q_{t'}$ assigns to $j_{t'}$.[16]

This is already a fairly precise and technical account of the central mechanism of action-commitment implementation, even though it may be a much simplified model and leaves a number of complications aside. We want to stress, however, that *living up to a commitment* (i.e., wholeheartedly satisfying the associated imperative) does not characteristically consist in simply doing the right thing, but in a number of strategic decisions and estimations of circumstances, and in performing deeds according to these decisions and estimates. Let us illustrate these points by the following case:

CASE 1.1   John is bound to take out the garbage. For him to live up to this commitment is the same as to wholeheartedly satisfy the imperative: John, take out the garbage! The address-action-reduction principle says that, in order for this imperative (and hence for the corresponding commitment statement) to have a clear meaning, it must be clear—from the context, say—

what John is supposed to do (what garbage he is to put where
and when, and so on). Let us suppose that John made a
promise to Mary to put out the garbage before 7:00 A.M.,
when it will be collected. The alarm clock goes off at 6:00
A.M. What actions by John are compatible with his living up
to his commitment?

Certainly, he shouldn't jump out of his bed and catch
the 6:10 express for Vladivostok, leaving the garbage where it
is. (Unless John really thinks this to be a way to go about his
task and adopts it as a strategy. We shall not suppose this to
be the case.) But what John could do is get a little more sleep
and reset the alarm for 6:30. Then, as the alarm wakes him up
again, he may change his strategy once more and opt for
6:45. Presumably, this is still in keeping with his promise.
(Whereas resetting the alarm clock for 7:30 is not: this would
not be part of following any *partial i-strategy*.) What if tension builds up, and Mary is going to take out the garbage at
6:55, if John is still in bed at that time? Would it be all right
for John just to stay in bed? If John were simply bound to
make sure that the garbage is out at 7:00 A.M., perhaps this
could be a permissible strategy. But, since we have supposed
that John should *take* out the garbage, it is not. Neither is the
strategy of resetting the alarm for 6:56, at least not as long as
we suppose that John knows well enough what Mary will do
at 6:55.

Suppose John has reset the alarm for 6:30. What if
his son Bill, quite unexpectedly, takes out the garbage at
6:15? In that case we may say that John has lived up to his
commitment (has kept his word), even though the associated imperative was not extensionally satisfied. (In the
terminology we shall introduce later, he has *maintained* but
not *fulfilled* his commitment.) John may, at 6:30, go to
sleep for the rest of the morning (all partial strategies
are eligible), provided, of course, that he is informed about
Bill's action (and believes his ears). John was prevented from
taking out the garbage, but he has not reneged on his
commitment.

Neither is John delinquent if he (unknowingly) takes
out a garbage bag stuffed with sweaters that Bill put in the
place where the garbage used to be. But if John accidentally
takes out the garbage, being under the impression that these
are some sweaters he abhors, then he has not thereby met the

commitment that he undertook. In the first case John has lived up to his commitment, in the second not (supposing that is all he does). The last case can in the present vocabulary be described as one in which the imperative is *extensionally* satisfied , but it is not *fully* or *wholeheartedly* satisfied.

Now, take the case where Mary gets sick at 6:30 and John takes her to the hospital. There is no time to bother about the lesser problem of the garbage. We cannot say, then, that John has lived up to his commitment: he did not adopt any *partial i-strategy* after 6:30. So we must say that John was delinquent at least as far as the garbage is concerned. Even so, who would say that John *wrongly* reneged on this commitment? Indeed, there were other, and more important, commitments that took over. So in undertaking to meet the total of his commitments, in this case John acted correctly.

Finally, what if at 6:30 John has simply forgotten about the garbage? As this would probably prevent him from adopting an *i*-strategy, we would not say that he is living up to his commitment (even if later he decides to be nice, and for once take out the garbage, so that the imperative gets extensional satisfaction). Forgetfulness, may, however, in some cases be excusable, depending upon circumstances.

We discussed the subject and the object of a commitment, but it remains to (briefly) inquire into ways subjects are bound, or into the nature of *commitment bonds*, as we shall say. Just as, with imperatives, one may distinguish commands, requests, advice, and so on,[17] there are commitments with varying forces or strengths:

13. a. *X* is not in a position to omit *A*.
    b. *X* is supposed to do *A*.
    c. *X* is told to do *A*.
    d. *X* is under the (moral) obligation to do *A*.
    e. *X* is forced to do *A*.

It seems that an explanation of the nature of these various bonds would have to go into a whole background of, say, command structure, moral codes, legal codes, social codes, and affiliations. A trenchant and useful, though perhaps perfunctory, way to gain some understanding of these matters is to ask, in each case, for the *sanction*. What exactly would happen if the subject of the commitment does not live up to it? Would he or she be ridiculed? Blamed? Censured? Banished? Executed? Go to the back of the line? Lose four hundred dollars? Or would the subject incur other specific commitments? Or fail to meet certain standards? The better we can answer these sanction questions, by setting a specific penalty in a particular case, the better we seem to understand the nature of a given commitment bond.

Though the sanctions may, in a particular case, be partially or simply ordered according to strength, and we may thus speak of stronger and weaker types of commitments, this does not imply that commitment is a scalar notion. As noted above, having a commitment is a yes or no affair. One does not gradually shift from one type of commitment to the other becoming more and more committed. What is meant, when people use the expression "*getting more deeply committed*" is either a shift to another stronger type of commitment, or a deeper involvement. Involvement, as opposed to commitment, is a matter of degree. We can speak of stronger and weaker commitments. We can't speak of having a commitment only partially, or to a certain degree.[18]

Let us now go back to 3, the lexical definition of commitment given by Webster's. It defines commitment as a state of the subject, for instance the state John is in when he is committed to take out the garbage. We can continue to use the word *commitment* in this way, provided we do not for *state* silently substitute *mental state*. We must rather think of a state here as a definite set of circumstances (legal, moral, social, etc.). A person's various commitments (the specific states he or she is in) together determine the (total) commitment (the state the person is in). This latter state determines what the person is committed to doing, and sets the various sanctions if he or she fails or falls short. We may call this state a person's *agenda*. A somewhat simplified model of an agenda of a subject X may be constructed in the following way. For each sanction S, there is a *sanction set* $C(S, X)$, the members of $C(S, X)$ are sets of partial strategies for X. Think of each of these latter sets as a set of *partial i-strategies*, where i is an imperative associated with some simple action-commitment statement: X is bound to A, with sanction S. The sets $C(S_1, X)$, $C(S_2, X)$, and so on, together give us a language-independent (concept and) model of an *agenda*. If Q is an element of $C(S, X)$, we may call Q *an object of S-commitment of X*, or simply an *S-commitment of X*. If Q gives the objective content of an imperative: $X, A!$, we may also say that "doing A" is an S-commitment of X (though one would hardly say that doing A is a part of a state of X).

The model can be enriched by giving more structure to the various sets (hierarchical orderings, etc.), but we shall not go into that here.

1.2 Propositional Commitment

It is time to explain what we mean by the term *propositional commitment* and to connect this notion with what has been said on action commitment on the one hand, and with rules of dialogue on the other. Let us look at some cases:

CASE 1.2   On the evening preceding the setting of case 1.1, John asks Mary: "Where will you put the garbage for me to take out tomorrow morning?" Mary answers: "Behind the door, as usual." Mary has now promised to put the garbage behind the door, so she's now committed to that course of action. There are several propositions associated with this commitment, for example, "Mary will put the garbage behind the door" (describing what, ideally, should happen), or "The garbage will be behind the door" (describing the desired result). But we shall not, for this reason, call Mary's commitment to putting the garbage behind the door a "propositional commitment." Mary's commitments, however, are not restricted to putting the garbage behind the door. She has also incurred some commitments that are more intimately connected with propositions. For instance, Mary is now bound not to deny (at least not without due explanation) that she will put the garbage behind the door, or that it will be behind the door, or that there is any garbage. These we shall call Mary's *propositional commitments*. Notice that, in ordinary circumstances, these propositions are not challengeable; that is, it would be odd to ask Mary for reasons or evidence for them.

CASE 1.3   John is about to take the garbage out. He asks Mary: "Where did you put the garbage?" Mary answers: "Behind the door, as usual." In this case Mary has not committed herself to do anything about the garbage, but she has incurred a propositional commitment with respect to the proposition that she has put the garbage behind the door. She cannot (without more ado) deny this proposition, and perhaps it wouldn't be entirely out of place to ask for evidence ("Are you sure?").

CASE 1.4   John is about to take the garbage out. He asks Bill where Mary put the garbage. Bill answers: "On the roof." Bill has incurred a propositional commitment to the proposition that

Mary has put the garbage on the roof. It seems quite acceptable to challenge this proposition. A dialogue may start.

CASE 1.5 Mary is the city's environmental specialist. She announces
that the city's output of waste will, over the next ten years,
increase by 5 percent per annum, if no measures are taken to
prevent this. She mentions some undesirable effects of this.
She then goes on to suggest some measures the city government should take. Mary has expressed opinions on matters of
fact, on what is desirable, and on what should be done. On all
three accounts she has incurred propositional commitments.
Living up to these commitments, would, in this case, mean
that Mary should try to argue for her tenets, to defend them,
when challenged. This holds not only for propositions on
matters of fact, but also for value judgments, normative statements, and injunctions. Clearly Mary is committed to certain
courses of action in some possible dialogues.

It should be clear, from these examples, that whoever makes a
declarative statement thereby commits himself to some course of action,
depending upon the context. In this respect asserting (but also denying,
conceding, doubting) is rather like making a promise: it puts something
on the speaker's agenda. (And, usually, it puts something on the listener's
agenda as well.) Suppose X asserts that P. Depending upon context X
may then become committed to a number of things, for example, holding that P, defending that P (if challenged), not denying that P, giving
evidence that P, arguing that P, proving or establishing that P and so on.
And, in various contexts, these commitments may be differently spelled
out. Ultimately, X becomes committed to some (sets of) partial strategies. But the reason that we speak of *propositional* commitment here is
that all X's commitments (as defined by the strategies he is committed
to) center on the proposition P, or perhaps even on X's particular formulation of P. Moreover, the various courses of action are *dialogical*, that is,
of such types as one would expect to occur in dialogue. We shall say in
this case that X *is committed to* P, meaning that X is committed to a set
of partial strategies centering on P.

To sum up then: *propositional commitment* is (1) a kind of action
commitment whose (2) partial strategies assign dialogical actions that (3)
center on one proposition (or a formulation thereof).

As we saw, commitments may be of various strengths, and for that
reason, we split a subject's agenda into a number of different compart-
ments, or sanction sets, one for each sanction: $C(S_1, X)$, $C(S_2, X)$, and
so on. It is no different with propositional commitment, but in order not

to complicate matters we shall only consider two sanctions: 1. failure to comply with the basic constraints that hold for the particular type of discourse in which the commitment is incurred, and 2. failure to perform well in this type of discourse.

In our view of commitment then, the way one is bound to follow the rules for a type of dialogue differs from the way one is bound to optimize behavior within the compass of the rules. If one goes against the rules of a type of dialogue, one is open to a particularly strong form of censure or criticism. Such a failure to realize the speech event of the assigned type is a serious kind of deviation that is highly inappropriate, unless the move is acceptable for external reasons, agreed to and approved by the other party. However, if one follows a weak strategy, but one that conforms to the rules, this type of internal failure is generally not quite so serious. However, one does run the risk to lose the exchange; for example, in a persuasion dialogue, one may fail to persuade the other party.

If, as we shall from now on assume, the type of discourse is one of rule-governed dialogue (a dialogue game), the first sanction may be formulated as quitting the dialogue by breaking the rules (in some dialogue games that would mean a loss or even a dishonourable loss), whereas the second sanction would amount to choosing a legal but bad strategy (this may lead to an honourable loss, if the other party chooses a good strategy). We shall call the sanction sets corresponding to these sanctions $C_1(X)$ and $C_2(X)$.

The inclusion of the second type of sanction reflects our point of view that in dialogue one should not just conform to the rules (e.g., defend one's assertion, if required) but perform to the best of one's abilities (e.g., give one's strongest arguments, etc.).

Thus, we get corresponding to X's assertion that P, at time t, in the context of a dialogue game two objects of commitment for X: a set $Q_1(P, X)$ and a set $Q_2(P, X)$ of partial strategies for X ($Q_1(P, X)$ is an element of $C_1(X)$ and $Q_2(P, X)$ is an element of $C_2(X)$). The rules of the dialogue game in question prescribe that X, from t on, stay within the confines of the partial strategies $Q_1(P, X)$, whereas, for X, it would be a matter of optimizing his strategy to stay within $Q_2(P, X)$. (If there is just one optimal strategy for X, $Q_2(P, X)$ will contain just that strategy.) Notice that, generally, X's adversary in dialogue, Y, will incur commitments, too, on account of X's assertion at time t: $Q_1(P, Y)$, $Q_2(P, Y)$. Each of the sets $C_1(X)$ and $C_2(X)$ contains a number of sets of partial strategies for X, one set for each commitment. And each "object of commitment" $Q_1(P, X)$ or $Q_2(P, X)$, starting to be operative at t contains a number of partial strategies for X. Evidently, these partial strategies and hence X's agenda are very complicated objects. We shall, therefore, as we introduce models of dialogue, not describe them directly but go about it in another way: we shall formulate rules of dialogue and a codification of the history of dialogues in such detail that these rules, together with a given codified history, completely determine the content of each set $Q_1(P, X)$ or $Q_2(P, X)$ that is, the action reductions of each person's propositional commitments. Thus the rules determine not only a participant's legal actions on account of a propositional $(Q_1(P, X))$, but also what constitutes good strategy $(Q_2(P, X))$, even though it may be hard to determine the latter in a given case. And they determine not only such actions as flow from a participant's assertions, but also such as are required by his or her opponent's assertions and by challenges, utterances of doubt, questions, and so on.

As to the codification of the history of the game, what we need primarily to lay down is what propositions a participant is committed to. We shall for that purpose introduce commitment stores (or sets) of several types.[19] For instance one commitment set may list a participant's assertions, another his concessions, and so on. Moreover, some commitment sets will contain formulated propositions, that is, sentences instead of the propositions themselves. Finally, nothing prevents us from including within certain commitment sets propositions that are not connected with any speech act within the dialogue. As we shall see in the next section, there are other ways of incurring commitments than by speech acts.

We shall end this section by making a short remark on the notion of a fallacy. Both actions diverging from those assigned by $C_1(X)$ and those diverging from those assigned by $C_2(X)$ could, perhaps, be called fallacies. We shall, however, prefer to use the word *fallacy* only in the strongest sense, that is, that of diverging from $C_1(X)$. A fallacy then is an infraction of some dialogue rule. For the other sense ("bad strategy") the words *blunder* and *flaw* seem appropriate, whenever strong terms are needed. A consequence of this stipulation is that what constitutes a fallacy in one game of dialogue does not need to constitute a fallacy in another (it could be just a blunder, or even be entirely all right).[20]

1.3 Problems to Be Solved

Commitments were analyzed into subject, object, and commitment bond. There remain many problems with respect to each.

With respect to the subjects of commitment: when does a set of people qualify as a collective; that is, when is it possible for a set of people to incur commitment? For instance, a group of people in a room does not normally constitute a collective, but if someone walks by and ask them to leave the room tidy, and if some of them say yes, it appears that they are committed as a collective. A further investigation would bring us into social philosophy (cf. the reference to Spit in note 6).

Normally, it is convenient to think of the individual person as the main subject of commitment. However, some odd cases challenge this preconception. In split-brain or multiple personality cases, the same person (or at least the same body) may be committed differently, so that it may be best to speak of several distinct subjects of commitment. Defining the subject of commitment in such a case could be a substantive problem for the philosophy of mind and for philosophical psychology.

In a mundane type of case, it may initially seem best to see a person who is deliberating an hour to act in a problematic situation as a single subject engaging in monological (i.e., nondialogue) reasoning. But if she is weighing the pros and cons of two opposed viewpoints, and perhaps is playing devil's advocate by hypothetically adopting the one viewpoint as a means of criticizing the weak points of the other, it may be better to see this as a case of two subjects of commitment engaging in a dialogue with each other. This is a problem of how to identify subjects of commitment in relation to the kind of dialogue theory developed in chapter 4. In dialogue theory, we may try to analyze monological reasoning as a type of interpersonal dialectical reasoning, that is, as an internal dialogue in which the reasoner functions in two distinct dialectical roles and, consequently, takes on commitment, not absolutely, but relative to these roles (self-criticism). Thus we would enter into problems regarding the best way of identifying subjects of commitment in a given case.

With respect to objects of commitment: in our analysis these are very complicated objects (sets of partial strategies). Could they be reduced to something more manageable? For instance, do all possible histories of the world have to be taken into account if I want to describe your commitment to volleyball, or could we do with a subset of these and a selected part of each history? How about the notion of a deed (atomic action)? Can it be given a viable meaning that does not depend on metaphysical preconceptions? Also, the notion of knowledge (about the history of the world as well as about the effect of following a certain strategy) needs further analysis, and so does the notion of "making an estimate." Further problems that could be investigated are the relations between the objects of commitment and the notions of intention, goal, obligation, duty, ideal, and so on.

An especially important problem is whether the notion of commitment in dialogue can be used to help define the notion of intention.

Intentions are often difficult to determine, but commitment to one notion or proposition is surely a good way to think of an intention. According to Segerberg: "The best way to think of intentions is perhaps as commitments on which the agent acts; he acts so as to bring about, make true, realize that to which his commitments commit him—to implement the intentions . . ." [21] The reader might like to look at Segerberg's account, where intention is defined as a subspecies of commitment.

With respect to the nature of the commitment bond one may wonder whether other approaches than that by a characterization of sanctions could be fruitful. Can one give a classification or hierarchy of sanctions and thus give more structure to the concept of an agenda? Can the idea of an agenda be worked out to yield a theory of personhood?

Many puzzles are provided by complex commitment statements. Hamblin (in a chapter on grammar-logic) discusses a number of complex and/or puzzling imperatives, which yield as many puzzling commitment statements, such as conjunctive, disjunctive, and conditional imperatives of various kinds. [22]

The concept of 'living up to a commitment' (wholeheartedly satisfying the associated imperative) is in need of some empirical links. What evidence can we use to establish that someone would have acted in that or that way had such and such been the case? What analysis of counterfactuals is appropriate in this context?

The problem of wavering (mentioned in note 16) is this: if someone, X, is committed to a set of (partial) strategies Q, and is living up to that commitment, this does not exclude X's changing strategy all the time in a way that systematically and perversely obstructs the possibility of reaching external satisfaction of the associated imperative. For instance, if the imperative is not to allow a draft in the sickroom, and if both the door and the window happen to be open, X could waver between the strategy of closing the door and that of closing the window, both of which would be in Q. After having taken one step toward the door X could change strategy and take two steps toward the window, then again change strategy and take two steps toward the door, and so on. How can we exclude this as a case of living up to one's commitment without excluding bona fide changes of strategy as well?

The present analysis does not take into account the possibility that a person's knowledge or belief with respect to the history of the world and with respect to the effects of certain deeds may change as time passes. How could our analysis be modified so as to take these factors into account?

The problems mentioned thus far pertain to commitment in general. As to commitment *in dialogue*, we note, at this stage, the following two special problems:

1.   Is every commitment in dialogue propositional? Or are there some
      nonpropositional commitments that are nevertheless dialogical?

2.   We introduced, for dialogue theory, just two types of sanction,
      and two "negative" qualifications with respect to moves within
      dialogue: fallacy and blunder. How about distinguishing more
      than just these two sanction sets, and, consequently, more than
      two "negative" qualifications? This would, obviously, influence
      the weighty question of how to define a viable concept of 'fallacy.'

1.4 Summary

The term *commitment* has many lexical uses, but our central interest in
this book will be with those commitments that can be expressed by
(simple) action-commitment statements: X is bound to A. Basically,
commitment has three aspects: a subject (X), an object (A), and the
special nature of the commitment bond (the way X is bound to A).
The subject is a person, or any well-structured institution or organization that can act or take responsibility. The object is the course of
action to which the subject is committed. In the general form "X is
bound to A," "X" stands for the subject of commitment and "A"
stands for the object. An example is "John is bound to take out the
garbage." Associated with this (simple) action-commitment statement
is the imperative, "John, take out the garbage!" Our way of approach-
ing commitment is an application of Hamblin's action-state semantics
for imperatives (systematically developed for our purposes in the appendix). In his account, wholehearted satisfaction of an imperative is defined in terms of a subject's partial strategies, each of which assigns a
set of deeds to each possible history of the world at a given point in
time. Living up to a commitment (wholeheartedly satisfying the associated imperative) must be distinguished from merely doing the right
thing. Rather, whether a subject is living up to a commitment must be
judged in light of that subject's estimations of circumstances, strategic
decisions, and deeds, not only in the actual world, but also in
counterfactual situations.

   Propositional commitment is a kind of action commitment whose
partial strategies assign dialogical actions that center on one proposition.
For example, if Mary asserts the proposition "There is too much garbage
in Hamilton," then she will become committed to a set of partial strategies centering on this proposition. But what she will be exactly committed to depends on context. For instance, if the proposition is challenged

by John, with whom Mary is engaged in a critical discussion about garbage disposal, Mary becomes committed to defending it.

Commitment bonds are the different ways subjects are bound to the objects of commitment. A useful way to understand the nature of a commitment bond in a given case is to identify its sanctions, the penalty the subject would incur if he did not live up to his commitment in that case. The agenda of a subject represents the totality of his commitments, along with the various sanctions if he fails to live up to these commitments.

Our primary concern is with commitment in dialogue, and so with propositional commitment. Here we consider only two types of sanctions, failure to comply with the rules of dialogue, which might amount to a kind of loss of the exchange, and failure to perform well in the dialogue. Correspondingly, we distinguish between fallacies and blunders. This orientation will be important later, in chapters 3 and 4, where our primary concern will be with how propositional commitments are gained or lost in a context where two parties are reasoning with each other by exchanging arguments.

2 The Dynamics of Commitment

A person's commitments are not given as a fixed trait of her character. This chapter addresses the origins of commitments, their relations and interactions, their vanishing. Commitments are incurred in various ways (section 2.1). They are then maintained or reneged, or retracted, or cancelled (section 2.2). Moreover, commitments enter relationships and interact (section 2.3) and may even clash (section 2.4).

2.1 Incurring of Commitment

Commitments do not have to be taken on by a specific, single, overt action at a particular time. But when they are, several ways of incurring commitments stand out as especially significant. Perhaps the most obvious way is for a speaker to incur a commitment through his own direct or indirect speech act. The most obvious speech acts of this sort are oaths and promises of various kinds.

Assertions also fall into this category. We saw that to assert a proposition is to become committed to that proposition. For instance, in some circumstances, to assert a proposition may amount to becoming committed to subsequently defending the proposition, if one is challenged to do so by another speaker in dialogue.

Table 2.1 below summarizes the various, distinctive ways commitments are incurred, as the subsequent discussion will elaborate. Notice that incurring a commitment through one's own direct or indirect speech act is category B.I, which comes under the more general category (B) of incurring a commitment by the subject's own action. The incurring of commitments by oaths or promises (mentioned above) comes under the subcategory B.I.2 of table 2.1.

All the ways of incurring commitment mentioned so far occur through the action of the subject. However, as table 2.1 indicates, commitments can also be incurred by a subject through someone else's action (category C). For example, my lawyer, or other representative, may commit

Table 2.1   Ways of Incurring Commitments (Propositional or Others)

A. By social position:

    A.I   By relationships.

    A.II By affiliation.

B. By the subject's own action:

    B.I   By a (direct or indirect) speech act:

        B.I.1 In dialogue:

            (a) by asserting a proposition;

            (b) by conceding a proposition;

            (c) by other speech acts in dialogue; e.g., by asking a question one may get committed to its presuppositions.

        B.I.2 Not in dialogue, e.g., promises, oaths, etc.

    B.II Other actions by the subject; e.g., making a decisive moral personal choice.

C. By the actions of actors other than the subject:

    C.I   By a (direct or indirect) speech act:

        C.I.1 In dialogue:

            (a) by being questioned;

            (b) by being challenged;

            (c) by other speech acts in dialogue.

        C.I.2 Not in dialogue; e.g., someone makes a promise on behalf of the subject or someone orders the subject to do so and so.

    C.II Other actions by others.

me to certain actions or courses of action—see category C.I.2 in table 2.1. Another example would be a team sport, where being put in a certain position by another player—say, by passing the ball—could commit me to certain types of actions, to certain kinds of partial strategies. Since passing the ball is not a speech act, this would fall under category C.II.

It may be less obvious that asking a question may commit the questioner to certain propositions. For example, in some cases, asking a question may be rightly held to commit the questioner to propositions that are presuppositions of the question. Consider the following question asked in the context of a parliamentary or congressional debate: "Why did your party's feeble efforts to contend with the debilitating inflation, which was allowed to undermine the economy, fail so miserably?" This argumentative question commits the questioner to several propositions— that there was inflation during a certain period, that it was "debilitating," that it was allowed to "undermine" the economy, and so forth. This way of incurring commitments would come under category B.I.1(c) in table 2.1. Also, asking a question may commit the respondent to certain propositions, if he does not immediately reject these propositions before attempting to answer the question. This falls under category C.I.1 (a) in table 2.1. For example, with regard to the parliamentary question above, if the respondent does not reject the accusations posed by the asking of the question, it will certainly appear that he is acknowledging these incriminating propositions and thereby incurring commitments of some sort to them. From what we know about political debate, it is likely that the questioner's follow-up attacks will be based on such presumptions, unless the respondent makes it clear that he does not accept the commitments alleged by the question.

Commitments can also be incurred by nonlinguistic actions, as we saw in the team sport example. Indeed, nonlinguistic actions and speech acts can be combined in the taking on of a commitment. Moreover, omissions to act can also be ways of incurring commitments. Perhaps we could simply include omissions as types of actions that can make one incur commitments.

In the following case, a commitment is incurred by a combination of a person's omission to act and somebody else's speech act. Categories C.I.2 and B.II are combined.

CASE 2.1   The commander of a besieged fort draws his whole complement of defending troops up in formation in the public square at high noon and announces: "I have decided to defend the fort against the assault expected tomorrow. Anyone who wants to leave can do so now."

In this case, anyone who fails to take advantage of the commander's invitation to leave, just then, has committed himself to taking part in the subsequent defence of the fort. His failure to act, taken in conjunction with the commander's speech act, has committed him to something thereafter.

Commitments do not necessarily have to be incurred through actions. Some commitments arise through relationships. For instance, in some countries children are legally bound to support their parents, and vice versa. The following case combines categories A.I and C.II of table 2.1.

CASE 2.2   In Dutch law, a parent may not be held legally liable for the consequences of the actions of his or her child. For example, if the child breaks a school window, the holder of the parent's liability insurance policy may point out that the parent does not, legally, have to pay for damages, and that, consequently, the insurance company is entitled to reject the parent's claim for compensation. However, the parent may nevertheless feel that he or she is (as a matter of common decency) committed to paying for the broken window.

In this case, the commitment may not be legally binding, but a commitment may nevertheless have been incurred by the parent through the child's action.

Another way commitments can be incurred by a person is through his affiliation with, or membership in, a group (A.II). Such groups are widely varied and may include political parties, denominations, professions, unions, and corporations. In some groups, commitments are codified in an oath that is required in order to join the group. For example, in the medical profession, taking the Hippocratic oath makes the new physician incur commitment. This type of case involves categories A.II and B.I.2 of table 2.1.

A group membership taken in conjunction with subsequent actions, assertions, and relationships may lead to the incurring of specific commitments in a particular case. The following case combines categories A.I, A.II, B.I.2, B.II, and C.II. It is the most complex case considered so far.

CASE 2.3   A physician takes on a particular patient for treatment. Thus a physician-patient relationship has been established and the physician has taken on certain commitments regarding the care of that individual person who has become his or her patient.

Once a physician has initiated a course of treatment for a particular patient, the physician cannot (straightforwardly) then cease treatment halfway through, or "abandon" the patient. In some instances this commitment can be legally binding, as well as a binding commitment according to medical ethics. In this type of case, the incurring of commitment has arisen through a combination of professional affiliations and promises (oaths), relationships, and actions. The physician and the patient each incur commitments that arise both through their own actions and the actions of the other party.

Another interesting aspect of case 2.3 above is that the physician may have general commitments to broad types of actions which may become operationalized in a much more specific way in a particular case. For example, once he has taken on a particular patient, the physician's commitments may then come down to highly specific actions in relation to this patient (cf. section 2.3 on specification).

An interesting fact about the incurring of commitments is that a person may come to take on commitments, freely but possibly with reluctance or hesitation, through critical questioning of his position on an issue by another person, in dialogue.

CASE 2.4   George is a committed Socialist but frustrated by the continual postal strikes, and he argues that the post office should be taken over by private enterprise. His friend Bob replies: "How can you say that, George? After all you are a Socialist, and Socialists do not think that state functions should be run by private enterprise."

In this case, George's position seems to be in danger of a conflict, for his general commitment seems to clash with the particular stance he has taken up on the post office issue. Reasoning out the difficulty in further dialogue with Bob, George may be led in one of two directions. He may either refine his version of socialism to allow for some private enterprise in some cases, or he may retract his commitment to private enterprise in the post office case. But in both cases George will have modified or refined his position in some respects. That is to say, he will have incurred some modified or refined commitments. Since both questions and answers play a role here, this case combines at least the categories CI.1 and BI.1.

People may be reluctant to submit to questioning of their most dearly and deeply held commitments. But such critical questioning of commitments can have the valuable maieutic function of articulating and clarifying them by bringing them forth from an unconscious level where they exist in a vague and general form, and sharpening their formulation. For example, in case 2.4 above, George's commitment to socialism may be clarified, and put into a more consistent and specific form, by discussing it in relation to the specific issue of post office management.

In the process of questioning that performs this maieutic function of clarifying commitments, the relationship of one commitment to another, within a person's store of commitments, is very important. Of particular importance is the type of situation where one of these commitments appears to be in conflict with another one. This may suggest a weakness or uncertainty in a person's position which calls for clarification, or even for retraction of commitments in some cases.

This brings us to the subject of how commitment can be retracted or withdrawn. More generally, this subject concerns the ways of losing commitments, since commitments can sometimes cease to exist as part of an individual's store of commitments, without necessarily having been explicitly withdrawn by an action.

2.2 Loss of Commitment

Commitments are not always permanent. Sometimes, they can be withdrawn or retracted. On the other hand, commitments tend to be "sticky." They cannot always be retracted without some explanation, criticism, or penalty. Retraction is often possible, but in some cases it is much more difficult and involved as a process than in other cases. In other words, commitment is often a matter of priorities. A more deeply held commitment may be more difficult to retract than a lightly held one.

Hamblin outlined various formal games of argumentative dialogue.[1] Some of them allow for retraction of commitments, and others, like the medieval Obligation Game, do not. In the terminology of Woods and Walton, the latter are called *cumulative* games of dialogue.[2] Many recognized games of dialogue in the literature allow retraction only under certain restrictions. Hamblin and Mackenzie have games where any participant is allowed to retract propositions that may even be logical consequences of previous commitments. However, in Mackenzie's games, if a participant retracts a proposition that is an *immediate* logical consequence of previous commitments, he may by a "resolution demand" be forced to either reassert this proposition or retract at least one of the previous commitments.[3] (An immediate *(direct)* consequence of a set of propositions is a proposition that follows from that set by means of a single application of one rule of inference of the game.) At any rate, Hamblin generally seems to think that "certain very immediate consequences" of a proposition that is a commitment of a participant in dialogue may also be regarded, for that reason, as commitments of that participant, unless he specifically objects or "changes his mind," as indicated by a subsequent locution in the dialogue.[4]

Just as it is simplistic to think that commitments are always and only incurred by frank, overt, and explicit declarations, so too it is an error to think that commitments are always lost by explicit declarations. In some cases, commitments can fade or become weakened without a subject being clearly aware of it until he is challenged by a critical discussion or a need to act.

Let us say that a commitment has *lapsed* if extensional satisfaction of the associated imperative either has been obtained or by the actual course of events has become unattainable. Assuming that the subject is aware of this, nothing he does can any longer affect his living up to that commitment.[5] Thus one's commitment to get to the station by 4:00 P.M. has lapsed at 4:00 P.M, whether one has made it to the station or not.

One way to discharge a commitment is to live up to it until it has lapsed. In that case we shall say that one has *maintained* it. Notice that one can maintain one's commitment to be at the station at 4:00 P.M. just by trying to be there to the best of one's ability. Actually reaching the station is not implied. If one has lived up to one's commitment and has gotten external satisfaction of the associated imperative (reached the station in time) as well, we shall say that one has *fulfilled* the commitment. A second way to discharge a commitment is for the person who has incurred it to *retract* it afterwards. Other ways of losing commitments, we shall call *cancellations*. For example, another person may withdraw a commitment on your behalf, or one may fail to live up to a commitment until it has lapsed. Various combinations of these ways are possible. For example, a physician and a patient may jointly agree to terminate a course of treatment, thereby removing the physician's commitment to continue treating this particular patient.

The three ways of losing a commitment in table 2.2 represent a very global schema of classification which is more finely detailed in the more complex schema of table 2.3, below. In table 2.2, the category of "getting cancelled" covers any commitment that is lost other than by having maintained it or by retraction. This category is necessary because, in many instances, a commitment can become "nonoperational" or no longer applicable, for various other reasons. For example, it might be excluded by an overriding (or prior) commitment and then lapse. In such a case, we shall say that the commitment has been cancelled.

In some cases, a commitment can be retracted very easily. For example, in some cases, merely saying, "I retract it," is enough to eliminate

Table 2.2   Schema for losing commitments

One may lose a commitment in one of three ways:	$\Big\{$ (i) by having maintained it, (ii) by retracting it, (iii) or by getting it cancelled $\Big\{$ •by one's own (in)action, •by the action of others, •by circumstances, or •by overriding commitments.

a subject's commitment. However, in other cases, it may be difficult for a subject to retract his commitment to a specific proposition or action. Indeed, in some instances, there is no possibility of retracting a commitment once it has been made. In this type of case it is appropriate to speak of *nonretractable commitment*.

Sometimes the term *commitment* is used in a strong sense—so strong, indeed that we regard this usage as understatement—to refer to an action that is absolutely irrevocable, once undertaken. A case in point was Caesar's crossing the Rubicon. Once the river was crossed, Caesar had embarked on a military adventure from which he (supposedly) would not have been able to turn back. In this case the term *commitment* really refers to nonretractable commitment. According to the laws or rulings of the Roman senate, it was forbidden for a Roman army to cross this river. So, having crossed the river, Caesar had already overstepped the bounds of law: the die was cast. Or, consider the jeweler's case:

CASE 2.5   Mr. S., a jeweler, acquired a 900-carat rough, gem-quality diamond. This diamond, when cut, could potentially be transformed into the largest finished diamond on earth. The largest existing cut diamond, the Star of Africa, is 530.2 carats. This rough stone, owned by Mr. S., could, if cut to a shape approximating its natural shape, produce a 531-carat cut diamond. However, if cut to a more aesthetically pleasing shape, a conventional pear shape for example, the final diamond would be much smaller and would not be the world's largest cut diamond.

Mr. S. starts cutting the rough diamond. It is narrow at one end, bulky at the other end. His approach is to start roughly cutting it and then try to let its natural shape emerge when he begins to see its potential. He makes a plastic model of the diamond to try to see how it would look if different kinds of cuts are made. He draws lines on the plastic model to visualize the effect of each cut. He is concerned about what he calls "committing the stone." Producing a conventional pear shape would require cutting many carats off the diamond, but this is a commitment he resists. Yet, after many discussions with his co-workers and with potential buyers of the diamond, he gives priority to beauty over size. The Tinal diamond is a beautiful triangular shape, but it weighs only 407.5 carats.[6]

Having made his initial cuts which give the stone a rough outline, Mr. S. reached a point where he could go no further without "committing the stone." Once he had made the next cut, he could then only proceed along one path and the other path was forever given up (closed off). For example, once he had decided to go for the beautiful shape which he ultimately chose and made some cuts towards this end, it was too late to go back to the idea of having the world's largest cut diamond. At this point, he was committed—or, in gem-cutters' parlance, "the stone was committed." What this really means, however, is that the commitment for the one shape and against the other was nonretractable.

In this strong sense then, the term *commitment* really means nonretractable commitment. It refers to a step that, once taken, seals off some alternative possible path of action beyond recall. In judging similar cases, however, we often see that nonretractibility is nonabsolute and is a matter of degree, even if retraction may be very hard or severely sanctioned. With propositional commitment, for instance, much may depend on the prior context of dialogue and on how deep or fundamental to the subject's expressed position a particular commitment happens to be.

For example, if a man has been deeply committed to a strong kind of socialism all his life, and often expressed Socialist tenets in political speeches, it may be difficult for him to try to explain why his actions, undertaken for his own personal profits in private enterprise schemes, do not really contravene his Socialist commitments. If he then tries to retract his Socialist commitments in order to justify his own profits in his private case, his audience may not be prepared to allow this retraction so easily.

CASE 2.6   A member of a Socialist party is a minister of finance in a government. This person has long been a critic of the conservative opposition party's allowance of "tax dodges" by the rich and privileged, arguing long and hard that these tax evasions are a "hardship on the backs of the workers." However, when this minister is accused of taking advantage of this very type of tax dodge himself, he retracts his opposition to them, arguing that they are acceptable in some cases.

The minister has left his personal integrity open to severe critical questioning by withdrawing a commitment that was, apparently, for him a deeply held and fundamental part of his political position. This raises the question of whether he is the deeply committed Socialist he appeared to be, or whether he is simply a political opportunist who lacks principles and scruples. Here retraction is not so easy given this man's political history and the responsibilities that go with an important political position.

In other cases, however, a commitment may be comparatively easy to retract. If Bob was formerly committed to painting his living room walls gray, but then changes his mind and becomes committed to painting them white instead, his retraction may be allowed without further problems or discussions arising. In some cases, commitments are easily and immediately retractable and there is no sanction incurred or explanation required.

A commitment that is easily retractable in one case, however, may not be so easily retractable in another situation where agreements or relationships have made the commitment firm.

CASE 2.7   Bob decides to paint his living room walls gray. Suppose that once they received Bob's message that he had committed himself to painting the living room gray, the interior decorators went ahead and ordered the right quantity of the right shade of gray paint to be mixed and delivered. Suppose further that the paint cannot be returned, once mixed in a specific shade and quantity and delivered to the site. Suppose even further that Bob's wife, Sarah, not only agrees with Bob's decision to paint the living room gray, but, after talking to several of her friends, has come to the conclusion that gray is the perfect color for the living room.

In this case, Bob's commitment to painting the living room gray is (perhaps) still retractable. But it is not so easily retractable. If he does retract it, he must be ready and able to pay the additional cost for the gray paint, and he must be able to persuade his wife that the white living room would be an alternative that would be acceptable to her.

In other cases, retraction becomes superfluous, because a commitment is lost, disappears, or becomes cancelled through factors external to the subject's action. If Bob's house is destroyed by a hurricane, for example, his commitment to painting the living room walls gray has become cancelled in this sense.

In the language of negotiation dialogue, sometimes a distinction is made between binding and nonbinding agreements. It is tempting to infer that a parallel distinction can be made between binding and nonbinding commitments, where the latter type is retractable and the former is not. However, this is an illusion. For there are no nonbinding commitments since the term *commitment* means that you are bound to something.

Of course, a commitment can be retractable in some cases. But even a retractable commitment is binding (until it is successfully retracted). From our point of view then, it is odd to speak of a nonbinding commitment.

In the language of international negotiations, binding results of negotiation are agreements and treaties (these are legally binding). Nonbinding results are UN-type resolutions, declarations, and agreed press communiqués. (These are not legally binding.) Moreover, according to Kaufmann, an agreement can be binding to one party to a negotiation, but not to another. For example, a decision that is an outcome of a negotiation could be binding for an international secretariat, but nonbinding for governments.[7]

It need not follow, however, that there must be such things as nonbinding commitments. Instead, the distinction in negotiation between these two types of commitments relates to the discussion at the end of section 1.1, where we saw that commitments can be binding in several ways. These ways are primarily characterized by the sanctions attached. So in the case of binding versus nonbinding agreements in negotiation, there are two different commitment sets, with a different type of bond for each set. One has a legal sanction, the other does not. But clearly these two types of commitment differ also in their possibilities and techniques of retraction.

It would not make sense within the framework of the analysis of commitment introduced in chapter 1 to say that a commitment is nonbinding. But it makes perfectly good sense to say that a commitment is *legally* nonbinding. Thus the language of binding and nonbinding results in negotiation dialogue is perfectly comprehensible once you understand that, in this type of case, you have two different types of commitment sets, each with a different type of bond, different sanctions, different possibilities of retraction. Even a UN-type resolution with no legal standing can be a commitment (and, therefore, binding) for those who have signed it, provided some sanction (like disapproval of the other parties to the resolution) is attached to it.

Notice that different types of infractions go with different commitment sets. For instance, a treaty can be broken, but a resolution can only be ignored or laid aside. It may be interesting to recall in this connection that failures to live up to a commitment in dialogue have already been divided into two types, corresponding to the two sanction sets set out in section 1.2. One kind of failure is the violation of a rule of dialogue—this we called a "fallacy." The other is the failure to do well in dialogue. This kind of shortcoming does not involve breaking a rule of

Table 2.3   Ways of Losing Commitments (Propositional or Other)

A. By getting out of a social position (these are *cancellations* or *retractions*):

  A.I By breaking off, or getting out of, a relationship, e.g., resigning from office.

  A.II By leaving a group, institution, etc., e.g., tearing up one's membership card in public.

B. By the subject's own action:

  B.I By a (direct or indirect) speech act:

   B.I.1 In dialogue:

    (a) by a speech act that *fulfills* the commitment, e.g., by defending a challenged proposition (i.e., by supporting it with arguments), or by giving a direct answer to a question, or by challenging the other party's thesis;

    (b) by a speech act of *retraction.*

   B.I.2 Not in dialogue:

    (a) by a speech act that fulfills the commitment, e.g., by passing on certain information, as promised;

    (b) by a speech act of retraction.

  B.II Other actions by the subject:

    (a) living up to a commitment until it has lapsed, thus having *maintained* or even *fulfilled* it;

    (b) getting a *cancellation*, e.g., by inaction until the commitment lapses.

C. By the actions of others (these are *cancellations*):

  C.I By a (direct or indirect) speech act:

   C.I.1 In dialogue, e.g., by getting a point conceded (so that no further defense is called for).

   C.I.2 Not in dialogue, e.g., by getting released from a promise.

  C.II Other actions by others.

the dialogue, and we call it a "blunder" or a "flaw," that is, an infraction of *good* dialogue.

It may also be interesting to note that in persuasion dialogue parallel to Kaufmann's case, a proposition can be binding for one party in a different way than it is binding for the other. One party, who has put forward a particular proposition in a dialogue, may be committed to defending it, whereas another party, who has merely conceded or granted it, is only committed to refraining from critizing that proposition.

To sum up this section, table 2.3 represents the ways of losing commitments comparable to the ways of incurring commitments given in table 2.1.

2.3 Relations between Commitments

In this section, we shall examine three ways in which commitments in a subject's agenda can be related: *implication, specification,* and *priority.*

Suppose that Q and Q' are (objects of) commitment, that is, sets of partial strategies (starting at a certain time t) for a subject, X. Let it be the case that for each time $t' \geq t$, history of the world $j_{t'}$ and strategy $q_{t'}$ in Q there is, for each deed d in the set $q_{t'}(j_{t'})$, a strategy $q'_{t'}$ in Q' such that d is an element of $q'_{t'}(j_{t'})$, that is, such that $q'_{t'}$ assigns the same deed (d), for X, to $j_{t'}$. We shall then say that the commitment Q *implies* the commitment Q'. If X acts according to Q, he cannot help but act according to Q' as well (even though X may be quite unaware of this). (See also the appendix.)

Note that whether one commitment implies another depends on what histories of the world are deemed possible. For instance, if we exclude from our realm of possibilities any course of events in which a green salad is prepared without washing the salad, commitment to preparing the salad would imply commitment to washing it. But otherwise, it need not. Certainly, cooking a dinner would imply preparing food. So, if Krister is committed to cooking a Christmas dinner, this implies a commitment to preparing food. Again, if he is committed to preparing a specific menu, comprising green salad among other dishes, this would, normally, imply a commitment to washing the salad. The same relation occurs among propositional commitments. Thus, in most dialogue games a commitment to (defending) a conjunction, if challenged, implies commitments to each conjunct, and a commitment to a universal proposition implies commitments to all of its instances.

It is tempting to conclude, on the basis of the examples adduced, that whoever is committed to Q is thereby committed to every commitment implied by Q. But should we accept that for all cases? The question is whether the following argument schema is generally valid:

(*) Q implies Q'
      X is committed to Q
      _____
      Therefore X is committed to Q'

Thus Krister being committed to cooking the Christmas dinner, would be committed to preparing the food, and so on. Indeed, the conclusion sounds innocuous in this particular case, but sometimes it may seem strained. For instance, Krister's commitment to cooking the Christmas dinner may, under circumstances, imply a commitment to go to a shop in Pakuranga, at the other end of town, since all the neighborhood shops closed up early.[8] Suppose Krister to be unaware of this when he promises to cook the dinner. Would we say that he has promised (by implication) to go to the distant shop? Would we count going to that shop as one of Krister's commitments, on a par with that of cooking the dinner? Clearly, it depends on how we use the term *commitment,* and the issue could be settled either way by a stipulative decision. But, since there seems to be a distinction to be made between the two types of commitment, we should not blur that distinction from the outset by a blanket acceptance of schema (*). We should refrain from inferring commitments from other commitments in this fast and easy way.[9]

The following, revised version of (*) seems unobjectionable:

(**) Q implies Q'
      X is (in some way) committed to Q
      _____
      X is at least implicitly committed to Q'
      (X got Q' as a subcommitment)

Here two types of commitment are distinguished: full (or explicit) commitment and a kind of implicit commitment, which we shall call *subcommitment.*[10] In the premise commitment can be of either type, but one can conclude to a subcommitment only. Another way to salvage some of the applications of (*), would be to put an immediacy condition on the first premise, reading it as "Q immediately implies Q'." But this presupposes an explication of immediacy.[11] Perhaps it will be more perspicuous to stick to (**) and add conditions under which we may from a subcommitment again conclude to a full commitment.[12]

Each commitment implies many others. Consequently, once a commitment has been incurred, one has acquired many subcommitments as well. Some of these subcommitments are of little interest in a particular case, like Krister's subcommitment to prepare food. But in some cases, where the realm of possibilities (set of possible histories of the world) is duly restricted, the ways to fulfill a certain commitment may narrow down, and more interesting or surprising subcommitments may arise for consideration, such as Krister's subcommitment to go to the distant shop.

The relation of implication between commitments is essentially a static one. Given X's commitment Q, his subcommitments are already there, and no concept of development or change is involved thus far. However, the turning of subcommitments into commitments is a dynamic process. It can be one of the results of dialogue as in case 2.4, section 2.1, where George may be made aware of certain subcommitments implied by his commitment to socialism, and, consequently, be made to accept them as explicit commitments.

The relation of *specification*, on the other hand, is dynamic from the start. A general commitment to cook a Christmas dinner would not commit one to any specific one among several suitable menus. So a few days before Christmas there are still many partial strategies available. But suppose that, later on, a menu has been fixed and menu cards have been written out, foodstuffs bought, and so on. These new data, together with the general commitment to cook the dinner, make one incur the more specific commitments involved in preparing this specific menu. Thus we say that a commitment Q (starting at t) is a *specification* of a more general commitment Q' (starting at $t' < t$) whenever Q is incurred on the basis of the subject's original commitment Q' and his perception of the history of the world up to t (j_t).[13] This way of incurring new commitments can be combined with any of the ways of incurring commitments listed in table 2.1 (section 2.1). Note that especially a subject's own actions many narrow down a range of options and thus lead to more specific commitments. Typically, the specific commitment is related to the general one as a commitment to a specific means is related to a commitment to further certain ends.

There are several ways in which the relation of specification holds between propositional commitments in dialogue. Thus a commitment to defending a disjunction may narrow down, in the course of dialogue, to a commitment to a specific disjunct, and a commitment to an existential proposition may narrow down to a commitment to a specific instance.

During dialogue, your commitment can become more and more specific. For example, Bob might declare that he is committed to equality between the sexes. But under critical questioning by Marcia, it may become much clearer exactly what Bob's commitment amounts to on this question. Also, George (case 2.4) may be brought, in dialogue, to specify his commitment to socialism. That is, he may be brought to admit more than what his original commitment to socialism actually implies. In this case the specific commitments would be related to the general one as commitments to a concrete implementation are related to a commitment to a global perspective or point of view.[14]

When the rules of dialogue are spelled out in the opening stages of a discussion, your commitment tends to be made more specific as well, for when precise rules of argument are spelled out, the means you can use to defend your point of view are narrowed down.

Another feature of many specifications of commitment is that they bring one to a more detailed level of action description. Thus as one's general commitment to cook a dinner narrows down, one may move from a level where menus are considered to a level of recipes, and further on to a level of foodstuff-modifying techniques, and even to a level of particular bodily movements. The importance of such specification levels for the theory of action was pointed out by Segerberg.[15] It is instructive to compare his notion of a *routine* with the notion of a partial strategy (derived from Hamblin's) used here. According to Segerberg, "a routine is a procedure which in principle can be carried out by somebody."[16] We already exploited his culinary example:

> To compose a menu is to select a routine which, if run under appropriate circumstances, will result in a meal. A recipe is a routine which, if run under appropriate circumstances will result in a prepared dish or component of a dish. A food stuff modifying technique is a routine which, if run under appropriate circumstances, will modify food stuffs in a certain way.[17]

Segerberg then points out the different ways routines can be combined and their organization into different levels:

> One important feature of routines is that they can be combined, simultaneously or sequentially. Routines which are in a certain sense independent can be run at the same time; but, more importantly, often they can be run in sequence, one after the other. Thus a complicated routine, like putting on a big dinner, is made up of a great number of simpler routines, just as a house is made up of a great number of units of building material (bricks, beams, nails, etc.). As our culinary example makes clear, routines depend on perspective. At the level of menus, recipes of individual dishes are routines. At the level of recipes, techniques for food stuff modification are routines. At the level of those techniques, certain bodily movements are routines.[18]

We may look upon a given routine from two sides. From one side it is itself a partial strategy to reach some end, from the other side it is a

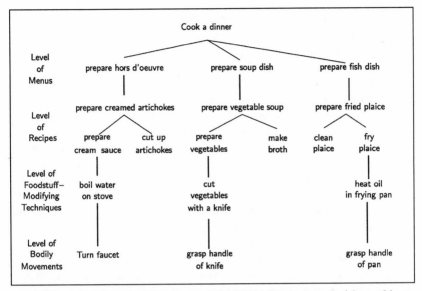

Figure 2.1   This tree structure elucidates Segerberg's idea of how routines are organized on different levels

basic building block (a basic action or deed) in the construction of a higher level strategy. Thus a technique for foodstuff modification, like a certain way of washing the salad is both itself a type of action composed of certain bodily movements, and a component basic action (deed) in the context of a recipe. In this sense a routine links more general commitments to more specific ones. For instance, the routine of washing salad links the commitment to preparing a salad to commitments to perform certain bodily movements. Similarly, a recipe for creamed artichokes links the general commitment to cook a dinner to specific commitments to apply certain foodstuff-modifying techniques.

The tree structure shown in figure 2.1 will elucidate Segerberg's idea of how routines are organized on different levels.

Of course figure 2.1 could be filled out in much more detail. There is no upper limit to the number of nodes one might want to add to the tree. Notice that in each branch of the tree, there are different levels. Cooking a dinner is a general commitment. One step in carrying out that commitment might be to prepare a hors d'oeuvre, and for this one may choose a recipe for a creamed-artichokes dish. Following this recipe may call for a sequence of specific actions (a routine). Part of this routine (what we may call a *subroutine*) might be preparing the cream sauce. And, in turn, one step in that subroutine might be adding a certain quantity of hot water. Notice that commitment to a routine would, according to the terminology of this section, be said to *imply* a commitment to its subroutines and to the steps out of which these are composed. Thus on each level of figure 2.1, commitment to the whole implies commitment to the parts. Between levels, however, the relation is not implication but specification. Commitment to cooking a dinner specifies to a commitment to preparing an hors d'oeuvre, only after a choice of an outline of a menu. Commitment to preparing an hors d'oeuvre, again, specifies to a commitment to preparing the cream sauce only after one has settled on the artichokes recipe, and so on. As we go down the tree the commitments become more and more specific. For example, in order to get hot water, one may become committed to boiling water on the stove, and this may lead to a commitment to certain very specific hand movements as one turns the faucet and so forth.

Since commitments to actions are naturally connected with routines that are ordered, by specification, from the more general to the more specific, it also makes sense to speak of commitments that are more general or more specific, but that are not specifications (or implications) *one* of the *other*. For example, the commitment to move the knife to cut up the vegetables is more specific than the commitment to prepare the fish (and, on the tree, it occurs at a lower level). But these two commitments are not related by specification or implication. So it is possible to say that one commitment is more general or abstract than another, without saying that the second commitment is a specification or implication of the first.

A third relationship between commitments arises when one commitment is given *priority* over another. In terms of sanctions: one commitment is placed in a sanction set with a more severe sanction. Typically, this would happen when commitments tend to conflict. On a very general level, however, the stating of a priority does not, in itself, mean that there is a conflict between the two commitments. For example, I might say that for me, philosophy has priority over volleyball. I can just sit in my chair and say that, without being committed to specific actions or having any specific conflict of courses of action arise. Yet with specific actions, a situation may arise where one action is more urgent than another. If the volleyball team urgently needs a player to fill in at short notice, I may take that urgency into account in deciding on a specific action this afternoon.

The following case combines all three ways of ordering a subject's agenda.

CASE 2.8   Professor G. is committed to teaching on the subject of informal fallacies. Accordingly, arrangements have been made for
him to give a lecture on this subject in Leiden on a certain
Friday at 11:00 A.M., and he has agreed to give this lecture at
that time. Professor G. is in Wassenaar at 10:00 A.M., on the
Friday in question, and there are only two ways that he can
get to Leiden in time, by bicycle or by bus. Professor G. starts
to bicycle down the Maaldrift Road, along his usual route to
Leiden. By 10:15, it is too late for him to bike back to
Wassenaar and catch the bus that would get him to the University of Leiden at 11:00 A.M., where his lecture is to be
held. He is now, as we would say, *committed* to continuing by
bicycle.
　　　　It is an extremely windy day on this Friday, and as
Professor G. rounds a corner on the Maaldrift, he sees a large
tree that has been blown over by the wind and has fallen
across a field by the road. He also sees a police officer who
signals him to stop and then points at another large tree at
the side of the road which is dangerously swaying in the wind
in such a way that it could easily fall over, onto the road.
There are canals at both edges of the road, so the only way to
get to Leiden in time, known to Professor G., would be to
bicycle past the tree. Now the question becomes one of
whether Professor G. is still committed to bicycling down the
Maaldrift on his route to Leiden. This is a question, because
G. is committed to preserving his life and health, as well as to
giving the lecture at 11:00 A.M. in Leiden. And the problem is
that the swaying tree could very well be a threat to G.'s life
and health, as the police officer has pointed out.

　　In case 2.8, Professor G. is confronted with a problem, for
whether he opts to cycle past the leaning tree or to turn around and go
back down the Maaldrift to Wassenaar, he fails to fulfill one of his
commitments.
　　In case 2.8, the commitment to the preservation of life is, in one
way at least, a prior or overriding commitment. For a significant risk of
loss of life would override the commitment to give the lecture, and
thereby cancel the latter commitment, in the sense outlined in section
2.2. On the other hand, if the threat to life is judged by Professor G. not
to be significant enough to cancel the commitment to give the lecture,
then G. is committed to cycling past the tree. Here it is up to G. to

weigh the strength of his commitments against the possible consequences of the actions required to carry them out and to arrive at a conclusion on where the weight of his commitment should lie.

Note that in case 2.8 Professor G. starts out with a general commitment to teaching on the subject of informal fallacies. It is through this general commitment that he is led to commit himself to the specific action of giving a lecture on the informal fallacies in Leiden on a particular Friday at 11:00 A.M. This, in turn, leads to other, even more specific commitments, like his commitment to continuing to ride down the Maaldrift on his bicycle at 10:15. The problem for Professor G., when he confronted the situation of the leaning tree, arose through the conflict between two of his commitments, relative to this specific situation. At any rate, it seems important that some commitments are more general and abstract for a subject, whereas others are much more specific and directly tied to particular situations and deeds for that subject.

Normally, Professor G. has a standard way of going to Leiden on his bicycle. This process is a regular sequence of actions that G. has learned to carry out as a matter of routine. He takes the elevator down to the bicycle shed in the basement, unlocks the lock on his bicycle, opens the basement door, and sets out by getting on his bike. Normally G. does not need to think very much about all these actions. But each of them represents a subcommitment, and the whole sequence of subcommitments could be spelled out in an ordered sequence of steps in a chain of routines. This whole sequence could be written out as a list, and it would constitute an account of a strategy of G. for carrying out his commitment to give his lecture in Leiden. As the strategy unfolds in time, as individual deeds in it are carried out by G., specific actions described by the list become commitments of G., relative to his initial commitment of giving the lecture. Accordingly, we can recognize a hierarchy of commitments. Some commitments are initially set or undertaken, in the ways described above in section 2.1, and other commitments are then incurred along the way, so to speak, as partial strategies for realizing these initial commitments adopted by the subject.

Thus a particular commitment brings with it a whole sequence of other commitments, all related to an item in a subject's agenda. But there may be other items in a subject's agenda as well. For example, Professor G.'s commitment to riding past the swaying tree arises (in the context of a particular strategy) from his commitment to giving the lecture in Leiden. But G.'s commitment to self-preservation may be a separate commitment from either of these other two. In fact, his strategies for self-preservation may even appear to run contrary to the hierarchical sequence of commitments formed by these other two commitments and their related partial strategies.

These two commitments of giving the lecture and self-preservation, although they may appear independent at first sight, are also related to each other in a way. For if, at any point, these two commitments appear to conflict—if one appears to negate or undermine the realization of the other—the resulting quandary may force an assessment of priorities of commitments, and questions of risk and likelihood will enter the picture as well. Clearly, self-preservation is a commitment that generally has a high priority, but if the risk is judged to be minimal enough, other commitments can take priority over it.

Case 2.8 also reveals the dynamic nature of commitment, because at different moments of time, certain partial strategies had to be cancelled out. Initially, there was a bicycle strategy available to Professor G. and also a bus strategy. At that point, he could have changed his mind and tried the bus strategy. But once he was on the Maaldrift at 10:15, it was too late to go back and take the bus. He was, at that time, committed to the bicycle strategy, and the bus strategy was cancelled out.

Our view of commitment is a dynamic one, because partial strategies, by their nature, have to be carried out by a particular date. Moreover, your commitment set can change with each action, and partial strategies can disappear at certain moments. There may be choices of (sub)routines that branch out toward the subject's future, but as in the case of G., these choices of (sub)routines may narrow down as a routine is run.

Significant problems of deliberation can arise when a particular situation poses a clash or conflict arising from two different (global) commitments. With certain types of very general commitments, you can expect a clash to arise. For example, consider someone who is strongly committed to both his family and his job. However, at the general or global level, there is no conflict. It is in a particular situation requiring action that such clashes manifest themselves, leading to quandaries. Quandaries do arise because multiple commitments, at the general level, are connected (through routines) to specific commitments that clash.

A case of directly clashing commitments is exhibited by the situation of Antigone.

CASE 2.9   Antigone's brother, Polyneices, was slain as he assaulted Thebes, his native city. According to her family obligations, based on divine law, she was bound to bury Polyneices. But, as a citizen of Thebes, she was also bound to obey orders from the city's king. The king ordered that no one was to bury Polyneices.

In this case, Antigone had two general commitments, one to abide by the laws of the gods, and one to obey the king's orders. As such, the two commitments (*qua* general commitments) did not clash, although they had the potential to clash. However, in the specific situation of the king's denying her brother a proper burial, Antigone was put in the tragic position of being unable to fulfill both commitments. Deciding to give priority to divine law, Antigone strew dust and poured a drink offering on the body of her brother and was executed for this act.

Thus the different ways of ordering commitment provide a background against which the subject of clashes of commitments can begin to be better understood. In the next section, we turn to a fuller consideration of this subject.

2.4. Clashing Commitments and Inconsistency

A person confronted with clashing commitments is somehow trapped. Clearly he has taken on too many commitments. But he may have gotten into this situation by a natural course of events, without any spot on which to lay a finger and say: "That's where you went wrong." Also, he may be hard pressed for an assignment of priorities to his commitments that would allow him to disregard or retract some of them. In these respects he may be compared to a victim of Socratic *elenchus,* caught in the act of contradicting himself.

In this section we shall first define clashing commitments in terms of clashing partial strategies. Next, we shall study clashes of propositional commitments in dialogue, primarily clashes between commitments to mutually inconsistent propositions such as P and *not-P.*

Let q_1 and q_2 be partial strategies for X. We shall say that q_1 and q_2 *clash* at a certain moment of time t, and given a particular course of events j_t, if and only if there is no deed for X that both strategies assign to j_t (i.e., if and only if the intersection of $q_1(j_t)$ and $q_2(j_t)$ is empty). Similarly for more than two strategies: q_1, q_2, q_3, . . . (In definitions such as the preceding we assume that j_t is in the common part of the domains of definition of the strategies, i.e., time t must be within the period of time over which the strategies are operative, and j_t must not be a course of events that is impossible, or ruled out beforehand. See also the appendix.)

Take, for instance, the case of Professor G. (case 2.8). Let q_1 be the bus strategy and q_2 the bicycle strategy. Suppose that Professor G. stays at home until time t: this course of events constitutes j_t. Suppose further that at time t it is no longer possible to postpone a decision between the two strategies. Then q_1 and q_2 clash at t, given j_t.

As may be clear from the example, a person's partial strategies can clash without there being any clash among his or her commitments. Commitments *clash*, we shall say, when any choice of partial strategies in accordance with these commitments confronts the subject with clashing strategies. Formally, let Q_1 and Q_2 be commitments of X, that is, sets of partial strategies for X. Let j_t be some course of events belonging to the common domain of the strategies in Q_1 and in Q_2. Then Q_1 and Q_2 clash at time t, given j_t, if and only if for every pair q_1, q_2, where q_1 is an element of Q_1 and q_2 is an element of Q_2, q_1 and q_2 clash at t, given j_t. Similarly, for more than two commitments: Q_1, Q_2, Q_3, . . .

Turn to the case of Professor G. again for an example. As he is hesitating in front of the swaying tree, his commitment to give the lecture clashes with his commitment to the preservation of life, assuming that a decision to cycle past the tree can no longer be postponed. But, according to our definition, we would not say that these commitments clash irrespective of this particular situation. Similarly, in the case of Antigone (case 2.9), we wouldn't say that her commitments to divine law and to the laws of the state clash *simpliciter*, but only that they clash at a particular time, given the course of events up to that time.

Yet, even before the king gave out his particular order that made Antigone's commitments clash, there was, one might say, a certain tension between her commitments. We need other terms, then, to describe a set of commitments that do not (or not yet) actually clash, but that will or may clash given certain further developments. If there is at least one possible history of the world in which every commitment of certain class is fulfilled, we shall say that these commitments are *compatible*, otherwise that they are *incompatible*. Thus, Professor G.'s commitment to give the lecture is compatible with his commitment to the preservation of his life. There wouldn't have been a clash of commitments if the swaying tree hadn't been there. Similarly, Antigone's commitments are compatible, because they mightn't have clashed, but for the king's particular order. On the other hand, if Professor G. were also committed to giving a lecture in Amsterdam, at the same time as the one in Leiden, he would be faced with incompatible commitments.

Clearly compatible commitments may lead to a clash all the same. We need a term for commitments that are safe in this respect. Let us say that the commitments of a certain class are *consonant*, if they will in no event yield a clash, otherwise, if there is some risk of a clash, we shall say they are *inconsonant*. Thus Professor G.'s commitments, as well as

Antigone's, though compatible, are still inconsonant. It should be noted that these notions (just like the notion of implication between commitments), are always to be understood against a background of courses of events that are deemed possible. Commitments that are consonant with respect to a restricted class of possible courses of events need not be so if more possibilities are taken into consideration. (The appendix to this book spells out the notions of compatibility and of consonance within the framework of *action-state semantics.*)

If a person's commitments clash in a given situation, we may say that they pose a *quandary,* or a *prima facie quandary* at least. A quandary can often be resolved by priority considerations. Among these considerations we may distinguish those that take the particular situation into account (as in Professor G.'s case) from those of a more general or abstract nature, such as 'safety first,' or 'divine laws have precedence over human laws.' These latter considerations can be represented by the partial ordering of the sanction sets in a person's agenda. Some quandaries posed by, say, two commitments from distinct sanction sets can then be resolved by giving precedence to the commitment in the sanction set that ranks highest in this ordering, that is, the commitment associated with the severest sanction. If such global priority considerations suffice to resolve a quandary we shall speak of a *spurious quandary,* as opposed to *real quandaries* that cannot be resolved in this way. Note that even with a spurious quandary there is a real clash of commitments.

For an instance of a spurious quandary turn to the case where John is committed to taking out the garbage, but also to taking his wife to the hospital in case of an emergency (case 1.1). These commitments are compatible, but inconsonant. A clash occurs as the emergency arrives before the garbage is taken out. This poses a *prima facie* quandary for John. But we may suppose that John has set his priorities in such a way that the quandary is spurious.

Even a real quandary may be resolved. Let us assume that Professor G., in front of the tree, is faced by a real quandary. Commitment to the preservation of life when confronted with small risks is not, in his agenda, ranked higher than commitment to giving the lecture, nor are those commitments ranked the other way around. He can, nevertheless, assign or reassign priorities to his commitments in the light of the particular situation in which they clash. In this way he may resolve his quandary, but this, one might say, involves a change or refinement of his agenda.

Let us now turn to propositional commitment and clashes between commitments in dialogue. In section 1.2 we distinguished two sanction sets for each party X participating in rule-governed dialogue: $C_1(X)$ and $C_2(X)$. Actions running counter to commitments in $C_1(X)$ are infractions of some dialogue rule. These we decided to call "fallacies." Actions running counter to commitments in $C_2(X)$ constitute bad strategy within dialogue. These may be called mere "weaknesses," "blunders," or "flaws" if strong terms are needed. We may assume that commitments in $C_1(X)$ always take priority over those in $C_2(X)$. (It may even be argued that courses of events in which a fallacy is committed fall wholly outside of the scope of applicability of the commitments in $C_2(X)$, and that, therefore, clashes between these two types of commitment are impossible.) Consequently, if a quandary arises from a combination of commitments of these two classes, whereas the $C_1(X)$ commitments by themselves do not clash, it must be a *spurious* quandary.

For instance, suppose that the rules of a certain type of dialogue stipulate that a party X should answer a certain question in a straightforward manner, but that each possible answer would be very detrimental to X's position in the dialogue, so that good strategy would dictate silence on the issue. Then X should nevertheless answer the question, since, according to the assumed priority of $C_1(X)$ over $C_2(X)$, it is always better to blunder than to commit a fallacy.

Next, we have to consider clashes of commitments within each of the two classes $C_1(X)$ and $C_2(X)$. Such a clash would pose a real quandary. First, consider $C_2(X)$. Suppose X is committed to the defense of two contradictory, or at least contrary, propositions P and R. $C_2(X)$ would then contain the commitments $Q_2(P, X)$ and $Q_2(R, X)$; that is, X is to put forward an optimal defense for both of the two propositions. This, however, X cannot do, since each argument in favor of P would damage the defense of R and vice versa. The defenses X puts forward cannot both be optimal. Hence the commitments in $C_2(X)$ are incompatible and will lead to a clash at some point. This is probably a type of quandary we shall have to live with in serious dialogue: it is not always possible to act optimally with respect to all one's preceding utterances in a dialogue.

One could suggest that, in order to preserve the possibility of optimal behavior, some dialectical rule should stipulate that the disputants avoid getting committed to inconsistent propositions: "Be consistent!" (Inconsistency would be a fallacy.) But if the advice is to be practicable it must be obvious, or easily checked, whether a position is inconsistent. And that is simply not the case.[19] Consider, for instance, the well-known *Barber Pseudoparadox:*

CASE 2.10 (B) In a certain village there lives a barber who shaves exactly those inhabitants of the village who do not shave themselves.

Does the barber shave himself? He/she does if and only if he/she
doesn't. Proposition (B) is self-contradictory. (It is not a paradox, since
the village in question does not exist.) The inconsistency in such riddles
is not "obvious," otherwise they would be no fun.

Perhaps one might say that in cases like (B) it is easily checked
whether there is an inconsistency. So a viable dialectics could ban (B) and
its cognates. If so, change the example to any desired degree of complexity. Frege's system in *Grundgesetze der Arithmetik* was shown to be inconsistent by Russell (Russell's paradox). Certainly this was not obvious,
nor was Frege's system easily checked for consistency. For rich languages
(predicate logic and beyond) consistency is an undecidable concept (i.e.,
no mechanical test can exist for it) and therefore totally unsuitable for
figuring in the formulation of dialectical rules.

It may be noted that, traditionally, inconsistency is seldom
counted among the fallacies. Exceptions are Gautama in the *Nyaya
Sutra*,[20] Mackie,[21] Johnson and Blair,[22] and Rescher.[23] But Rescher rejects a simple characterization of inconsistency as a fallacy. Mackie and
Johnson and Blair do not discuss dialectical rules, and consequently
cannot draw a dialectical distinction between 'blunder' and 'fallacy.' If
their treatments were put in dialectical terms, inconsistency might, with
these authors, come out as a blunder rather than a fallacy.[24] Thus
tradition seems to put 'inconsistency' apart from the subject of fallacy.
This is not surprising, for one of the aims of dialectic is to unearth
hidden inconsistencies. And how could this be done if inconsistencies
couldn't be expressed within the dialogue? So we cannot expect the
rules to proscribe all inconsistencies. For instance, in case 2.4, George
and Bob may start a discussion. As the discussion gets on, it may
become clear to both Bob and George that certain Socialist tenets to
which George is deeply committed do indeed conflict with George's
uttered position. These dark-side[25] commitments of George may come
to the light in the course of, and as a consequence of, the discussion.
Finally, George may have to withdraw his uttered proposal, or modify
his commitment to socialism. Yet all the time George and Bob could be
arguing without committing any fallacy.

We may conclude that a dialectical rule stipulating consistency
would be both undesirable and impracticable. There is, however, another
way to restore the possibility of choosing an optimal strategy and thus
avoid quandaries with respect to $C_2(X)$. That is to give up to the idea of
separate commitments connected with different propositions and replace
them by just one commitment: choose an optimal strategy! In this way a
disputant that fails with respect to the defense of one of his assertions

may still be fulfilling his unique commitment in $C_2(X)$. Assuming that the quality of a performance is measured by a finite range of values,[26] there will always be some optimal strategy.

Finally, we have to consider quandaries posed by clashes of commitments within $C_1(X)$. Such a quandary would mean that X is confronted with conflicting rules of dialogue. This is certainly something we wish to avoid. When formulating a dialectical system one should take care that such situations are excluded, at least as long as no party commits a fallacy. It is, therefore, required that $C_1(X)$ be a consonant set of commitments (as long as the parties stick to the rules). This *postulate of consonance* should hold for each party X. Perhaps one may require a dialectical system to comply with an even sharper postulate of consonance, that is, one against a wider background of possible courses of events, including fallacious moves. Ideally there should be some higher order rules that allow one to move legally even after fallacies have been committed. For instance, to avoid quandaries one could have a rule to the effect that a fallacy should be pointed out as soon as it is committed and that the responsible party should in such a case withdraw its last move and substitute a legal one. Thus one would always have a legal move at his or her disposal (legal at the level of these higher order rules).[27]

It is instructive to compare our postulates of consonance with Hamblin's description of four "kinds of quandary-freedom" a set of imperatives may possess.[28] Translated to quandaries that arise from $C_1(X)$-commitments in dialogues, we get the following list of degrees of quandary freedom a set of dialogue rules may guarantee (we have added 2a):

1. *Absolute Quandary Freedom:* The rules of dialogue do not allow quandaries to arise under any circumstances. This is a strong postulate of consonance (against a wide background of possible courses of events). Of course one cannot *stipulate* quandary freedom in the rules. The rules must be carefully formulated (and, if necessary, assigned priorities) in order to provide a legal (nonfallacious) act for each disputant in every possible situation (even if fallacies are essential for getting into that situation).

2. *Legislative Quandary Freedom:*
   a. *Personal:* As long as a party acts legally (does not commit any fallacy) this party will never be put in a quandary (even if the other party commits fallacies). A somewhat weaker consonance postulate.

b. *Collective:* If all parties act legally (avoid fallacies), no quandaries will arise at all. This is the first postulate of consonance for $C_1(X)$ (for each party X) formulated above. It is weaker than 2a.

3. *Strategic Quandary Freedom:* For each party there is at least one legal strategy that will keep this party out of quandaries. Somewhat stronger than mere compatibility.

4. *Minimal Quandary Freedom:* It is possible for all parties to act legally and in such a way that no quandaries will arise at all. This is merely compatibility.

It seems desirable for the rules of a system of dialectics to guarantee a high degree of quandary freedom with respect to commitments in $C_1(X)$. This degree should be one corresponding to a consonance postulate, certainly 2b, but preferably 2a or 1. We do not want quandaries, because fallacies run counter to the ends of the dialogue (ends the rules should help us to achieve), and quandaries leave no option but to commit a fallacy.

Since we cannot stipulate consistency, we must take care that the rules of dialogue can handle commitments to inconsistent positions without posing a quandary with respect to $C_1(X)$. Above we argued that complex or hidden inconsistencies cannot be ruled out in good dialogue. But even commitment to P and to *not-P* (or to *P-and-not-P*) must not be ruled out. First, this is the type of position to which a position containing a hidden inconsistency is reduced in dialogue. A party thus committed may suffer a loss immediately after, or may be forced to retract some statement, but the position itself should not be declared illegal. Second, such a position could even be tenable in at least some systems of dialectic (e.g., minimal dialectics[29]). Third, an explicit contradiction *(P-and-not-P)* could be used as a provocative thesis, that is, a thesis not reflecting the position of its proponent, but the proponent's point of view that its adversary should, given its position, accept this thesis.[30] A provocative thesis *P-and-not-P* is equivalent to a claim that the position of the other party is inconsistent. It is essential that such claims be admitted in dialogues. Sometimes a particular dialectical constant *(absurdum, falsum)* is used for this purpose. Thus Russell, confronting Frege as the author of the *Grundgesetze,* may be called a proponent of the absurd.

A provocative thesis need not be absurd or self-contradictory. Even if it is not, it may contradict the position of its proponent. Take Haddock's conclusion as an example:

CASE 2.11 Thomson and Thompson doubt whether Captain Haddock did accurately calculate the ship's position. They show the captain some improved calculations of their own. Haddock: "You are right . . . I have made a mistake. Gentlemen, please take off your hats . . . " [takes off cap, and stands in prayer for quite some time]. [. . .] Thomson: "But Captain, tell us what you mean. . . . " Haddock: "I mean, gentlemen, that according to your calculations we are now standing inside Westminster Abbey!"[31]

Haddock's provocative thesis, confronting Thomson and Thompson in their capacity as calculators, determines the ship's position as inside Westminster Abbey. This is what the captain should defend, if challenged, starting from the other party's concessions, in this case the improved calculations made by Thomson and Thompson. Obviously, Haddock himself does not hold the ship to be in that position.

Let us return to quandaries. We want, on the one hand, the rules of a dialectical system to guarantee at least collective legislative quandary freedom (with respect to commitments in the first sanction set). On the other hand, we want to admit explicit inconsistencies as legal positions in dialogue. The consequence is that the dialecticians should take care that situations in which a party is committed both to P and to not-P do not lead to quandaries. If a party is to defend both P and not-P one would expect the rules to stipulate which defense takes preference. This can be done quite simply by stipulating that one should defend first whatever statement is challenged last. In general, if more than one defense obligation is allowed to be in force at one time, these obligations should be ordered.[32]

Sometimes inconsistent statements are so mutually isolated that they cannot interfere one with the other. For instance, in certain systems of formal dialectic a concession P in one chain of arguments does not interfere with another concession not-P, if the latter should take place in a different chain of arguments.[33] In such a case there is no fallacy, no blunder, no quandary. Perhaps one should say there is no real inconsistency.

Another case, where the isolation is less evident, is provided by the preface paradox:[34]

CASE 2.12 An author has completed a learned work containing propositions S_1, through S_m. He adds a preface containing the statement *(P):* "In view of human fallibility and the complexity of the present work, there is no doubt that I must have erred somewhere. Consequently, not all assertions that follow can be correct, however much I tried to avoid error." Clearly P implies that S_1, through S_m cannot all be true (given that S_1, through S_m are the assertions that follow[35]). Let S be the conjunction of S_1, through S_m. Then P implies that not-S. The book *cum* preface is, therefore, inconsistent. What is the paradox? On the one hand the author displays a *reasonable* modesty. After all, there may be very good reasons to hold P. On the other hand the author's position is obviously inconsistent and for that reason often deemed *unreasonable*.

The preface paradox is usually discussed from the point of view of reasonable belief or acceptance.[36] From the point of view of dialogue all we can say is that the author's position is weak. He can be refuted. Yet, from this point of view, it can be reasonable to be in a refutable position.[37] However, it may also be possible to isolate P from S by claiming that here we have two different fields or areas of discussion (epistemology and whatever the book itself is about). P and S would then no longer interfere with each other, at least not without more ado.

A final example of presumed isolation is the following:

CASE 2.13 A social worker in a regional hospital has to deal with patients from all walks of life. Two patients, both seriously ill, are very upset by the prospect of death. It is urgent that the social worker should have a word of comfort for each of them. However, in view of their difference in outlook, this cannot be the same word. Discussing death with the first patient she stresses that one may look forward to eternal bliss hereafter. Involved in a dialogue with the second patient she points out that "as long as we are present death is not, and once death is, we are not."[38]

We may assume that both dialogues are free of fallacies and blunders. Since the two statements occur in distinct dialogues, our social worker feels sure they will not lead to a quandary. Unfortunately, the two patients meet shortly after in the hospital's conversation room. They get into a serious discussion on death and afterlife. The social worker happens to walk in, and both parties claim her support. What should she do?

2.5 Problems to Be Solved

We have briefly reviewed some processes by which commitment can be incurred or lost, but many of these processes are yet to be studied in detail. Within dialogue especially the functioning of presuppositions is important as a means by which commitments are incurred. For instance, in asserting a proposition the speaker does not only commit himself to that very proposition but also, indirectly, to its presuppositions. According to Manor, these commitments build up as a speaker progresses through a series of speech acts that together constitute a speech. What exactly the contribution of each speech act is must be determined from the context (taking into account, in particular, those speech acts that went before). Also, she points out that some presuppositions (P-presuppositions) are tied to the sentence expressed in a speech act, whereas others (C-presuppositions) that equally contribute to commitment depend on further features of the speech act, such as gestures.[39] One circumstance that has to be taken into account when determining commitment is whether the sentence expressed occurs in the context of an argument. If so, the speaker will incur commitments to all the various elements (premises, conclusion) of the argument. Van Eemeren and Grootendorst show how unexpressed premises in an argument can also be attributed to a speaker as commitments she is obliged to defend in a critical discussion.[40] Both presuppositions and unexpressed premises represent ways of incurring commitment that are more subtle and complex than the kinds of more simple and clear cases we have emphasized.

Problems of retraction in dialogue are studied further in chapter 4 (esp. section 4.3.3), and the reader should go on to that point, to consider these problems in detail.

Among the relations between commitment we mentioned (viz., implication, specification, priority), specification seems most in need of a detailed analysis, both in order to further the general theory of action and to get a more detailed and realistic view of action in dialogue.

We need practicable tests to check whether proposed sets of dialectical rules are quandary free (in several senses).[41]

The theory of isolated areas of discussion which we mentioned at the end of section 2.4 needs to be developed further in such a way that an adequate assessment of case 2.13 can be made.

2.6 Summary

The ways of incurring commitment are summarized in table 2.1. In some cases, commitments can be incurred simply because of one's relationships or affiliations, but in many cases they are incurred by the actions of oneself or others. In chapters 3 and 4, the concern will be with commitments incurred through different kinds of speech acts in a dialogue where two parties are engaged in argumentation with each other. We use the general phrase *losing commitments,* despite its somewhat awkward sound, because retracting a commitment is not the only way something can cease to be one's commitment. One could live up to it until it has lapsed, or it could simply be cancelled, for example if one failed to live up to it until it lapsed. Table 2.3 sums up the various ways of losing a commitment.

The idea that some commitments are nonretractable is very important, as in the case of Caesar's nonretractable embarkation on a military adventure once he had crossed the Rubicon River. 'Commitment' often means nonretractable commitment, as in the case of Mr. S.'s commitment to the beautiful shape of the diamond, as opposed to having the largest diamond, once he made certain cuts to the rough stone.

We define 'commitment' as a kind of bond, and all commitment is, in a sense, binding. Even so, the same propositions could be morally binding but not legally binding, because (on our analysis) these represent two different bonds. Also, some commitments are more binding than others, at least in the sense that some are much more easily retractable (i.e., the sanction is less severe) than others.

In section 2.3 we studied three relations among commitments. One commitment implies another if the subject cannot help but act according to the implied commitment once he acts according to the primary (nonimplied) commitment. For example, if Krister is committed to cooking a Christmas dinner, he has an implied commitment to preparing food. Subcommitments are implicit commitments derived by implication from explicit commitments.

Implication is a static relation, while the relation of specification is a dynamic relation, as shown by the case of the routines used in cooking a dinner, exhibited in figure 2.1. For example, commitment to cooking a dinner specifies to a commitment to preparing an hors d'oeuvre, but only once a choice of menu has been made. As one goes down the tree in figure 2.1, the commitments become more and more specific. These levels of specification are connected by routines (Segerberg), that are standard kinds of procedures that can be carried out by somebody.

Another kind of relation between commitments is that of priority, which most commonly comes to the fore when commitments conflict. In the case of Professor G., the situation of the leaning tree posed a conflict of commitments between G.'s commitment to teaching on fallacies and his commitment to the preservation of life. This case also reveals the dynamic nature of commitment generally, in problems requiring deliberation.

A case of clashing commitments is the case of Antigone (case 2.9), where, in a specific situation, Antigone is unable to fulfill both commitments. Generally, commitments are said to clash when a choice of partial strategies confronts the subject with clashing strategies (which means that there is no deed available that conforms to every one of these strategies). If a subject's commitments clash in a given situation, we say that they pose a quandary. A real quandary as opposed to a spurious quandary, is one that cannot be resolved by priority considerations alone (set by ranking the sanctions in order of severity).

One type of quandary singled out for attention is that it is not always possible to act optimally with respect to all of one's preceding utterances in a dialogue. This quandary arises because of the impracticability of a dialectical rule that would prescribe consistency. Hence inconsistency (by itself) should not be defined as a fallacy. Any fallacies that arise depend on how one reacts to inconsistency (of oneself or another) once the inconsistency arises or is revealed in the dialogue. It is useful, however, to avoid conflicting rules of dialogue. A system of dialectics should comply with a postulate of consonance, which stipulates (minimally) that if all parties act legally (avoid fallacies), no quandaries with respect to the rules of the system will arise.

3   Dialogues: Types, Goals, and Shifts

In this chapter, we shall investigate how propositional commitments depend upon a context of dialogue. There are many different normative models of a dialogue, each of which has its own distinctive goals and rules. Accordingly, it is possible to distinguish several important, characteristic types of dialogue. Each type of dialogue has different kinds of rules for the management of commitments (section 3.1).

An important feature of this chapter is a case study of a *complex dialogue,* an extended sequence of dialogue where there is a shift from one type of dialogue to another (section 3.2). A complex dialogue is a single speech event, but within the event itself, there is a shift from one type of dialogue to another. It is important to be able to identify these shifts, and we need rules for determining whether such a shift is legitimate or not, and for settling the concomitant shifts of commitment (section 3.3). As we shall see, shifts can be reasonable and licit, but also illicit. Many illicit types of shifts connect with traditional fallacies. Understanding these dialectical shifts helps one to understand why fallacious moves in dialogue may often seem reasonable (section 3.4).

3.1 Types and Goals of Dialogue: A Sketch

A scientific dispute, a parliamentary debate, negotiations on the terms of a surrender, an investigation by a committee, a consultation of one's

Type	Subtypes	Initial Situation	Main Goal	Participant's Aims	Side Benefits
I Persuasion Dialogue (Critical Discussion)	Dispute Formal Discussion Discussion of Proposals	Conflicting Points of View	Resolution of Such Conflicts by Verbal Means	Persuade the Other(s)	Develop & Reveal Positions Build Up Confidence Influence Onlookers Add to Prestige
II Negotiation	Bargaining Making a Package Deal	Conflict of Interests & Need for Cooperation	Making a Deal	Get the Best out of It for Oneself	Agreement Build Up Confidence Reveal Positions Influence Onlookers Add to Prestige
III Inquiry	Scientific Research Investigation Examination	General Ignorance	Growth of Knowledge & Agreement	Find a "Proof" or Destroy One	Add to Prestige Gain Experience Raise Funds
IV Deliberation	Means-End Discussion Discussion of Ends Board Meeting	Need for Action	Reach a Decision	Influence Outcome	Agreement Develop & Reveal Positions Add to Prestige Vent Emotions
V Information-Seeking Dialogue	Expert Consultation Didactic Dialogue Interview Interrogation	Personal Ignorance	Spreading Knowledge & Revealing Positions	Gain, Pass on, Show, or Hide Personal Knowledge	Agreement Develop Position Influence Onlookers Add to Prestige Vent Emotions
VI Eristics	Eristic Discussion Quarrel	Conflict & Antagonism	Reaching a (Provisional) Accommodation in a Relationship	Strike the Other Party & Win in the Eyes of Onlookers	Develop & Reveal Positions Add to Prestige Gain Experience Amusement Vent Emotions
VII Mixed	A. Debate (Persuasion & Eristics)	Conflicting Points of View in Front of a Third Party	Accommodating Conflicting Points of View	Persuade or Influence Each Other & a Third Party	Develop & Reveal Positions Add to Prestige Amusement
	B. Committee Meeting (Mainly Deliberation)	Conflict & Antagonism & Need for Agreement in Practical Matters	Working out a Policy & Endorsing It	Influence Outcome	Agreement Build Up Confidence Develop & Reveal Positions Air Objections
	C. Socratic Dialogue (Mainly Inquiry)	Illusion of Knowledge	Healing the Soul from This Vice to Get Ready for Real Knowledge & Virtue	Refute & Avoid Being Refuted Agreement	Develop & Reveal Positions Gain Experience Amusement

Figure 3.1   Types of Dialogue

doctor, these exemplify different types of dialogue. Types of dialogue may be grouped according to various differences and resemblances. We shall not attempt to establish a full-fledged taxonomy of dialogue types, but in figure 3.1 we have, provisionally, grouped a number of types under seven headings, or general types. Thus a type may be more general or more specific. General types have more specific types as subtypes. For instance, both pseudo-academic-wrangling debate and domestic quarrel are subtypes of eristics.

At the most specific level, in order to fully characterize a type of dialogue, one should lay down its primary goal and its rules. The rules are such that they guarantee or at least facilitate the reaching of a goal in each particular case of application. Together, primary goal and rules constitute a *normative model* of the type of dialogue in question. At this level, types of dialogue coincide with particular *dialectical systems* or *dialogue games*.

At a more general level, one can do no more than adumbrate the kind of goal and the kind of rules that figure in dialogues of the type. Notice that the various subtypes mentioned in figure 3.1 are still at a general level. We shall not get to particular systems until chapter 4. The structures of dialogue proposed here can be thought of as dialogue games, in the sense that two participants take turns making moves and that they have goals and strategies in making their moves. But the main point is that these structures or systems of dialogue are normative models that represent ideals of how one ought to participate in a certain type of conversation if one is being reasonable and cooperative. It is important not to confuse this with an account of how participants in argumentation really behave in instances of real dialogue that take place, or that are recorded in some text of a dialogue exchange between participants in a speech event. This is quite a different matter. In chapter 5, in section 5.1, we will take up some questions relating to how our normative models of dialogue apply to real conversational speech events.

We must distinguish between the primary or main goal of a type of dialogue and the aims of the participants of a dialogue of that type. Thus the primary goal of negotiation could be characterized as "making a deal." By entering into negotiations the parties implicitly subscribe to this overall purpose. But, besides, each party pursues, within the dialogue, the particular aim of getting the best out of it for oneself. It wouldn't be negotiation if they didn't. In figure 3.1 the primary goal of each type is indicated in the fourth column. In each case there is a particular kind of initial situation and the goal is to change that situation in specific ways. The next column lists the internal aims of the participants of a dialogue of a given type, which are constitutive of that type. Finally, in the last column, we list some side benefits, some of which are often important motives for entering a dialogue of a certain type.

The classification of types of dialogue given by figure 3.1 is by no means complete. But it does sketch out six main types of dialogue and a category of mixed types all of which are required to be identified in order to begin to study commitment in dialogue. There are many types of mixed (complex) dialogues not discussed in this section, but the three examples indicated in figure 3.1 give the reader an idea of how mixed dialogues can arise from the social practices of conversation.

Our main interest lies with persuasion dialogues, and we shall discuss these first and somewhat at length. After, we shall briefly sketch the other main types of dialogue.

The initial situation of a *persuasion dialogue* (or *critical discussion*),[1] is a clash or conflict of points of view. The main goal is a resolution of the initial conflict by verbal means. This means that if the dialectical process is to be successful at least one of the parties involved in the conflict will have to change its point of view at some stage in the dialogue. The internal aim of each party is to persuade the others to take over its point of view.

In extant normative models of persuasion dialogue, there are generally two parties. Initially, there are one or more questions at issue (propositions) toward which the parties take different points of view. A point of view can be positive (for), negative (against), or merely one of (critical) doubt.[2] In the initial conflict situation at least one party must have expressed a positive (or negative) point of view with respect to a proposition. Since a negative point of view toward a proposition P can usually be equated with a positive point of view toward the proposition *not-P*, we may restrict our attention to the case where the points of view taken are either positive or of (critical) doubt. Positive points of view, however, may again differ in type. Clearly each expression of a positive point of view toward a proposition (P) makes the speaker incur certain propositional commitments in the dialogue that ensues. But this may be either a commitment to defend P against criticism or merely a commitment to allow the other participant to make use of P in his defense of some other proposition, say Q. In the first case P is really (one of) the question(s) at issue and may be designated as a *thesis*, or an *assertion* (or *expressed opinion*) of the speaker. In the second case P is merely something taken for granted (for the sake of argument or otherwise) and may be called a *concession* of the speaker.[3] Whether or not such concessions are initially part of the conflict from which the dialogue starts, there must always be at least one participant holding a thesis toward which the other participant expresses some doubt. The participants must "have committed themselves in different ways to the expressed opinions under discussion."[4]

Subtypes of persuasion dialogue can be classified according to five types of criteria.

1. The Type of Initial Conflict from Which the Dialogue Starts. According to Van Eemeren and Grootendorst, "a discussion may centre on *a dispute of greater or lesser complexity*."[5] (*Dispute* is their term for the initial conflict situation.) *Single disputes (conflicts)* have to do with only one expressed opinion (thesis), whereas *multiple disputes (conflicts)* have to do with more than one question which is at issue. In a *simple dispute (conflict)* only one positive (or negative) position is taken with respect to each question at issue, whereas in a *compound dispute (conflict)* one participant takes a positive and the other a negative point of view toward at least one question at issue. (That is, if we reduce negative points of view to positive ones, one participant holds that *P*, and the other holds that *not-P*.)[6]

Barth and Krabbe concentrate on *pure* (or *simple*) conflicts, which are similar to the simple and single dispute in the terminology of Van Eemeren and Grootendorst. Conflicts in which both participants have expressed doubt as to the other participant's thesis they call *mixed*.[7] However, in one respect the notion of a 'pure conflict' allows for more structure in the initial situation than that of a simple single dispute: in a pure conflict there may be initial concessions. In a mixed conflict there may be initial concessions on both sides.

Clearly, different types of conflicts introduce different constellations of commitment sets. Thus, with the most complicated type, the mixed conflict, the discussion starts out with at least four commitment sets: a set of theses (expressed opinions) and a set of concessions for each participant. Presumably, each participant's set of concessions contains his theses as a subset. Other types of conflict can be characterized either by requiring certain sets to be empty or by a restriction on their contents. With simple single disputes (conflicts) all sets are required to be initially empty, except for one participant's set of expressed opinions which contains the unique thesis. With compound single disputes (conflicts) there is one proposition *P* such that *P* is the unique thesis of one participant, whereas *not-P* is the unique thesis of the other. (There are no sets of concessions involved in the description of such a conflict.)

We prefer to use the term *dispute* for a persuasion dialogue ensuing from this last—compound single—type of conflict. Thus, in our usage, the term *dispute* will stand for a type (a subtype) of dialogue, rather than for a type of conflict. In the strictest sense only dialogues arising from *conflicts of contradictory opinions* (*P* versus *not-P*) are called "disputes." It will be convenient, however, to extend the term to cover dialogues arising from certain *conflicts of contrary opinions*. These are compound *multiple* conflicts in which each participant has a unique thesis (*P* versus *Q*), such that these theses are not contradictory but *contrary* (*P* and *Q* are incompatible, but *not-P* and *not-Q* are not). For example, one participant may hold that jogging is (in a certain respect) good and the other that jogging is (in the same respect) bad. Jogging can't be both good and bad in the same respect, but it could be neither.[8] We shall, however, only speak of a conflict of contrary opinions (and of a dispute issuing from it) if the contrariety is conventionally obvious (and has not to be discovered by subtle logical methods). It must be obvious to the participants, as members of a particular company which adheres to particular conventions, that a positive point of view with respect to P implies a negative point of view with respect to Q and vice versa.

The remaining four criteria (according to which one may classify persuasion dialogues) can be treated more briefly.

2. The Nature of the Subject Matter Discussed. It is possible to have dialogues on matters of fact, questions or problems of theory, ethical problems, practical problems, aesthetic issues, or the proper use of words. As the subject matter changes, interesting shifts can be observed. For example, a dialogue may shift to a discussion of the fine shades of meaning in the terminology being used in the discussion, instead of focusing directly on the original problem.

3. The Degree of Rigidity of the Rules. Some dialogues are more conversational in nature, and their rules are formulated in a permissive manner. Typically, at each stage there is a large supply of options available in how a speaker may make contributions to the dialogue. Other dialogues are more rigorous in that the number of options is narrowed down.

4. The Preciseness of the Procedural Description of the Dialogue. Sometimes the description of a system is informal and is not meant to specify all the options. It just gives a rough sketch of what is expected in that type of dialogue. On the other hand, some dialogues exhibit a system of formal dialectics in that they are governed by precisely formulated rules of procedure.[9] Ultimately, the rules may define a "game" in the sense of mathematical game theory.

5. Admixtures from Other Types of Dialogue. In some instances, a specimen of dialogue can have a flavor or overtone of another context of dialogue. For example, a persuasion dialogue can have an "eristic flavor" if it partially becomes a heated fight or a contest where one party is trying to attack and defeat the other party with a greater intensity than normal. In other instances, a persuasion dialogue can take on the flavor of a rhetorical debate, for example, in a political discussion where the participants, though seriously committed to their points of view and really trying to persuade each other, may yet be influenced by the fact that their audience consists of potential voters.

A flavor of the *expert consultation dialogue* is expected as soon as one participant in a discussion is an expert on the subject of the discussion and the other person is not, for this introduces a certain asymmetry into the dialogue. And the dialogue may not be properly understood unless this asymmetry is taken into account. For example, in case 1.5, it may help us to understand a dialogue between Mary and John on the subject of garbage disposal if we take into account that Mary is the city's environmental specialist while John is a layperson in this field.

As we shall see in section 3.4, the admixture of various flavors often relates to fallacies. For instance, repeated *ad hominem* attacks are sure to introduce an eristic flavor; whereas the *argumentum ad verecundiam* may stress an asymmetry in the dialogue (with respect to expertise) and thus introduce the flavor of an expert consultation dialogue. An appeal to pity *(argumentum ad misericordiam)* often involves an admixture of the bargaining (negotiation) type of dialogue, in certain respects. The introduction of an overtone may have important implications for evaluating what an argument is and whether it may justifiably be judged to be fallacious or open to various kinds of criticisms.

Common to all the subtypes of persuasion dialogue, the normative model of persuasion dialogue has certain basic structural characteristics. One of the main characteristics is that of the participants' commitment sets. A persuasion dialogue is made up of a coherent sequence of speech acts, and at each individual speech act advanced by a participant, propositions are added to or deleted from that participant's commitment sets, according to the commitment rules appropriate for the type of persuasion dialogue in question.

In Hamblin's formal dialectic, a log or repository of every proposition a participant has become committed to during the course of the dialogue is kept, and this collection of propositions is called the participant's *commitment store* (commitment set).[10] According to one type of rule, if a participant makes a statement, the propositions expressed by that statement are automatically added to the commitment store. In some kinds of persuasion dialogue, retractions can also be made, meaning that propositions can be deleted from a participant's commitment store when he or she advances the appropriate kind of speech act.

Persuasion dialogue generally takes the form of a sequence of questions and replies, or attacks and defenses, where each side takes a turn to make a "move". A *move* is a sequence of locutions advanced by a participant at a particular point in the sequence of dialogue. For example, a move could be a statement which is a reply to the question posed by the other party, followed by a question directed back to the other party. The *locution rules* of a dialogue define the permissible locutions, like statements, questions, inferences, and so on. The *structural rules* define the order in which moves can be made by each participant. The *commitment rules* define the insertion and deletion of propositions from a participant's commitment store, as a consequence of his or her moves. If there is more than one type of commitment store, we need commitment rules for each type. The *win-loss rules* determine the conditions under which a player wins or loses the game.[11]

These four kinds of dialogue rules characterize not only persuasion dialogues, but many other important types of dialogue as well. The goal of *negotiation* dialogue is to make a deal. Each participant aims to maximize his share of some goods or services which are in short supply. This aim is carried out by a process of self-interested bargaining where the strategy is directed to finding a compromise that will be attractive to both parties. In carrying out this strategy of making a good deal, persuasion may be of secondary importance and is sometimes even irrelevant to the business of bargaining. Persuasion may be involved, however, in setting up an agenda for negotiation and in various aspects of the dialogue that aims toward a settlement of the issues of a negotiation. It would be a mistake to think, however, that persuading the other party that your point of view is right (true, based on logical reasoning or good evidence) is the primary goal of negotiation.[12]

Normative models of negotiation dialogue share many features with those of persuasion dialogue. Thus, in a negotiation dialogue both participants have a commitment store containing their *concessions*. There must be *commitment rules* to regulate the insertion and deletion of concessions from a participant's commitment store. In general, the possibilities for retracting a concession, once made, will be severely restricted in negotiation dialogue. Again there must be *structural rules* to determine turns in asking (or granting) concessions. In contrast to concessions in persuasion dialogues, however, these concessions need not be *propositional* commitments: in general they may be commitments to any course of action.

One side benefit of negotiation dialogue is that it builds up confidence and cooperation, opening up channels of communication, a benefit which accrues from some other types of dialogue as well. The *inquiry* is a type of dialogue that strives to establish or "prove" propositions in order to answer a question (solve a problem) in such a way that a stable and general agreement on the matter at issue results. In its focus on propositions (expressed by declarative sentences), inquiry seems closer related to persuasion dialogue than to negotiation. But it differs from persuasion dialogue in that it does not start from a conflict of points of view, but from an open problem. No party needs to have a positive or negative point of view on the matter at issue to begin with. On the other hand, if the inquiry is to have been successful, all participants must wholeheartedly subscribe to the same conclusions at the end.[13] Consequently, if one of the participants reaches a (final or intermediate) conclusion before the others, it is of paramount importance for the success of the inquiry that she convinces her fellow inquirers. The obvious instrument for this is the persuasion dialogue. We may, therefore, expect to find persuasion dialogues embedded, as subdialogues, in any given inquiry.[14]

Conversely, a persuasion dialogue may reach a point where some matter of fact has to be settled before the discussion can proceed. The participants may then agree to conduct an inquiry to settle the matter. Thus inquiries can be embedded, as subdialogues, in a persuasion dialogue.[15]

Negotiation dialogues may profit both from inquiries and from persuasion dialogues as subdialogues, but not the other way around. A shift from a persuasion dialogue or from an inquiry to negotiation seems always to obstruct or at least impair the original dialogue. We shall return to this in section 3.3 (fallacy of bargaining).

Many people identify the inquiry with the process of scientific investigation of a hypothesis. Certainly it is true that the inquiry has the goal of assembling the relevant "facts" in a domain of research and then drawing the conclusions from these facts. However, this type of dialogue is not always purely or narrowly scientific in its methods or orientation. For example, the Warren Commission Report into the death of President Kennedy was the report of an inquiry. Yet this inquiry was not a scientific investigation, in a narrower sense of the term at any rate.

The inquiry is characterized by the goal of establishing a cumulative process of argument which builds on "established facts" in order to "prove" conclusions beyond reasonable doubt. Thus the burden of proof in an inquiry is characteristically set at a high standard of proof.

Deliberation as a type of dialogue is similar to inquiry, and different from both persuasion dialogue and negotiation in that it starts from an open problem, rather than from a conflict of opinion. The problem in this case is a practical one, and the goal is a decision on how to act. Agreement, which is a main goal of inquiry, is here classified only as a side benefit, for the final decision may be taken by an authority or by a vote without general agreement on the outcome. Every participant, however, tries to influence the outcome during the deliberation process. The discussion typically turns on means and ends. Of course, if one of the participants gets to defending a particular proposal, we are back to a subtype of persuasion dialogue: discussion of proposals. Such persuasion dialogues are usually embedded in what at large is not a persuasion dialogue but a deliberation in the present sense.

Deliberation arises out of a need for action and is concerned with the future. An agent has to consider different options and different possible ways the world might go as an outcome of both the agent's option and the way things are now. The agent has to try to visualize the future and look at the various possible consequences of his actions given certain plausible developments. Deliberation is often hazardous and difficult because of the uncertain nature of the future and the fact that many things are not in an agent's control, typically. Therefore, deliberation involves speculation and guesswork about plausible occurrences that might happen.

Deliberation also involves the formation of plans and a survey of contingencies that may need to be continually revised or updated, in relation to an agent's knowledge and updating of an evolving situation. Deliberation often takes the form of a two-person discussion, but it is sometimes a solitary process where an agent poses questions to himself and then tries to answer them by being "devil's advocate," or his own critic. In still other cases, deliberation can be a vast group discussion which involves corporate or institutional planning and policy making.

The kind of argumentation that is most central to deliberation is *practical reasoning,* a kind of goal-directed, knowledge-based reasoning where an agent considers different means of carrying out a goal in a particular situation, as he understands or knows it. Practical reasoning ends in a conclusion that indicates the prudential or practical action (or *partial strategy*) to take to fulfill a goal in a given, particular set of circumstances.

In a practical inference, there are two types of premises. One describes a particular goal or intention that an agent is committed to. The other postulates an action, or type of action or partial strategy, that is a means for the agent to carry out this goal in the given situation, as the agent sees it. The conclusion expresses a practical "ought" which directs the agent to carry out the action or strategy postulated in the second premise, if he wants to achieve the goal described in the first premise.

Practical reasoning is a chaining together of a sequence of practical inferences which can be organized into a hierarchy of goals, subgoals, actions and subactions, strategies and substrategies, according to routines. Typically, for example, an agent may start out with some very general goal and then search around for some specific means of carrying out that goal in his given circumstances. Practical reasoning occurs in different contexts of dialogue. It can occur in advice giving by an expert source to a layperson who has consulted the expert, for example, or it can occur in critical discussion where one party defends the soundness of a particular proposal *vis-à-vis* real or supposed objections. But the point is that practical reasoning is also typical for a context of "pure" deliberation, without expert advice necessarily being involved, and without a present commitment to any particular proposal.[16]

The *information-seeking dialogue* arises from an initial situation where one participant has some knowledge, or is in a position to know something, and the other party both lacks and needs that information. Thus the initial situation for the information-seeking dialogue is asymmetrical. The goal is some kind of spreading of knowledge. This is not true of inquiry, where both (or all) parties are ignorant.

Suppose, for example, that Doug's ballpoint pen cannot be found, but Doug knows that Erik has a habit of absentmindedly picking up this particular type of pen during their discussions. Doug might ask Erik, "Do you know where my pen is?" and a dialogue on the question of identifying and locating ballpoint pens may ensue. This type of discussion would be typical of the information-seeking type of dialogue, because Doug needs to find his pen, and he has reason to think that Erik may be able to give him information that might enable him to find the pen.

The inquiry and the information-seeking type of dialogue are different, because the inquiry seeks proof. In the example above, Doug and Erik are not so much interested in proving that the pen has a certain location. It is enough for Doug to find it, and that is his goal in initiating the discussion. Once he has found the pen, he has no further need to collect evidence proving that it was in a certain location or that it is definitely the same pen that was lost, and so on. If the pen had been a murder weapon, however, an inquiry into its finding might need to consider such things.

The *expert consultation* and the *didactic dialogue* are two subtypes of the information-seeking dialogue. In the expert consultation, one party is an expert in a particular domain or field of knowledge, and the other is not; that is, the other is a layman. By asking questions, the layman tries to elicit the expert's opinion (advice) on a matter on which the layman himself lacks direct knowledge. By this kind of dialogue, the questioner can arrive at a presumptive conclusion which gives a plausible, expert-based answer to his question. This may be very useful if the questioner has no direct access to knowledge of the matter himself.

The didactic dialogue is similar to expert consultation in that one party is an expert and the other is not. However, instead of being centered on a problem of the layman, the purpose is to turn the layman into a kind of expert himself. In such a dialogue both parties ask questions and give answers.

Other subtypes of information-seeking dialogue are the *interview* and the *interrogation*. The interview is a kind of opinion probe which arises out of interest in the position of the subject of the interview. The subject may be a famous person, for example, or someone who has an interesting story to tell. The subject's position is (partly) unknown, and therefore curiosity is typically the motivating position of an interview. The skill of the interviewer is to facilitate the subject's bringing out of the story, by asking the right questions in the right order.

Similar skills are needed by the questioner in interrogation, where the purpose is to get evidence on some specific matter from the answerer (suspect or witness). As long as the answerer is fully cooperative, this leads to no more than a formal or rigorous type of interview. But when the answerer tries to hide certain parts of the evidence which the questioner is after, we meet with a special subtype of information-seeking dialogue that has some interesting similarities to the more rigorous types of persuasion dialogue. As in persuasion dialogue, each answer adds a proposition to the answerer's commitment store. Finally, the answerer may contradict himself, the commitments clash, and the questioner wins (part of) the dialogue. This procedure is to be compared with the way a proponent of a thesis may win a rigorous persuasion dialogue by forcing the opposition into the contrary dialogue attitudes of conceding and challenging the same proposition (section 4.4).

Examination is similar to interrogation in that one party may not be willing to yield all evidence. However, the overall purpose of an examination is not the spread of knowledge and information. The purpose is to find out whether the examinee disposes of a certain level of abilities and knowledge in a certain field. To start with one cannot suppose the examinee to have a good estimate of this himself. So the examination dialogue is a subtype of inquiry rather than of information dialogue.

Let us now turn to *eristics*. Under this title we have assembled all types of dialogue, such as acrimonious verbal exchanges and private quarrels, that serve primarily as a substitute for fighting (tournaments or duels) as a means to reach, provisionally, an accommodation in a relationship. As in a fight, the participants are foremost trying to win. What constitutes winning may differ but is often defined in terms of effects on onlookers or referees.

The *quarrel* is a type of eristic dialogue that gives vent to repressed emotions. Each party aims at striking or hitting the other party verbally. The initial situation of the quarrel is that of a feeling that one has been unfairly taken advantage of by another party. Sometimes, too, the quarrel arises from a kind of truculence or from self-pity, which results in a desire to get attention. Thus the quarrel often has a theatrical aspect. It is a series of controlled explosions.

From a point of view of its logic, the quarrel is not complex, but simple. In fact, it is characterized as a kind of anarchy of dialogue, where logical rules of procedure are cast aside. The context is strongly adversarial, and the more usual rules of good dialogue are abandoned in the direct attempt to attack the other party. The quarrel generates more heat than light, as the saying goes. And its function is all too often that of distracting from more reasoned argumentation by bringing in irrelevant appeals to emotion.

Notice, however, that the main goal of eristic dialogue is not to defeat the other party—a sort of verbal combat where the aim is victory at all costs. It is important to notice that even the quarrel has a co-operative element, for it is based on the philosophy that it is better to have verbal activity than it is to engage in physical fighting. Even in a quarrel, the participants agree to stay around and have some verbal exchanges, rather than simply leave or engage in other forms of struggle against each other.

Of course, in one sense—from the single point of view of the participant—the goal in the quarrel is to verbally strike out at the other party and to defeat or humiliate the other party as much as possible. But in another more global sense, the goal of the quarrel, as a type of dialogue, is to engage in some form of exchange aimed at reaching an accommodation, and, moreover, a form of exchange that is verbal rather than physical. Thus, contrary to what one might initially think, the quarrel often can have a very valuable function. By giving vent to powerful emotions, it can serve as a valve to release powerful, repressed feelings that could otherwise cause constant disruptions and violent physical demonstrations of unrest and frustration. Although quarrels often seem silly and pointless to onlookers, arising from what appears to be trivial conflicts, something that seems trivial to one person may be deeply important to another person who is emotionally involved in a situation at the time. Hence a certain degree of tolerance for the quarrel—indeed quarrels that seem pointless or that arise out of extreme positions that may appear juvenile or radical—can turn out to be highly beneficial and educationally sound in the end, even if the extreme views voiced during the quarrel often appear highly distasteful, excessive, and emotionally loaded at the time they are expressed, to those not involved.

The initial situation of the quarrel is the conflict or antagonism between two parties, each of whom has hurt feelings, or a grudge against the other side, on the grounds of a complaint about some perceived harm or deprivation brought about by the other party. The quarrel is a verbal means of dealing with this situation by allowing the grudge or hurt feelings to be expressed openly and recognized on both sides. Once the conflict has been openly expressed, the goal in a favorable kind of quarrel is to move towards an accommodation whereby each party expresses a willingness to behave in a more sensitive and considerate way in the future, or at least to be sensitive to the feelings of the other party on the issue.

The closing stage of the quarrel is a kind of making up where both parties agree to cease quarreling and, ideally, give assurances that they will try to be more sensitive and considerate in the future.

The "argumentation stage" of the quarrel is characterized by *counterblaming*, where each party attacks the other as personally blameworthy for some alleged fault or culpable act(s) committed in the past. *Ad hominem* argumentation is typical of, and closely associated with, this stage of the quarrel.

The quarrel has often been equated with a kind of anarchy of argument where all rules of dialogue are cast aside. But there is turn taking in a good quarrel. The goal of the quarrel can only be achieved if both parties take turns in allowing the other side to respond. A caricature of this turn taking in the quarrel is found in Laurel and Hardy, who apply the norms of the quarrel to an actual fight. Hardy may tweak Laurel's nose, for example, and Laurel might reply by kicking Hardy in the shins.

As mentioned above one of the most important benefits of the quarrel, however, is to provide a verbal substitute for physical fighting. It is a way of resolving antagonism without harming either party badly or in an irreparable way. Examples of this kind of substitution for fighting is common in animals, for example, where two sheep will butt heads to establish which is the stronger in a way that is less likely to cause serious harm than an outright fight.

As a type of dialogue, the quarrel comes under the general heading of "eristics" (from the Greek word for "strife"). The goal of eristics is to reach a provisional accommodation in a relationship between two parties who are (initially) in a situation of antagonism. The quarrel is perhaps the most common and typical type of dialogue in everyday argumentation, but there is also another type of eristic dialogue that is worth mentioning. The *eristic discussion* is a type of dialogue where two participants engage in verbal sparring to see who is the more clever in constructing persuasive and often tricky arguments that devastate the opposition, or at least appear to. The initial situation in this type of dialogue is an unsettled intellectual hierarchy, prompting a need to test out verbal skills of argumentation to see who is the more masterful. The goal is to settle the intellectual hierarchy by having a verbal contest of arguments. A classical example of this type of dialogue is the series of exchanges in the Platonic dialogue *Euthydemus,* where the Sophists Euthydemus and Dionysodorus use all sorts of deceptive tricks and verbal fireworks to try to get the best of Socrates and other adversaries in argumentation. But Socrates himself did not shun eristic moves.

Needless to say, the eristic discussion is quite different in its methods from the critical discussion, where the goal is to resolve the initial conflict of opinions by rational means. Yet the eristic discussion is closer to the critical discussion than the quarrel is. In its execution, an eristic discussion may resemble a rigorous, or tightened up, persuasion dialogue, but the ultimate purpose to resolve a conflict (by logic and argument) and serious attempts to convince the other party are lacking. Instead, one tries to trick one's opponent by strategems that would be fallacious from the point of view of persuasion dialogue. In the eristic discussion, an outrageous fallacy may be the best and most successful technique to persuade your audience.

The quarrel is one of those neighbouring types of dialogue into which the persuasion dialogue can shift (sometimes at a moment's notice). This type of dialectical shift from persuasion dialogue to quarrel, may be signaled by a prominence of *ad hominem* argumentation. One party may attack the other as a "liar" or "hypocrite," signalling a descent of the level of dialogue from that of persuasion to that of quarrel. If the other party responds in kind *(tu quoque),* the dialogue may shift to a full-blown quarrel. This type of shift is (from the point of view of logic), a negative shift, or deterioration of reasoned dialogue. We shall return to the subject of dialectical shifts in section 3.3.

According to the survey given thus far, there appear to be many different kinds of dialogues, and naturally, therefore, the question arises whether the set of six basic types of dialogue given here can be proved to be complete in the sense that any other types of dialogue can be shown to be subtypes or composites of these. While, at this time, we can make no claim for completeness, we are able to present a systematic survey of dialogue types (figure 3.2) which gives a matrix of main goals and initial situations for the six basic types of dialogue we have identified.

Persuasion dialogue (critical discussion) always arises from a conflict of opinions, and its goal is to resolve the conflict, to arrive at a final outcome of stable agreement in the end. In both regards, critical discussion is inherently different from the deliberation dialogue.

Initial Situation / Main Goal	Conflict	Open Problem	Unsatisfactory Spread of Information
Stable Agreement/Resolution	Persuasion	Inquiry	Information Seeking
Practical Settlement/ Decision (Not) to Act	Negotiation	Deliberation	
Reaching a (Provisional) Accommodation	Eristic		

Figure 3.2   Systematic Survey of Dialogue Types

Deliberation can, of course, arise out of a practical conflict, that is, a clash of commitments or quandary, as in the deliberations Antigone may have undergone when she tried to decide what to do about burying her brother (case 2.9). However, a deliberation does not always or characteristically arise out of a conflict. It often arises out of a problem of having to proceed with some action, even without the pressure of practical conflict. Deliberation is necessitated by a need to act in the face of some situation posed by the so-called real world because even doing nothing (not acting) will have consequences in relation to the given problem, and therefore constitutes a kind of action. Although deliberation is often beset with conflict, it does not necessarily have a conflict (either a practical conflict or a conflict of opinion) as its initial situation. And although a stable agreement would be a desirable outcome, for sure, the primary purpose of this type of dialogue is rather a kind of action-directed practical agreement for the time being.

Inquiry, as a type of dialogue, is like persuasion dialogue (and unlike deliberation) in that it aims at a stable agreement. However, it resembles deliberation (and differs from persuasion dialogue) in that it arises from a problem rather than a conflict: something is not known definitely to be true or false. This not knowing can be a problem where it is useful to clarify or establish one way or the other whether something can be proved or not, according to standards of proof appropriate for the particular context of the inquiry. Thus, in scientific research, problems are posed which researchers try to bring scientific methods to bear on.

The negotiation is like the persuasion dialogue because it arises out of a conflict, but it is like deliberation because the goal is to arrive at a decision as a basis for action. Thus both deliberation and negotiation

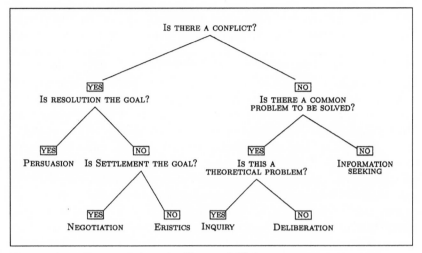

Figure 3.3   Determining the Type of Dialogue

are inherently practical types of dialogue, geared to action in order to enable practical affairs of life and human commerce to go ahead.

In this regard, the information-seeking type of dialogue is different from negotiation or deliberation because its aim is to correct or eliminate an asymmetrical distribution of information between two (or among more than two) parties—one party needs knowledge or information that the other party lacks direct access to. What is resolved, however, is not a conflict between the parties in the dialogue. Moreover, even though the initial situations may be described as "problematic," this must not be understood in the narrower sense in which both inquiry and deliberation start from "problems," that is, from lack of knowledge or lack of resolve on all sides. The knowledge is already there, and the problem is to communicate it from one party to the other.

The eristic dialogue, finally, evidently starts from a conflict as initial situation, but is more modest in its aspirations than any other of the main types.

In deciding whether a verbal exchange in a particular case belongs to one type of dialogue or to another, a good deal of evidence of the text and context of discourse may have to be judged. Figure 3.3 gives a key to arriving at this sort of decision.

In many cases, the evidence may be incomplete, so it may be most useful to arrive at a conditional decision to look at the case, consecutively, from the points of view of different types of dialogue.

We shall end this section by a brief discussion of the three mixed types listed in figure 3.1. We have already discussed two ways in which types can be blended with each other: (1) by adding a flavor (discussed in the context of persuasion dialogues) and (2) by embedding dialogues of a certain type as subdialogues into a structure of some other type. Of these two ways, the second can presumably be rendered in normative models of dialogue. The term *flavor*, however, points to aspects of real-life dialogue that may be hard to model or even describe very accurately.

A normative model of dialogue is an abstract conception which exists as a type of dialogue that is a discrete entity in itself. However, discussions that occur in everyday experience are complex speech events that can be difficult to classify and can be mixed composites of more than one normative model. It follows that a real discussion or text of argumentative discourse can be primarily of one type of dialogue, yet have overtones (flavors) of another type of dialogue mixed in with it in the same speech event. From an abstract, or purely formal point of view, a structure of dialogue is either that of a persuasion dialogue or an inquiry, for example, and cannot be both at once. But from a practical or descriptive point of view of classifying a speech event as one type of dialogue or another, such an exclusive and clear-cut decision would, in some instances, be an erroneous over-simplification of what is really going on.

Hamblin explained this dichotomy very well when he made the following distinction. The study of dialectical systems can be pursued *descriptively* when one examines "the rules and conventions that operate in actual discussions,"[17] for example, parliamentary debates. But the study of dialogue can also be pursued *formally* by setting up abstract systems which represent normative models of types of dialogue which track the properties of the sequences of dialogue that could be played out in accord with the rules for that type of dialogue. Both the formal (abstract) and the descriptive types of study of dialogue are useful and necessary, and they should ideally be integrated in a study of commitment and other aspects of dialogue.

From a descriptive point of view, a particular speech event can exhibit two (abstract) types of dialogue throughout that same speech event without there being an explicit shift from one type of dialogue to another. When this is taking place, we sometimes say that there is one type of dialogue along with a *flavor* of another type of dialogue, meaning that the one type of dialogue is more explicit and dominant, while the secondary type of dialogue is present in a more subdued or less explicit form. But often it is hard to tell which type of dialogue is dominant, especially as flavors are shifting back and forth throughout the speech event. In that case we shall prefer to assign the dialogue to one mixed type or other, without forcing an assignment to one of the six main types.

In figure 3.1 our first example of a mixed type is the *debate*. The debate is a kind of dialogue that initially may appear to be an eristic exchange very much like a quarrel, because the goal of each debater is to win victory over his opponent. Indeed, the debate was largely portrayed as this kind of win-at-all-costs dialogue by Woods and Walton.[18] However, new light can be cast on the debate as a distinctive type of dialogue once we make the subtle but important distinction between the aims of the individual participants in a debate and the over-all goal of debate as an institution or practice which has a purpose in its own right as a collective activity.

The debate is an institutionalized social tool to make society possible. The debate makes it possible to have a political culture instead of living in a state of quarreling, repression, and/or revolution where viewpoints are constantly in an eristic power struggle for dominance. The goal of the debate is not to be sought exclusively in terms of the goals of the individual participants in it.

The debate has, moreover, two distinctive features that make it essentially different from the quarrel. One is that its participants aim at persuading, or at least influencing, a third party: either an audience of onlookers (hearers) or a judge or referee. The other is that the debate has rules, rules which are often highly institutionalized. For example, in a debate on a legislative bill in the House of Commons of Canada, there are constitutional rules, codified in *Beauchesne* (the handbook of rules of debate) and enforced or guided by the speaker of the house. Or to take another example, a debate in a university debating society will have well-codified rules that the debaters are guided by. In these two types of debates, the rules might be quite different. And in general it is characteristic of debates that their rules are highly sensitive to an institutional context.

Although the debate does have rules, it can very easily slip into an eristic discussion. And indeed, the debate does have a strong eristic element because the goal of each participant is to win out over and defeat his adversary by any means that is allowed by the rules or will successfully persuade the audience or judge that this goal has been accomplished. On the other hand, the debate also has an admixture of the persuasion dialogue, because logical rules of consistency and reasonableness are often appealed to in the debate and are often paid serious attention to in judging the arguments. Even so, the debate is not all that deeply logical or reasonable, and a debater who tries to build up his own side of a case or to attack his opponent's position using carefully formulated rules or principles of logical reasoning may well lose his case. For very often, an audience's attention in a debate is captured by a colorful metaphor or emotional appeal, much more strongly than by a dry sequence of careful logical reasoning to a conclusion. Indeed, depending on the audience, reasonable argumentation may be a serious deficit of strategy in a debate, and use of emotions or *ad hominem* attacks—see the quarrel, above—may be a far more effective strategy to win. Much depends on the rules in a debate, on how intelligently they are enforced, and on the level of knowledge and intelligence of the audience (or judge).

Yet the debate can be a noble thing. At its best it displays the good qualities of a critical discussion which brings out the positions and strongest arguments of both sides on a hotly controversial issue of national or international importance. Therefore, it is best to say that there can be gradations in the quality of debate, ranging from excellent to low. The debate is, in many respects, midway between critical discussion and eristic dialogue, and it is important not to fall into the error of classifying it exclusively at one extreme or the other. In realistic practice, the debate has both aspects, and it needs to be evaluated in relation to the material specifics of its institutional context.[19]

The *committee meeting* is a type of mixed dialogue in which the goals of persuasion, negotiation, inquiry, information seeking, and even eristics all show up. It is a generic type of dialogue which also has many subtypes, with particular combinations of purposes. For example, one type of committee meeting is that of the planning committee, which has the goal of forming a collaborative, agreed-upon plan to carry out action for a purpose. The objective of the committee meeting generally, as a type of dialogue, is to make recommendations that are forceful and binding. Thus, as a stage of planning for action, it is to be classified as a subtype of deliberation dialogue. However, there is a greater stress on reaching agreement, since it is better to have unanimity on the issue than to take a vote. Another purpose may be to delay or inhibit criticism—for example, Royal Commission Reports in Canada often have this purpose. Yet another one may be to lead to a wider group discussion of an issue, which will influence public opinion. The goal of the committee meeting is not simply to reach agreement, but also to give those parties who do not agree with a proposal an opportunity to air their objections. Thus a committee meeting is a mixed dialogue in several senses: it usually contains a number of embedded dialogues of a different main type (e.g., proposal discussions); it serves several purposes at the same time; and, consequently, it will exhibit a number of flavors.

Another interesting case is the *Socratic dialogue,* which evidently was intended to be primarily a kind of inquiry, but which clearly has some elements of the persuasion dialogue. According to Robinson, the goal of the Socratic dialogue is to make people virtuous.[20] For Plato and Socrates, virtue is a kind of knowledge. The dialogue typically starts from a problem of the type "Is $x\,y$?" or "What is x?."[21] Thus globally what we have is inquiry starting from an open problem, and presumably with a high standard of proof.

Despite this high standard set for the dialogues as a kind of philosophical inquiry which results in knowledge, one can see by examining the texts of the Socratic dialogues that there is a definite admixture of persuasion dialogue and even eristics to be found in them. We see that Socrates has the technique of getting his codiscussant to commit himself to a particular thesis as that discussant's point of view to be defended. Socrates then proceeds to question, and often even to refute, this thesis by trapping his adversary in contradictions and other absurdities. Thus we meet with a number of subdialogues of the persuasion type. As the argument goes back and forth, a flavor of eristics can often be detected.

Elenchus (refutation) would appear to be a kind of inquiry which strives to furnish proof of a contended hypothesis by the negative route of showing the discarded hypotheses to be false. However, elenchus is more personal than that: it aims at cleansing the spirit, and, ultimately, at moral improvement: "In order to make men virtuous, you must make them know what virtue is. And in order to make them know what virtue is, you must remove their false opinion that they already know. And in order to remove this false opinion, you must subject them to elenchus."[22] Thus a flavor of education, of didactic dialogues, is also present. Enough has been said to illustrate that, at the descriptive level, it is possible and indeed commonplace to have a text of dialogue that combines one primary type of dialogue with the flavor or secondary existence of another type of dialogue within the same discussion.

3.2   Complex Dialogue: A Case Study

In this section, an extended case study of a persuasion dialogue is presented. The case concerns the subject of a woman who has decided not to have an abortion even though she has been told by her physicians that her baby has a severe type of brain damage which means that there is no chance that it will survive. The persuasion dialogue takes place between two students, Wilma and Bruce, who are discussing this question. Bruce is the brother of the woman who has decided to have the baby.

Wilma and Bruce are not directly involved in the decision of whether to have this baby or not, so their commitments will not directly affect the outcome of the issue in any way. However, they both become directly involved in their discussion of this issue, and they differ in their positions on it. As the discussion continues, each develops arguments which imply very definite commitments. Moreover, these commitments evolve through the discussion in a way that makes the position of each of them on the issue quite coherent and distinctive. Each of them has a position that emerges as opposed to the other.

Another key aspect of this case study to watch for is that, at a certain point in the discussion, there is a kind of tightening up of the dialogue. At first, the dialogue has a kind of loose, exploratory character. But at a certain point the nature of the disagreement is sharpened and a more sharply argumentative posture is adopted by both parties. See if you can detect where this tightening up occurs.

The Discussion on Medical Ethics

[Wilma, a second-year medical student, is sitting in the Buffeteria, drinking coffee, waiting for her friend Bruce, a graduate student in sociology, to arrive. Bruce enters the Buffeteria, taking off his coat, and sits down across from Wilma.]

    B.: I had the most traumatic discussion with my sister, Ethel, and her husband, Karl, last
2   night when I had dinner at their house. You remember about Ethel's situation. Her
          baby was diagnosed as having some sort of brain damage, and the doctors said that
4   it has no chance of survival if she takes her pregnancy to term. I told you, I think,
          that she and Karl had decided not to have an abortion.
6 W.: Of course I remember. The fetus was diagnosed as anencephalic, meaning that most
          of the cerebral cortex of its brain is missing. This condition is known to be always
8   fatal. It is very sad for them. How are they coping?
    B.: Well, they were in pretty bad shape emotionally. But Ethel has decided to have the
10   baby, and she and Karl have asked the doctors at Ridgeview Memorial Hospital to
          keep the baby alive long enough for its organs to be transplanted to save the lives of
12   some other babies. They feel better after having made this decision.
    W.: Well, you know Bruce, to make conditions favorable for transplantation, the doctors
14   are likely to have to use mechanical support systems (like a respirator) on the baby.
          Would Ethel and Karl agree to that?
16 B.: They already have. And I think it's a good idea. I think it is very generous and life
          supporting for Karl and Ethel to make this choice, and they both feel very proud that
18   some part of their baby may save the life of somebody else's child.

W.: Well, hold on a minute Bruce. I know you are very close to Ethel and Karl and want
20   to be supportive of their feelings. But I don't think I can agree with your point of
view on this decision. I think the decision to put that baby on mechanical life-support
22   systems, solely for purposes of salvaging its organs, is wrong.

B.: Well, why? Don't you see that the purpose is to save the lives of other babies, who
24   would die without receiving those organs? Surely the purpose here is a good one,
both highly worthwhile in itself and also helpful to Karl and Ethel.

26 W.: Yes, I agree with all that. But my reservations are for different reasons. You see,
that baby, when it is born, will be a living human being, and if I were its physician, I
28   am not sure that I could justify the act of putting it on mechanical life-support systems
as an act of medical treatment.

30 B.: Well, it is an act of medical treatment because it will save the lives of the babies of
some other parents. This baby is one life to be considered, but other lives are
32   involved. We must have respect for all life.

W.: It follows, however, from what you say, that we must also respect this baby's life. But
34   there are other considerations at issue as well. This baby will be the patient of those
doctors who are caring for it when it is born. They have an obligation to the baby.
36   It is their patient. If they apply any drastic, heroic, or invasive methods of medicine
to that baby, these acts must be justified as medical treatment of the baby. Otherwise
38   they would not be medical treatment of the baby. Putting the baby on mechanical
life-support systems is not going to restore the baby to health or contribute to making
40   it better. That baby is going to die whatever they do. Putting it on a ventilator will
only prolong its existence for a time, in a way that could not conceivably be of any
42   benefit to the baby. Do you see what I mean?

B.: Well, Wilma, you are looking at it from the doctor's point of view. I can see your
44   concern, from that point of view, all right. But look at it this way. That baby is born
with a tiny brain and almost no cerebral cortex. It will not feel any conscious
46   experience. It will not know the difference one way or the other.

W.: That may be true, but that is not the real point. An anencephalic infant is not brain
48   dead, meaning that it is not legally or medically dead in the sense that its brain is
irreversibly destroyed. This means that ethically speaking, the baby will still be a
50   person and is entitled to the respect we have for a living, breathing human being.
In an anencephalic infant, the brain stem (the lower part of the brain, connecting it
52   to the spine) is still intact, and therefore this baby will likely be able to breath on its
own, as long as it survives.

54 B.: It all depends on what you care to call a "person." I am willing to grant all that
medical stuff: if breathing is considered all-important in medical ethics, perhaps I had
56   better just go along with your use of language. Anyhow, let's not quibble about
words, even though I would have much preferred to include conscious experience in

58   the definition. By the way, how come you are so sure that an anencephalic "person,"
      as you call it, lacks all conscious experiences?

60 W.: I'm not sure about it at all! You insisted on that point yourself!

   B.: Did I? I did not!

62 W.: You graduate students are always trying to browbeat us. Remember that you said
      that these babies will not know the difference one way or the other . . .

64 B.: Well, anyhow, you seemed to agree.

   W.: As a matter of fact, I only granted the point for the sake of argument. We really

66   know very little about it, and it is not unlikely that all conscious experience is absent.
      But even so, it seemed to me, your argument does not hold water.

68 B.: Are you still prepared to grant this for the sake of argument?

   W.: Well, Yeah.

70 B.: Then how can you deny that Karl and Ethel made the right decision?

   W.: What do you mean?

72 B.: Use logic! Your own position implies this!

   W.: It does not! But show me.

74 B.: Well, you agree that the purpose of putting the baby on the life-support machine—that
      the purpose of it is good. Remember?

76 W.: Yeah.

   B.: And, by your own concession, the baby would not suffer.

78 W.: I'll have more to say about that later. But go on.

   B.: So no one would suffer. Or do you think it might hurt someone else?

80 W.: Not really. But what's the point?

   B.: Well don't you see! If something is all for the good and hurts no one, then it's

82   simply a good thing to do.

   W.: You're subtle!

84 B.: But do you agree with the principle?

   W.: No. We discussed a similar case in class last Thursday. Certain drug experiments on

86   patients could yield very useful statistical information, provided these patients do not
      know about it. So trying these drugs out on patients is "all for the good." Also, in

88   some cases, the drugs won't hurt the patients. According to your reasoning, then,
      would it be all right to experiment on these patients without their consent?

90 B.: No. But then you're not really sure that the drugs would not hurt the patient. What
      else would the experiment be for? You need a better example.

92 W.: O.K. You'll have one. Just a minute . . . Stealing a little money from a rich doctor and
      giving it to a poor sociology student. That would be all for the good. Wouldn't you

94   say so? Certainly the rich doctor wouldn't notice, so it wouldn't hurt her.

   B.: Don't get sarcastic Wil. And let's get back to the case we were discussing. Surely if

96   a certain medical treatment is all for the good and hurts no one, it would be all right

to put it through? But my point is that the baby itself will not suffer any additional
98   pain on mechanical support systems, as far as we know. And the organs will not be
taken until the baby is certified as brain dead.

100 W.: Two points. First, we are not certain what this kind of baby feels or does not. And
I believe the baby should get the benefit of our doubt. Second, the problem I have
102   is with putting the baby on mechanical support systems in order to keep the baby
alive long enough for certification of brain death so the organs can be taken. The
104   sole purpose of using the support systems is to harvest the organs for the benefit of
someone else. The purpose could not be described as treatment of the baby.
106   Therefore, I think is is questionable to call it "medical treatment" at all.

B.: But even if it cannot be defined as medical treatment of the baby in a narrower sense,
108   it can still be described as a beneficial and life-giving medical procedure. Compare
it to the case where one sibling offers to give a bone-marrow transplant in order to
110   save the life of his brother or sister. This procedure does not have the purpose of
benefitting the donor (at least in narrower terms of medical treatment). But it does
112   benefit the recipient. And it does benefit the donor in the sense that he can be
proud of volunteering the gift of life at some cost and sacrifice of pain and suffering
114   to himself.

W.: Yes, I do concede your point that there can be a benefit involved to both parties.
116   But the medical procedure is still not for the purpose of contributing to the health
of the donor. In the sibling case, it is a gift volunteered by the donor. The difference
118   between the two types of cases is that the anencephalic baby is not freely volunteering
such a gift. He or she is not in any position to do so. The physician must look out
120   for the patient's well-being and health first and foremost. Therefore, putting him or
her on mechanical support systems, in this case, cannot be justified ethically.

122 B.: I disagree here, because the baby cannot make any real decision one way or the
other and is dependent on its parents. The parents must act as the guardians and
124   proxy decision makers for the child. Ethel and Karl have decided to go ahead with
this. They are proud that their baby will save the life of another child.

126 W.: To volunteer to save someone else's life at the cost of your own pain or suffering is
an act of saintliness or courage, beyond the requirements of duty. But each person
128   has to volunteer his or herself for this type of supererogatory act. You can't
volunteer for some hazardous act on behalf of someone else. That's absurd!

130 B.: Well, I am not convinced that the baby will suffer, or that this is a case of a
supererogatory act, or act beyond the requirements of duty in ethics. I think it is
132   questionable to speak as if the baby has "duties" or is "acting courageously" at all.
In this case, the baby has such a poor quality of life that I don't see how a major
134   degree of importance can be assigned to the baby's life in arriving at a decision.

W.: Hold on Bruce! Am I hearing you right? You are telling me now that this baby's life
136   is not an important commitment for you in this case? You already admitted that
           Ethel's baby is one life to be considered [see line 31 above]. It follows that, in your
138   view, Ethel's baby has a life to be respected. You can hardly take that back now, at
           this point. For it clearly follows from what you explicitly conceded, earlier in our
140   discussion.

B.: This is problematic. Let me make myself clear. I am not committed to a policy of
142   respect for life *per se*. That's kind of extreme, isn't it?

W.: The whole underlying position your argument has been based on is the importance
144   of saving human lives. It seems to me that respect for life is your basic commitment
           in this argument. You mean that you are now prepared to explicitly deny this principle?

146 B.: Well no, you're right. I have placed a lot of importance on this principle, and rightly
           so.

148 W.: Are you really maintaining that respect for life is your basic commitment, but the
           baby's life in this instance is not a factor to which a major degree of importance can
150   be assigned? I think we need to go into the implications of this apparent deep
           conflict in your position.

152 B.: Now, wait a minute. I'm not saying that the life of the baby is not important. It's just
           that there's so little prospect of saving the baby's life, in this case, that I think we
154   have to take into account the other lives that could be saved by organ donation.

W.: So you agree that the baby's life is important?

156 B.: Yes, but respect for life means respect for all persons involved. This decision affects
           a lot of people, including the parents, the physicians (as you have pointed out), and
158   other people whose lives could be at stake as well. This is a larger decision, and I
           think it should be up to the parents.

160 W.: I don't dispute that the parents should have some say in the matter. How do they
           really feel about this? I mean, why do they feel so strongly about it?

162 B.: Ethel and Karl feel that this possibility of organ donation has turned their personal
           tragedy into a gift. At first, they were overwhelmed that all their efforts and trials
164   over this were going to end in disaster. They had put so much into this and had such
           high hopes for the baby. But now they are hoping that their baby will be born alive
166   so that it can serve this highly worthwhile purpose. It is very helpful for them to feel
           that something good is going to come out of all their efforts.

168 W.: I respect their feelings, but Ethel and Karl have been through a lot, and I wonder
           whether they are in an emotional frame of mind to appreciate all the ramifications of
170   this type of decision. A physician can be more objective about these types of things.

B.: But surely physicians can have the same sorts of biases and emotional prejudices as
172   anyone else. In the end, it is the parents who have to live with the decision, or feel
           guilt about it.

174 W.: Yes, you have a good point. The parents have the right to put their point of view
forward and voice their concerns. But the doctor also has the right to ask to be
176   removed from the case if he or she feels that giving in to the parents' demands would
go against professional medical ethics. In this case, the physician might feel that he
178   or she should not be required or called upon to modify the treatment of a patient for
some purpose other than the medical treatment of that patient. Any course of action
180   of this sort deviates from the norms of medical ethics and thereby comes open to
question on ethical grounds. Can it be justified in this case? I think there is at least
182   room for doubt. Would such a course of action show lack of respect for this infant
as a human being? A doctor must be sure that the answer is "no" before proceeding.
184 B.: I feel that Karl and Ethel's decision does show respect for their child as a human
being, because the ultimate purpose served is the highly worthwhile one of saving
186   human life. I agree that whether or not the physician can go along with this decision,
consistently with professional standards of medical ethics, is another question. But
188   I think that the doctor has to consider not just one isolated person at a time, but to
remember that the ultimate goal of medicine is saving life and that sometimes saving
190   life involves sacrifice and a team effort for the greater good of all.
    W.: Well . . . Good heavens, Bruce! There's Albert! We're late for volleyball.
[They both hastily get up and leave.]

Analysis of the Dialogue

Bruce's reported conversation with Karl and Ethel presents the facts of
the situation, including Bruce's report of the decision that Karl and Ethel
have made. Bruce and Wilma were not (direct) participants in the situation. Although Bruce and Wilma both have commitments that emerge
through the course of their discussion, it is not their commitments that
will decide the outcome of the situation.

    A particular point of view is stressed at line 16 of the dialogue
when Bruce says, "And I think it's a good idea." This is Bruce's thesis in
the dialogue: he affirms that Karl and Ethel's decision is right.

    A confrontation stage is reached when Wilma says, "Well hold on
a minute Bruce," at line 19. This is an expression of disagreement.
Wilma's thesis is that Karl and Ethel's decision is wrong (lines 20 through
22). Wilma says that she doesn't think that she can agree with Bruce's
thesis, and, moreover, she thinks this decision is wrong.

    Here then we have an explicit conflict of points of view, the initial
situation for a persuasion dialogue. The respective theses of the two
participants have been stated, and the goal of each participant is to show
from the concessions of the other that she/he is right.

In this case, the two theses are stated as *contraries* of each other, meaning that both cannot be true, but it is possible for both to be false. The two points of view are represented by the dichotomy below:

| good idea / wrong |

One side expresses a positive ethical value, and the other side expresses that the decision has a negative ethical value. There is a possible middle ground in this case: the decision could have no ethical value. It could be neutral or of no morally significant value. Thus this dialogue starting from a conflict of contrary opinions is not technically a *dispute* in the restricted sense that the thesis of one side is the negation (contradictory) of the thesis of the other side. It is, however, a dispute in the larger sense admitted above. The initial situation would be classified as a compound multiple dispute (conflict) by Van Eemeren and Grootendorst and as a mixed conflict by Barth and Krabbe. Since the opposition between the two theses is obvious to all concerned (each implies the negation of the other), we may say that each party has actually (though indirectly) expressed a negative point of view with respect to the other party's thesis. At any rate, the participants are opposed in their points of view, and this provides the starting point of the dialogue.

When Bruce says "Well, why?" at line 23, he is expressing doubt about Wilma's thesis. Immediately following this, Bruce brings forward his first argument. Bruce is not asking questions here. He is making statements. He is *presuming* that Wilma is questioning his thesis and responding to the presumed questioning. It is interesting that in such a case a critic (the reader) cannot distinguish between a participant's arguments for his own thesis and his arguments against his opponent's thesis. Both have the same effect and make one incur the same commitments. Here Bruce is presuming there are doubts about his thesis, so he is answering (what he presumes) are the questions that would express these doubts.

At line 26, Wilma concedes quite a bit when she says, "Yes, I agree with all that." All Bruce's assertions will then go into Wilma's commitment store, but they are not propositions that she will have to defend. They are concessions that she freely incurs, but she does not regard them as a clincher for Bruce's side of the argument. In the language of Johnson and Blair, Wilma could be said to have agreed that Bruce's assertions are acceptable (and presumably relevant), but not that they are sufficient.[23]

Then Wilma goes on to give her reasons for her thesis (line 26 onwards). Her first premise is that the baby will be a human being. Her second premise is that she is not sure that she could justify the action A at issue (of putting the baby on mechanical life-support systems) as an act of medical treatment. Wilma's second premise is ambiguous and could possibly be interpreted in either of two ways. First, Wilma could be arguing that A cannot be justified in the way that medical treatments are justified. In other words, she could be conceding that A is a kind of medical treatment, perhaps, but not one that could be justified ethically. Or second, Wilma could be denying that A could even be classified as a medical treatment. On this second interpretation, she is arguing that A could not be justified because it is not a medical treatment.

Bruce interprets Wilma's argument in the second way and retorts that A is an act of medical treatment. He argues that A can be classified as a medical treatment because it will improve the health of some person (namely the organ recipients). At lines 33 through 42 however, it becomes clear that Wilma would reject this argument, for in order for A to qualify as "medical treatment" it must benefit the patient (in this case the anencephalic baby), not only other parties. Thus the discussion is centering on the second interpretation of Wilma's argument, and Bruce and Wilma are having a verbal disagreement about the meaning of the phrase *medical treatment*. Wilma (line 34) is beginning to interpret the phrase in light of the physician's requirements and obligations of medical ethics, on the principle that there is a physician-patient relationship involved. In other words, she is saying that the physician's obligation should be to the anencephalic baby. This move clearly has important implications for the discussion.

Wilma's long argument of lines 33 through 42 makes several assertions which go into her commitment store. Bruce has the option of attacking any of these commitments if he wishes, and Wilma would have to defend them. Wilma is not just making these concessions for the sake of argument. She is advancing them as commitments that reflect her own position on the issue. We begin to see Wilma's position emerge here. She considers the point of view of the doctors and phrases the issue in terms of their professional obligations. She is putting herself into the situation from the point of view of the doctor. It is interesting to see how Bruce responds at line 43. He passes over Wilma's assertions and does not attack any of the commitments (individually) that she has advanced in her long argument. Instead, he remarks, "Well, Wilma, you are looking at it from the doctor's point of view."

Bruce doesn't concede Wilma's assertions—certainly not as strongly as she conceded Bruce's assertions in his previous argument. Instead, he advances an *ad hominem* attack by suggesting that Wilma has shown a bias toward the physician's point of view. This type of move is known in fallacy theory as "poisoning the well." While it is true that Wilma did take up the physician's point of view, Bruce's innuendo could be very dangerous here, because of his suggestion that Wilma's argument could be biased. There could be an opening here for the dialogue to degenerate into a quarrel or negotiation. For example, Bruce could talk of physicians "playing God," or Wilma could suggest that Bruce was ignorant of medicine and therefore didn't know what he was talking about. But none of this happened. It was an opening that Bruce passed up (to his credit), and therefore it remained just another possible way that the dialogue could have developed.

At lines 44 and 45, Bruce repeats the fact (already asserted by Wilma at lines 6 and 7) that the baby has almost no cerebral cortex and will be born with a tiny brain. But he makes a new assertion when he says (lines 45 and 46), that the baby will not "feel any conscious experience." Here it is apparent that Bruce has been somewhat intimidated by Wilma's long exposition of the physician's point of view in her previous argument. Bruce does not feel very safe when the subject turns too strongly to areas of medical expertise, and he comes back to an earlier point in the dialogue, where Wilma had advanced a premise to the effect that the baby, when it is born, will be a living human being (line 27). Bruce's statement that the baby "will not know the difference" can be interpreted as a challenge to Wilma's argument that the baby is a human being after it is born.

At line 47, Wilma begins to respond to this challenge. She concedes Bruce's point that the baby may not "know the difference," but then goes on to support her previous statement that the baby is (or will be) a human being. At lines 47 through 53, she constructs a complex argument for that conclusion. No doubt this technical argument—expressed from a physician's point of view—will irritate Bruce. This brings out an aspect of the dialogue worth mentioning; namely, while neither participant takes the position or can claim the role of an expert on the issue of the dialogue, one participant (Wilma) has some medical training. Therefore, Wilma often begins to assume a kind of quasi-expert point of view which Bruce cannot share. Nevertheless, Wilma does not give in to the temptation to indulge in the *argumentum ad verecundiam* in any way that is seriously disruptive of good dialogue or that interferes with the exchange of points of view.

However, at line 60, Wilma advances an *ad hominem* remark that is a kind of tit for tat rejoinder to Bruce's *ad hominem* remark earlier at line 43. But Wilma's reply does have some legitimate basis in the dialogue, because Bruce had previously committed himself to the proposition (lines 45 and 46) that an anencephalic baby lacks "conscious experience." Now, at lines 58 and 59, he is questioning Wilma how she can be so sure that an anencephalic baby lacks all conscious experience. Bruce is engaging in a curious reversal of the roles in the dialogue, by trying to impute a commitment to Wilma that is really his own.

In this instance then, Bruce has made a challenge based on a presumption that Wilma has a certain type of commitment which (according to the evidence of the previous dialogue) she has not really incurred. This should be judged a kind of fallacy or unfair move on Bruce's part. For he puts it in such a way that the proposition is something that Wilma should have to give arguments for. Yet her previous dialogue moves do not justify this interpretation at all.

The error here is comparable to, or perhaps a new version of, the "straw man fallacy," but it is a subtle kind of fallacy in this instance. For Wilma's concession "That may be true," at line 47, does give some indication of commitment to Bruce's thesis that the baby does not have conscious experience. So Bruce did not just make up Wilma's imputed commitment to this proposition in his question at lines 58 and 59. He does refer to the previous evidence in the dialogue, which really exists. Hence the fallacy here is not the usual strong form of the straw man argument, which sets up an imaginary point of view as representative of the opponent's position and then refutes it. Instead, the fallacy in Bruce's case is a kind of misrepresentation of commitment or twisting of a commitment out of its proper context of dialogue. The fallacy, in this case, is not one of the propositional content of an argument, but a misrepresentation of an arguer's stance or position in relation to how he has advocated that position. It is a misconception of the pragmatic status of a proposition in a dialogue. In terms of commitment stores, an element of the class of Wilma's concessions is wrongly taken to be an element of her class of theses or assertions.

Wilma tries to correct the problem at line 60, by the higher level move of correcting Bruce and pointing out that the commitment in question is attributable to him, not to her at all (in the strong form that Bruce maintains, at any rate). Then following that, at lines 61 through 69, there is confusion about who asserted what and an attempt to clarify the commitments of both parties.

So Bruce's fallacy has some confusing effects on the dialogue. It should be noted here that confusion about who is committed to or has gone on record as saying what is a common source of disputation in dialogue. Participants will argue back and forth: "You said that before!," "No, I never did!" and so forth, and if no record of previous commitments is available, the dispute can be impossible to settle. Here then is a useful advantage of the device of a written or taped record of the commitment store in dialogue.

Wilma's rejoinder at lines 47 through 53 puts Bruce on the defensive. Rashly, Bruce denies (line 61) that he is even committed to the proposition that the anencephalic person lacks conscious experience. This too is a kind of fallacy, because Bruce is denying that this proposition is a commitment of his, but the previous text of dialogue clearly shows that it is.

What has happened here is that Bruce feels attacked, and as a result he rushes to deny things. But note that this is not a retraction (which could be perfectly acceptable, perhaps), but a denial. Here Bruce is involved in a kind of inconsistency or ambivalence in relation to a commitment. This could be described as a kind of error or fallacy, but it would not appear to come under any known genre among the traditional informal fallacies. Yet it is a serious and not uncommon kind of problem in dialogue argumentation.

Following this, Bruce says at line 64, "Well, anyhow, you seemed to agree," which is a kind of retraction of the denial at line 61.

At line 68, Bruce starts to tighten up the discussion by adopting a kind of Socratic style of attacking Wilma's commitments. As this shift takes place, the goal of developing the positions of the two sides recedes more and more into the background. Bruce apparently still thinks that Wilma has conceded the point about the baby not having any conscious experience. He seems to think that Wilma has a dark-side commitment (a subcommitment) that he can bring to light, and that would enable him to use logic to refute Wilma's rejection of the decision made by Karl and Ethel. But Wilma replies (at line 73), "show me," taking a reasonable attitude towards Bruce's argument attempt.

Bruce once again (line 77) tries to secure Wilma's commitment to the proposition that the baby would not suffer. But she tries to wiggle out of it without actually denying it, saying, "I'll have more to say about that later." Then Bruce proposes a new concession that no one would suffer (line 79), followed by a rhetorical question, as he moves towards a statement of his ethical principle. The general principle he proposes is that if something is "all for the good" and hurts nobody, then it must be a good thing to do (lines 81 and 82).

Wilma refuses to concede this principle (line 85). By itself, this refusal would not commit a discussant to hold and defend that the principle is false. However, Wilma volunteers to take on such a commitment by starting an argument against Bruce's principle (lines 85 through 89). In fact, she advances a counterexample to it, which (it appears) would refute it. Bruce in turn, however, rejects the counterexample (lines

90 and 91), but for a wrong reason. He denies one of the suppositions of the counterexample, rather than denying the relevance of the counterexample itself. This is not a good move, but it is effective enough to cause Wilma to look for another counterexample. An interesting question of rules of dialogue is involved here. How many examples should be allowed to prove a point? Clearly a million examples would be obstructive for good dialogue. Yet, in some cases, allowing more than one example (as in this case) might seem reasonable enough.

Wilma's second counterexample (lines 92 through 94) appears to cause Bruce to have some doubts. Anyhow, Bruce gives up trying to support his abstract principle in its full generality. At lines 95 through 97 he substitutes a more specific principle about medical treatment. Wilma doesn't push her analogy of the rich doctor very far, but it does seem to show some potential of throwing doubt on Bruce's principle. However, she does not really try to draw an explicit conclusion from it to refute Bruce's principle.

At lines 97 through 99 Bruce reverts to the point about the baby not suffering any pain. Wilma's reply (lines 100 and 101) retracts the concession that the baby does not feel anything. She now maintains that this is not a safe or permissible assumption in the circumstances, even though she does not deny that it may be true. This is a kind of reasonable *argumentum ad ignorantiam* by Wilma. She is in effect arguing that even though we don't know for sure whether the baby does feel pain or not, it is not permissible to draw the conclusion that the baby does not feel pain. Her reason is that the baby should get the benefit of the doubt. She argues as follows: we don't know that the baby does not feel pain, therefore we have to conclude (or operate on the presumption) that the baby does (or could) feel pain. This is an argument from ignorance, but it is a reasonable kind of argument, in this case, that serves to shift the burden of proof in making a decision of how to operate on a presumption in a situation of uncertainty (ignorance).

Wilma's second point (lines 101 through 106) reverts to a repetition of her original argument at the beginning of the dialogue, to the effect that A is not a medical treatment if the sole purpose of A is to harvest the organs. This is the old argument over again (without the reference to doctors, patients, and the doctor's medical duties toward the patient).

Bruce then replies with an argument (lines 107–14) that turns on questions about the meanings of words. Bruce uses the analogy of a bone-marrow transplant case to argue that an action could, at least, be legitimately called "medical procedure" if it benefits somebody (who is not necessarily the donor). The term *treatment* is here revealed as disputably ambiguous, and Bruce shifts to the term *medical procedure,* perhaps not feeling very confident about arguing with Wilma about the meaning of the term *medical treatment.*

Next, Wilma introduces a new argument (115–21), arguing that it would be all right if the baby volunteered. Here she concedes quite a bit. But, at the same time, she denies that the baby can be correctly described as a "volunteer" and argues that its situation is ethically different from that of a consenting, adult volunteer. This is an important new line of argument in the discussion, and the dialogue now takes a turn toward a new ethical issue. Bruce (122–25) introduces the idea of the parents as proxy volunteers, but Wilma (126–29) rejects this concept as untenable. The issue here is an interesting ethical problem in its own right.

Bruce wants to get away from the philosophical issue of whether one can volunteer on behalf of someone else, and his next reply at line 130 is a little beside the point (his remark that the baby will not suffer). He then brings up the baby's "poor quality of life" (130–34).

At line 135, the dialogue takes an important turn. Previously, Bruce and Wilma had been arguing about the subissue of whether the baby could be said to be volunteering in some sense. But then at line 135, Wilma asks, "Am I hearing you right?" citing an apparent inconsistency in Bruce's line of argumentation. Wilma cites line 31, where Bruce said that Ethel's baby is one life to be considered. She is drawing an inference here, by saying at lines 137 and 138 that "it follows" in Bruce's view, that Ethel's baby has a life to be respected. Wilma is confronting Bruce at this point, saying that, on the one hand, he can hardly retract his commitment to the proposition that Ethel's baby has a life to be respected, while on the other hand, he has just said (at lines 133 and 134) that he didn't see how a major degree of importance could be assigned to the baby's life. There is the appearance of a clash of commitments here.

At lines 141 and 142, Bruce tries to extricate himself from the apparent inconsistency in his position by saying, "I am not committed to a policy of respect for life *per se.*" But then, starting at line 143, Wilma follows up her attack by questioning whether Bruce is living up to his real position in the dialogue, in light of his previous underlying commitments. Wilma says, "The whole underlying position your argument has been based on is the importance of saving human lives," and asks whether Bruce is now prepared to explicitly deny this important commitment. Bruce concedes (line 146) that he has "placed a lot of importance on this principle," conceding that he does not want to deny that he has a fundamental, underlying commitment to the saving of human lives.

Now the apparent conflict of commitments has been revealed and fixed, Wilma (148–51) confronts Bruce with the inconsistency in his position. Is Bruce still prepared to maintain that the baby's life is not a factor to which a major degree of importance can be assigned, or is Bruce serious and sincere in sticking to his underlying commitment to respect for human life? At line 144, the technique of revealing or "pulling out" an implicit commitment was used to bring Bruce's underlying commitment forward. Now Bruce is being asked to make a choice—which way is he prepared to take? At lines 150 and 151, Wilma asks him to resolve the conflict in his position.

At lines 152 through 154, Bruce sticks to his principles of respect for life as a commitment, but stresses that other lives are involved as well. He then evades further conflict by moving to the issue of who should make the decision. This is an internal subject shift, within the persuasion dialogue, away from the issue of whether the action A is right or wrong to the question of who should decide. This consideration is relevant, but it takes us somewhat away from the main issue. But following on the subject shift, there is a shift to a different type of dialogue at line 160, where Wilma asks why Karl and Ethel feel so strongly about the decision. Here the discussion shifts to an information-seeking dialogue where Bruce reports on the parents' feelings concerning their decision.[24] Is this a digression? Yes, to some extent it does take us away from the persuasion dialogue, but it is not a bad shift. It is what we will call a "licit" as opposed to an "illicit" shift. The shift has the constructive function of bringing useful information into the persuasion dialogue by anchoring the discussion of a moral issue to the specifics of a given case. At line 168, you can see how the internal information-seeking dialogue (160–67) functions in the larger persuasion dialogue in which it is embedded. From that point, they revert to the issue of who should decide such matters. This issue, as we said was brought in by a subject-matter shift from the main issue, but again it is a useful digression, which leads to the best speeches at lines 174 through 190, where both participants summarize their final positions. At lines 168 through 170, Wilma advances an *ad hominem* (poisoning the well) kind of argument, based on the information-seeking interlude, which suggests that the parents, Karl and Ethel, could have a biased point of view because of their "emotional frame of mind."

Wilma's concluding statements (174–83) present a mitigation of her original point of view. It appears to be a mild form of retraction. She is no longer prepared to assert that the decision to carry out action A is actually wrong. Instead, she takes the position that there is room for doubt, from the physician's point of view. So the original compound conflict reduces to a simple and single conflict and is partly resolved. This is a softening of the conflict to mere doubt rather than strict opposition.

Wilma's maintaining her doubt at this point in the argument is reasonable, because her argument up to this point has been fairly strong. She has successfully argued that action A is not medical treatment (in at least one sense), and she has shown that if the baby is a person, there are reasons for not going ahead with action A.

Wilma's final statement comes back to the point of view of the doctor's responsibility and sums up her position which has now emerged from the dialogue. She feels that the physician is obliged to have reservations in this type of case, because of the nature of the doctor-patient relationship, and because the physician must proceed with caution where there is doubt or uncertainty involved. Her rather modest position at the end is a kind of retraction or weakening of her original tighter position, even though, on the whole, her arguments have been dominant over Bruce's through the course of the dialogue.

In his final summation (184–90), Bruce reveals his consequentialist position in a more full-blown and general form. His position has emerged, in a more general and clearer way, as a result of the interchange of the dialogue.

Bruce is also conceding Wilma's point that the baby is a human being (or at least a being you can have respect for). Nevertheless, he has not weakened or reduced his original thesis and continues to maintain it at the end.

The dialogue began with a particular case that posed a conflict of opinion for Bruce and Wilma concerning the decision about the particular action A. However, by the end of the dialogue, Wilma's position had emerged as a general and abstract ethical point of view with a deontological cast. Her concern was the physician's norms of medical ethics, and especially the obligation of respect for a patient that is a human being. Bruce comes out of the dialogue with a general type of ethical position that could be called "utilitarian" (or "consequentialist") in nature. Their original opposition has not disappeared but it has taken an altered form.

3.3 Dialectical Shifts

During the course of a conversation between two or more parties there can be a change in the context of dialogue or a *dialectical (dialogical) shift* from one type of dialogue to another. Empirical studies of Gumperz[25] showed, for example, that students knew from a change of "register" when a conversation changed from classroom talk in an academic discussion to personal chat. You could detect the shift by a change of pace and attitude in the speech exchanges.

Another example of a dialectical shift would be the following case.

CASE 3.1 A union-management negotiation group finish their bargaining session and adjourn to the bar where they start arguing about who will have the best soccer team that year.

All the same participants may be taking part in both sessions, but the context of the argument has changed, as well as the topic. One dialogue was a negotiation, and the second could perhaps have been a kind of critical discussion on which team arguably has the best prospects.

In the union-management case, the first dialogue was properly closed off, presumably by the chairman or mediator who ran the meeting. Then there was a clear break, and even a change of venue, that marked the transition to the opening of the second dialogue. However, in some cases the transition is not so clearly marked. The one dialogue can be sandwiched between the prior and the subsequent parts of an enveloping sequence of dialogue of another type. Practical reasons can cause an interruption, but then the dialogue can quickly shift back to the original type.

In the following case there was a sudden dialectical shift from a critical discussion to an action-directed deliberation dialogue.

CASE 3.2 Karen and Doug were cycling along the bicycle path while having a conversation together. As they cycled along, they were discussing the pros and cons of living in a house versus living in a condominium. Doug said, "Sometimes the walls in those condominiums are pretty thin, and you can hear the neighbors." Karen replied, "Yes, but with a condominium it is easier to travel. You don't have to worry about cutting the grass or having the walk shoveled while you are away." Doug agreed, saying "Yes, that can be expensive." Just then they came to a junction in the road, passing a sign giving the directions to the next villages. Karen immediately said, "I think if we turn to the right, the path goes to Sassenheim. Do you want to go to Sassenheim?"

Just at Karen's last speech, there was a quick shift in the conversation, necessitated by a practical need to pay attention to directions. After they had returned to the junction, and started along the path to Sassenheim, the critical discussion of house versus condominium resumed.

But at Karen's last speech above, there had been a shift from the critical discussion to a type of deliberation dialogue which concerned a practical decision.

In this case, the shift from the critical discussion to the action-directed dialogue was interruptive. Karen shifted to a different type of dialogue by bringing up the issue of directions. But in this case, the shift was a legitimate (licit) one, because there was an immediate practical need to talk about directions. Once this question was settled, the conversation shifted back to the continuation of the critical discussion. Even though there was no formal closing off of the first dialogue, by a chairman or mediator, there was a good reason to close off the first dialogue, and since it could subsequently be resumed with no real loss except for a small inconvenience, there was nothing illegitimate or suspicious about the shift.

Some dialectical shifts are definite and sharp, where there is a *déplacement* of the one type of dialogue by the other. In other cases, there is a gradual shifting or *glissement* from the one type of dialogue to the other. In some cases, the two types of dialogue overlap, and we have a dialogue of mixed type.

In many cases, having a dialectical shift to another type of dialogue can enhance the quality of the original dialogue, because the second dialogue is functionally related to the argumentation in the first dialogue. When there exists such a functional relationship between two dialogues, we say one dialogue is *embedded* in the other. Some examples are found in section 3.1 where we discussed the inquiry. Consider the case of an appeal to expert opinion during the course of a critical discussion. Suppose a panel is having a discussion on whether or not to build a new nuclear reactor. Expert opinions are consulted on whether nuclear reactors are safe. Here, the intelligent solicitation and use of the expert opinions could greatly improve the critical discussion.[26]

In case 3.2, however, even though there are shifts back and forth between two types of dialogue, and even though these shifts are legitimate, there is no functional relationship between the two dialogues. Therefore, case 3.2 does not display an embedding of one dialogue in the other. This goes to show that not every licit shift is an embedding.

Some dialogue shifts are quite reasonable and legitimate and do not create problems or fallacies. Some dialectical shifts, however, are illicit, and these illicit shifts are often associated with informal fallacies. To judge whether a shift was licit or illicit in a particular case of argumentation, you first have to ask what the original context of dialogue was supposed to be. Then you have to identify the new context and ask whether the shift was licit or illicit by looking backwards and judging by the goals and standards of the original context. Is the new dialogue supporting those old goals, or at least allowing their fulfillment to be carried forward, or is it blocking them? Was the shift agreed to by the original speech partners, or was the shift unilateral, or even forced by one party? These are the kinds of questions that need to be asked.

The first dialectical shift that occurred in the case of the discussion on medical ethics (lines 68 through 73) in section 3.2 above was a kind of shift that occurred within the persuasion dialogue itself. The dialogue still continued to be a persuasion dialogue after the shift occurred, but it was a different kind of persuasion dialogue. Definitions, assumptions, and moves all had to be made clearly and explicitly after the shift. The dialogue tightened up, and then very strict attention was paid to the exact wording of a claim, and allowances for retractions or qualifications concerning how what one said previously was to be interpreted became much less permissive. In the tightened-up phase of the discussion, both parties were much more careful to phrase their contributions very rigorously and deliberately, for fear of being attacked on the implications of what they said, being subject to unfriendly interpretations, or even being accused of inconsistency in their commitments.

The basic rules of persuasion dialogue seem to carry over, from before to after the shift in this instance, but the rigor with which the rules are interpreted and applied—especially in drawing inferences from commitments—appears to have changed. Moreover, as we go on to show in chapter 4, some of the rules of dialogue do significantly change their character through this tightening-up process, and the resulting shift to a different structure of persuasion dialogue radically alters the nature of the very concept of commitment.

The tightened up part of the dialogue is clearly functionally related to the main dialogue. In the main dialogue several assertions are challenged and defended by argument. The tightened up part concentrates upon the one assertion that Karl and Ethel made the right decision (line 70). Bruce has to defend this assertion in the light of Wilma's position as it has developed thus far in the main dialogue. So clearly the commitments in the second (tightened up) dialogue originate in the main dialogue. Also the results of the second dialogue should be carried back to the main dialogue, or have some specifiable influence on the commitments in the main dialogue.

In the main dialogue there are, as the shift occurs, many assertions, arguments, and concessions on both sides. The dialogical situation is quite complex, and the possibility of easy retractions doesn't make it easier to make headway. In this context it may be a good idea to concentrate on one particular issue for a while—and not to allow retractions—

and reason it out. It is not hard to see that the second dialogue may further the goal of the main dialogue. So what we have here is an embedding of one type (subtype) of persuasion dialogue in another. (At least it could be described or modeled in that way.)

The examples of shift given thus far are all shifts from one type of dialogue to another. We shall discuss some more examples of this general type of shift. After, we shall briefly discuss the two other types of shifts: *internal shifts* and *shifts of flavor.*

1. Shifts from One Type of Dialogue to Another. A complex dialogue is a kind of sequence of dialogue made up of two distinct types of dialogue; that is, when there is a shift in a discussion from one type of dialogue to another. For example, suppose the Socialist minister of finance in case 2.6 goes on to argue that tax exemptions of the sort he has profited from should be allowed, at least temporarily, as acceptable, and should not be penalized. Suppose that this minister then goes on to propose that if his critics will abstain from moving for penalties for these exemptions, he will refrain from opposing a bill that these critics would profit from. In a case like this, what has happened is that there has been a shift from persuasion dialogue to a negotiation (bargaining) type of dialogue.

From the perspective of persuasion dialogue this is not a permissible move. The minister may be accused of a fallacy, since he reneges on his commitment, in this case his burden of proof for his position on the permissibility of tax exemptions. It is the fallacy of substituting an offer for an argument. In the context of a negotiation dialogue this could be acceptable, but from the perspective of persuasion dialogue we may call it the *fallacy of bargaining.*

Characteristically, in negotiation dialogue, one may propose to trade one concession for another. But in other contexts of dialogue this could be entirely out of place. The following example displays a dialectical shift from an expert consultation to a negotiation:

CASE 3.3   A doctor recommends that her patient quit both smoking and drinking, giving medical reasons for the recommendation.

Patient: O.K. I'll quit smoking, as long as you allow a glass of wine once in a while.

In this case the shift is from the main type of information-seeking dialogue to another main type: negotiation. For the rest, it is quite similar to that of the bargaining minister. One only has to replace the term *recommends* with *tries to convince* and the case would illustrate the fallacy of bargaining again; that is, it would show us a shift from persuasion dialogue to negotiation. Evidently, the study of fallacies as far as they are connected with shifts moving away from persuasion dialogue is part of a more general study of illicit transitions from one context of dialogue to another.

Shifts from negotiation dialogue to critical discussion are common in divorce dispute mediation, and mediators often try to encourage this kind of dialectical shift, because it can be a positive direction that fosters constructive agreement. For example, suppose a divorcing couple are arguing about child custody. It may be very positive if the dialogue shifts to a critical discussion on how well each party is equipped to look after the child. If both parties are working, who is free to look after the child? Who is best at providing a structured life for the child? Who has shown the most interest and support in looking after and spending time with the child in the past? Instead of trying to "score points" in hard-nosed bargainings, the participants are now posing questions that can be answered more objectively by looking at evidence. By engaging in a critical discussion, they come around to a more dispassionate, less personal type of exchange that is less close to quarreling. Of course, in this type of case, the quarrel is always lurking under the surface of the discussion, and it is all too easy for the dialogue to degenerate into a sequence of counterblaming and personal attack.

Referring again to the discussion of the extension of case 2.6 above, where the minister of finance commits the fallacy of bargaining, notice that this type of case is also interesting in relation to the *argumentum ad hominem*.[27] The minister's critics could accuse him of bias, partiality, and self-interest, claiming that he has abandoned the political issue as a disinterested discussant and has pushed for one side in order to support his own personal interests in the matter. Such a criticism is a species of *ad hominem* attack which can be a legitimate kind of argumentation in some cases, yet is notoriously subject to fallacies and abuses. Thus to understand the *argumentum ad hominem* as a species of informal fallacy, the ability to detect and understand a dialectical shift is crucial. This fallacy is further discussed in section 3.4 below.

In this case, the shift is from one type of argumentative (conflict-centered) dialogue to another. But in other cases of complex dialogue, the shift is from an argumentative type of dialogue to a different kind of speech event. One example is a shift from an argument to the telling of a joke or some other kind of banter that has nothing to do with argument.

Other examples of shifts from one type of dialogue to another have already been mentioned. A political debate, for example, can start out as a kind of persuasion dialogue and then degenerate into a quarrel, as the pressures of partisan politics escalate a demand to win by impressing a wider audience.

A *cascading effect* can occur when there are multiple shifts from one type of dialogue to another. For example, one of the partners in an inquiry may believe that she has already grasped the truth about the matter under investigation. She may then start a critical discussion to convince her peers. Next, the participants in this critical discussion may get more and more conscious of the presence of an audience. Thus they may be tempted to commit certain fallacies, such as appeals to popular passions *(argumentum ad populum)* and *ad hominem* attacks. But these are fallacies only from the perspective of persuasion dialogue. At a certain stage, one should say that the participants are no longer engaged in a persuasion dialogue but rather in a debate. Moves that were fallacious from the former perspective may now have to count as permissible and effective strategy.

However, in figure 3.4, that is not the end of the story. As the participants intensify their *ad hominem* attacks, getting more and more abusive, they may leave even the standards of efficient debate and cascade down into a personal quarrel. Typically, they then forget about their audience (a serious fallacy in the context of a debate!). And if they keep forgetting, a stage is reached where it no longer makes sense to say that the participants are involved in a debate. In this type of case, the dialogue started as a dispassionate and reasonable inquiry into an issue, but then moved downwards to the eristic level of appeals to popular passions, personal attacks, and recriminations, and thence to an outright quarrel.

On the righthand side of figure 3.4 another route is taken. As the participants deliberate about some issue they may get more and more aware of the practical consequences of adopting a certain position. They may take sides and move into a critical discussion. Next they may be tempted to move away from a principled discussion on the issue itself to a discussion of advantages and disadvantages for each involved. This may still be no more than a shift to another persuasion dialogue. But as concern over the outcome of the discussion deepens and overshadows concern of the quality of the argumentation on which the outcome is based, the participants may be tempted to resort to special pleading *(argumentum ad misericordiam)* and promises (a form of the *argumentum ad baculum*). Thus a persuasion dialogue may change into a negotiation dialogue. Negotiation again may cascade down from a level of reasonable give and take to a level of harsh threats, and then degenerate into a quarrel.

We discussed a number of shifts that take one from one of the six main types of dialogues, or a mixed type, to another (see figure 3.1).

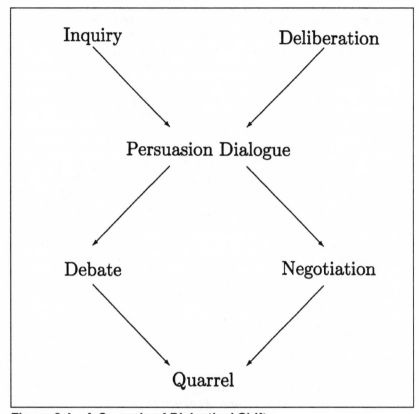

Figure 3.4   A Cascade of Dialectical Shifts

Other shifts take place within one and the same main type, but introduce another subtype of that main type. For instance, an eristic discussion may run down into an outright quarrel (within the main type of "eristics"), or an interviewer could maneuver an interview into an interrogation (within "information-seeking dialogue"), or a means-end discussion could shift towards a discussion of the ends themselves (within "deliberation"). Within the main type of persuasion dialogue, we already discussed an example of such a shift: the tightening up (lines 68 through 73) exhibited in the case study of the discussion on medical ethics. In this example, the type of dialogue—persuasion dialogue—remains the same, but the rigor and quality of the dialogue change significantly. When this tightening-up shift is fallacious, it is called *quibbling* or *logic-chopping*. However, as chapter 4 will show, such a shift is not always fallacious or illicit. It can represent a legitimate shift from one reasoned mode of dialogue to another equally reasoned mode of the same type of dialogue.

2. Internal Shifts. Internal shifts are shifts within one and the same type of dialogue. With such shifts there is no change of normative model: rules and goals remain the same. We mention three types.

The first type of internal shift is the change from a simple conflict to a dispute, within a persuasion dialogue. In this type of shift, one participant ceases to merely question the other participant's thesis and becomes actively opposed to it. What has shifted here is the one party's point of view, and such a shift can radically alter the nature of a persuasion or other type of dialogue. Generally, we may call such shifts, *shifts of attitude*. These shifts may be fallacious or not depending on the extent to which the rules of dialogue permit such changes of attitude.

A second type of internal shift is a change in the subject of a dialogue, meaning a change in the issue which was originally conceived as the subject to be discussed in the dialogue. This kind of shift, which we may call *shift of issue*, has to do with relevance and irrelevance of speech acts in a dialogue. The well-known reproach "you are changing the subject" points to fallacious instances of this type of shift. But sometimes a change of subject is licensed by the rules, or even called for by the internal dynamics of a discussion.

A third kind of internal shift has to do with taking sides on an issue as an argument progresses. For example, while two parties in a persuasion dialogue are discussing an issue, a third party, who was initially a neutral observer, could suddenly interject and begin to take part in the discussion by actively supporting the point of view of one side of the issue. This may be called a *shift of participation*.

3. Shifts from One Flavor of Dialogue to Another. In section 3.1 we introduced the concept of a "flavor." In the course of a dialogue, flavors may appear and disappear or change quality. That is, flavors may shift. For instance, a persuasion dialogue could, for some time, proceed logically and dispassionately, until a certain remark introduces an eristic flavor. This does not necessarily mean that the persuasion dialogue has stopped and that eristics takes over. But even if there is no shift of type of dialogue, something of eristics is blended in. Turn to the dialogue on medical ethics, lines 54 through 56, and notice how the eristic flavor is introduced by the very choice of words ("all that medical stuff"). The dialogue, however, does not shift to an eristic discussion or quarrel.

3.4 Illicit Shifts and Fallacies

A deeper understanding of many of the so-called informal fallacies can only be achieved through the realization that they characteristically involve dialectical shifts.

The *argumentum ad populum*[28] or playing on the popular sentiments, often involves a shift from persuasion dialogue to a type of discourse described by Perelman and Olbrechts-Tyteca[29] as the *epidictic
speech*, where the goal of the speaker is to heighten the adhesion of his
audience to some common ideal or values. In the epidictic speech, in
contrast to the persuasion dialogue, there is no thesis supposed to be
held in doubt by the audience and to be argued for by the speaker.
Instead, the speaker's goal is the exaltation of virtues that he and his
audience implicitly share, even though they have not been, or perhaps
could not be, stated explicitly as so many propositions. The goal of this
type of discourse is to strengthen the adherence to values already held
dearly by the group by bringing these values from a subconscious level
and articulating them in an emotionally moving manner. Moving and
poetic key phrases (sound bites) are the phrases used to evoke deeply
held values in this type of speech. For example, Ronald Reagan, in a
speech in March 1985, described the freedom fighters of Nicaragua as
"the moral equal of our Founding Fathers." This sound bite evoked
deeply held American values in a speech supporting the Contra movement in Nicaragua by drawing a memorable and moving comparison.
Judged from the perspective of epidictic speech this parallel may be
appropriate, or even clever. Much depends upon the audience. But from
the perspective of persuasion dialogue it may at the same time constitute
a fallacy, namely, an illicit shift to another genre, impeding the success of
the original persuasion dialogue.

Another emotional fallacy is the *argumentum ad baculum*,[30] or
appeal to force, which often involves the flavor of the quarrel (fight)
mixed in with a persuasion dialogue. Often the basic problem in sorting
out cases of *ad baculum* argumentation is to distinguish between the
speech act of an argument (to persuade) and the speech act of a threat,
which is part of an eristic quarrel.

During a negotiation type of dialogue, threats and appeals to
force or sanctions are characteristic. However, if the context is supposed
to be that of a critical discussion, the same kind of argumentation which
was appropriate enough in the negotiation context can become highly
fallacious. Being open to fairly considering the arguments on both sides
of an issue is very important in a critical discussion. In this context, the
use of the *ad baculum* argument is always highly suspicious and tends to
be at odds with the discussion, because it is a way of trying to force
closing off the free expression of one's point of view that is necessary for
critical discussion.

CASE 3.4   A union leader argues for a pay raise. He points out that the
workers may get very angry if they don't get the pay raise and

may go on strike with disastrous consequences for all. The president of the board retorts that, though he personally would be glad to grant the pay raise, his colleagues on the board would probably sooner close the shop.

The problem with this case is that the union leader's argument is in itself worthy of consideration. However, this union leader will himself be a major voice when the workers assemble to decide about a strike. So there is also a flavor of the threat in the argument. And this threat is paid back in kind by the president of the board. In this way, the context of critical discussion easily gets lost. Threats will not just intermingle with but actually take the place of arguments.

From this perspective, the *argumentum ad baculum* as an illicit shift from persuasion dialogue to negotiation is just a special case of the fallacy of bargaining. The same holds for the *argumentum ad misericordiam*, the appeal to pity, in which pleas take the place of arguments. The fallacy of bargaining again, together with other fallacies that substitute something else for argument, is a special case of the fallacy of *abandonment of discussion* (i.e., of persuasion dialogue).[31] What these fallacies have in common is that whoever commits one of them reneges on his original propositional commitments (burden of proof, etc.) in persuasion dialogue by moving to another type of discourse.

We are not implying that a movement away from persuasion dialogue is always fallacious. Sometimes it may be better to close off the persuasion dialogue and try to settle the matter by negotiation or some other means. The problem is that often the persuasion dialogue isn't closed off properly at all and the shift occurs without both parties being aware of it and agreeing to go along with it.

Neither do we want to suggest that movement toward persuasion dialogue is always an improvement and could never be illicit or fallacious:

CASE 3.5   Wife: I'll do the cooking if you'll wash the dishes.
            Husband: Why should I?

In this case the wife is, presumably, negotiating about the division of labor within the household. The husband shifts to a challenge, but there is no assertion to be challenged. Yet by the challenge itself the impression is created that there is an assertion to be challenged, namely, that the wife asserted that the husband should wash the dishes (she didn't). The fallacy is known as *straw man*. It's an illicit creation of propositional commitment. The shift is from negotiation toward persuasion dialogue.

Argumentum ad hominem is a technique of argument used to . attack someone's position by raising questions about that person's character or personal situation. The personal or abusive *ad hominem* alleges bad character for veracity, or bad moral character generally. The circumstantial *ad hominem* alleges a practical inconsistency between the person and his or her circumstances. A third type of *ad hominem,* the bias or "poisoning the well" variant, alleges that the person has a hidden agenda or something to gain and is therefore not an honest or objective arguer.

Whether an *ad hominem* argument is reasonable or fallacious, in a particular case, depends on the context of dialogue. For an attorney to raise allegations about the bad moral character or character for veracity of a witness he is cross-examining in court can be a reasonable kind of *ad hominem* argumentation. Yet in a scientific inquiry, for example, criticizing a scientific argument by attacking the scientist personally for his alleged bad moral character could be inappropriate and fallacious.

The *ad hominem* argument is characteristic of the quarrel, where it is well suited to the goal of the quarrel which includes airing personal grievances by fixing blame on the moral character of one's opponent. The *ad hominem* can be a reasonable argument as used in a critical discussion, but often it has a tendency to go wrong by causing the argumentation to shift by a *glissement* into a quarrel, as the exchange becomes more heated and personal. In such a case, the *ad hominem* fallacy can occur because the argument was originally supposed to be a critical discussion, and quarreling is a very poor and inefficient way of carrying out the goals of a critical discussion, perhaps even blocking it altogether.

When the bias type of *ad hominem* attack is used in a critical discussion, the allegation is that the respondent has illicitly and covertly shifted to a negotiation dialogue. The accusation is that he is only making a pretence of looking at both sides of the issue with an open attitude of looking at the evidence and that he began by being set to push for his own side for personal gain. For example, in a critical discussion on the issue of acid rain, one party accuses another of being a major stockholder in a coal company. The *ad hominem* attack alleges that his mind was made up so he never really (honestly) entered into the critical discussion at all. Generally with this type of *ad hominem* argument, an alleged shift from one context of dialogue to another is involved.

Shifts that go from another type of dialogue to a quarrel are always dangerous and often illicit. This type of shift is closely associated with the *argumentum ad hominem.* For example, the negotiation between the union and management of Eastern Airlines during the strike period of 1989 shifted gradually in a *glissement* from a negotiation dialogue to a quarreling type of dialogue.

CASE 3.6   The unions began to portray Frank Lorenzo, the chief execu-
tive officer of Eastern, as a symbol of greed and ruthlessness.
After Lorenzo had tried to cut costs by cutting back on wages,
the union adopted a tactic of making him the issue of the
dispute, by portraying him as a "brutal, unscrupulous auto-
crat." This approach was taken up with enthusiasm by the
employees of Eastern who booed and shouted, "There's the
slimeball!" when shown a picture of Lorenzo.[32] According to
a report in *Newsweek*, however, Lorenzo did not really de-
serve this kind of treatment—although he was said to be a
quiet and shy sort of person he was by no means the bad
person portrayed in these attacks. However, as this *ad hominem*
attack escalated, the workers became "obsessed" with it, and
the "fight became so personal that any possibility for compromise was lost," according to *Newsweek*.[33]

In this case, the gradual shift to the quarrel forced into place by
one side eventually destroyed the possibilities for constructive negotiation in time to address the problem. The outcome was a prolonged
deadlock, and the company went into bankruptcy.

The *argumentum ad ignorantiam*[34] is a kind of argumentation
that involves shifting a burden of proof in dialogue. This can involve a
shift from one persuasion dialogue to another. In some cases it can be
making a simple conflict of opinion into a dispute:

CASE 3.7   Wife: You should wash the dishes.
Husband: Why should I?
Wife: Why shouldn't you?

In this case there was a shift from a persuasion dialogue centering
on a single and simple conflict (there is just one proposition in dispute
and only the wife has a burden of proof) to a dispute (in which the
husband, too, has a burden of proof). The wife's move is presumably
fallacious from the perspective of the first persuasion dialogue. It may
easily lead to an indefinitely long series of interchanges of the same type,
until one of the parties accepts its burden of proof. The fallacy of an
argumentum ad ignorantiam in this type of case consists of an illicit
introduction of a propositional commitment and an illicit shift to another
persuasion dialogue.

In other cases, the *argumentum ad ignorantiam* is a fallacy of
wrong conclusion which involves a shift from a context of a practical,
action-guiding dialogue to that of an inquiry. The fallacy here is that of
requiring a high standard of proof for a conclusion when the proper

context of an action-guiding (practical) dialogue should require only a plausible presumption as an appropriate conclusion in relation to a practical problem.

CASE 3.8   There is no evidence that quintozene is dangerous to human beings.

Robinson[35] argues that this case is a fallacious *argumentum ad ignorantiam* because it is fair to infer the tacit conclusion that quintozene is not dangerous to human beings and the tacit premise that "bad consequences have been searched for, and would have been observed if they had occurred." But much depends on the context of dialogue. If the dialogue is that of an inquiry, the statement in case 3.8 could be the conclusion, backed up by careful findings. But then again, we do not know this, until more information is given. The same statement could have been made by a physician who is about to use quintozene to save a patient in a medical emergency.

Another fallacy worth noting in this connection is the fallacy of *many questions*, which characteristically, in many cases, involves a change of flavor from persuasion dialogue to an interrogation. Instead of allowing the respondent to challenge the presumptions of his question in a reasonable order appropriate for persuasion dialogue, the questioner shifts to a forceful (yes-no) mode of interrogation.

The fallacy of many questions is very sensitive to contexts of dialogue. The question, "Have you stopped beating your spouse?" could be nonfallacious if asked by a cross-examining attorney in a trial to a person who just previously admitted that he had beaten his spouse in the past.[36] Of course, in another context, asking this kind of question could be rightly judged fallacious. It depends on the context of dialogue in a particular case whether asking such a question is fallacious or not. In particular, it depends on the prior commitments of the respondent in the prior sequence of the dialogue in the given case.

The *argumentum ad verecundiam* is usually treated as a fallacy, but many appeals to expert opinion in argumentation are quite reasonable as arguments, provided the context of dialogue is appropriate. Generally with *ad verecundiam* argumentation, there are four participants and three contexts of dialogue involved. It is a mixed dialogue situation. Two primary participants are engaged in a critical discussion, and one accuses the other of not paying sufficient attention to an expert opinion that he (the first party) has brought forward to support his line of argument. Presupposed is a secondary dialogue exchange between the first party and some expert source that has been consulted or interpreted by this party to the critical discussion. This party is alleging that his opponent in the critical discussion has not been properly respectful to the authority that has been consulted and is therefore immodestly saying, in effect, that he "knows better" than the expert. The first party is therefore appealing to a fourth-party audience, arguing that they should not take the arguments of this second party seriously for, after all, he is a person who is so immodest and unwise that he thinks he knows better than the experts.[37] Thus the third context of dialogue is the dialogue between some fourth-party wider audience and the two original participants who are in a contest to persuade this audience.

Generally, the expert consultant dialogue is often mixed with the critical discussion in a way that is a highly positive factor in supporting the goals of the critical discussion. A critical discussion on the issue of whether nuclear reactors are good or bad, for example, might be not nearly so intelligent and revealing if it did not have input from expert opinions mixed in, as noted in the discussion of this type of embedding in the preceding section.

The *argumentum ad verecundiam* characteristically becomes a fallacy where there has been an illicit shift from a persuasion dialogue to a type of information-seeking dialogue. One participant attempts to treat the other as a "pupil" who should be eager to learn these new facts instead of contesting what an expert has said by raising critical questions.

A fallacy is traditionally said to be an argument that seems valid but is not.[38] But this slogan needs to be revised, or at least interpreted in a special way. By valid, not just deductive (semantic) validity should be meant. What should be referred to is the use of a technique of argumentation in a context of dialogue. The argument techniques we have referred to, traditionally known as fallacies, can be used reasonably to support goals of dialogue in some cases, and used fallaciously as sophistical tactics to block or subvert legitimate goals of dialogue in other cases. The job is to study the uses of these techniques to develop criteria to aid in sorting between the fallacious and nonfallacious uses of them in particular cases.

By seeming validity, not just what seems to be correct to the individual respondent, to whom the particular argument was addressed, should be meant. This psychologistic account of seeming validity should be rejected. Also, what the proponent or the respondent's motives were, whether he intended to deceive or had a guilty mind, are not requirements of judging the use of an argument as fallacious.

Two factors often make fallacious arguments seem valid—that is, they make the use of such argument techniques effective in a dialogue, even when it is not correct. One is that in many cases, perhaps similar cases in many respects, these argumentation techniques are used correctly to support legitimate goals of dialogue. The other factor is that there is often a dialectical shift involved. The use of this particular technique might be quite inappropriate and incorrect in one type of dialogue, running quite contrary to the goals of the dialogue, but if the context has shifted to another type of dialogue, the use of this same technique may now be quite appropriate. If the shift has not been perceived, or if it was a covert or unilateral shift, not made out in the open, or agreed to by both parties, the incorrect argument may appear correct on the surface to the uncritical respondent or observer.

The view of fallacies arising out of this analysis may not be popular with everyone, because it places a serious burden of proof on the would-be critic who is to go around declaring arguments fallacious. He can no longer simply declare: "Aha, that's an *ad hominem* argument; therefore, it's fallacious," or "That's an appeal to authority: therefore it's a fallacy." Since the uses of these argumentation techniques are sometimes quite reasonable in some types of dialogue, it is incumbent upon the critic to show why they are fallacious in a particular case. This puts a serious burden of proof on the critic to support a charge of fallaciousness by citing evidence of two types: (1) textual evidence from the given text of discourse in a particular case, and (2) contextual evidence showing the type of dialogue involved, including the existence of dialectical shifts.

What is important is the identification of the type of dialogue that the participants were supposed to be engaged in and the commitments of the participants, as revealed though their speech acts as verbal exchanges in the dialogue. But commitments are not beliefs or motives (psychological entities) of the participants. Commitments are inserted into the commitment stores of the participants in a dialogue in virtue of the rules of the dialogue.

In our view, many fallacies are illicit shifts from one type of dialogue to another. But the question could be raised, if one has stepped outside the scope of rules of a certain type of dialogue, how can one still be obliged to adhere to them? In other words, how can we ever pin down a charge of fallacy against someone, once that person has opted out of, say, a persuasion dialogue? It would no longer seem to make sense to apply the norms that pertain to this type of dialogue.

But this question is ill-conceived. One may as well wonder how a burglar can ever be said to have committed a crime if he uses the excuse that he has opted out of the conventional legal system. In fact, terrorists often claim this type of excuse.

Once a fallacy has been committed, it may not be fallacious from the norms of the new type of dialogue one has entered. The burglar's action, for example, may be condoned by the "code of the underworld."

Even though the move may be all right from that perspective, it can still be described as an error from the point of view of the norms of the original type of dialogue. The perpetrator may be said to have reneged on some commitment that he had in the original type of dialogue. For example, there could be an unfulfilled burden of proof or an unanswered question. And the other parties are justified in demanding that this party live up to the commitment in the original type of dialogue.

Whether an argument is to be judged fallacious or nonfallacious in a given case then is a matter of judging the commitments of both the proponent and the respondent as revealed by their performances in a context of dialogue. Such an evaluation involves applying a normative model of reasonable dialogue, perhaps even more than one model, to a particular case.

3.5 Problems to Be Solved

We briefly discussed only those types of dialogue that immediately interfere with persuasion dialogue. Actually there is a whole field of study here that includes many other types of dialogue. Many other mixed types could be adduced (we gave only three examples). The usefulness of the concept of 'commitment' is not restricted to the area we studied. For example, the functioning of commitment in negotiation should be compared with its functioning in persuasion dialogues. Commitment is a central concept in the normative model of negotiation dialogue given by Donohue, and it is instructive to compare his use of the concept with the analysis of it given in chapter 3.[39]

More clarification is needed of concepts relating to various dialogue attitudes, such as 'critical doubt.' Van Eemeren and Grootendorst define a critical doubt as an attitude one party in a critical discussion has toward the attitude of the other party.[40] Walton discusses different ways of defining critical doubt, then defines bias in argumentation as a species of failure of critical doubt.[41] It is an interesting problem to try to define bias of an argument in relation to commitment in dialogue and also to try to devise empirical criteria which could be used to identify bias in a given argument.

It remains to be investigated whether 'flavor' is a viable concept for use in the systematic description of dialogues and to devise empirical criteria to identify flavor shifts in given cases.

The distinction between *déplacement* and *glissement* indicates one approach to a further study of dialectical shifts. Anyhow, we do not think we have exhausted the subject of shifts and of fallacies as illicit shifts. For one thing, we still need procedural rules that may help to judge various types of shifts in dialogue and to evaluate their fallaciousness.

It would be useful to collect more cases of shifts, for example, shifts from a critical discussion to a quarrel, in order to study different ways these shifts

1. can take place

2. can be difficult to resist, and

3. can deceive the participants into being unaware of their existence, and thereby

4. lead them to commit fallacies.

The *ad hominem* is often a key indicator of the shift to the quarrel, and more casework on this fallacy would be helpful in better understanding how some very significant dialectical shifts work in practice.

3.6 Summary

Each of the main types of dialogue outlined in figure 3.1, and systematically surveyed in figure 3.2—persuasion, dialogue, inquiry, negotiation, deliberation, information-seeking, and eristic—is primarily characterized by its initial situation and its main goal. There is only a rough notion of the kind of procedures that would get one from the initial situation to a fulfillment of the objective of the dialogue. But on a more specific level types of dialogue are given as normative models of dialogue, meaning that they offer us ideal models that prescribe how one ought to act in order to fulfill the goal of that type of dialogue. Such normative models are not meant to be descriptive; for instance, argumentative models are not meant to describe how people actually behave when they argue.

In the persuasion dialogue, the aim of each participant is to persuade the other participant that her thesis is true (point of view is right), using only the commitments of the other party as premises of arguments for this purpose. Thus in a persuasion dialogue, it is crucial not only that the participants take turns, but also that they listen to each other and gain an accurate comprehension of what the commitments of that other party really are. Also, they must use this information, and abide by it, in their arguments.

Subtypes of persuasion dialogue can be classified according to five criteria:

1.   the type of initial conflict,

2.   the nature of the subject matter,

3.   the degree of rigidity of the rules,

4.   the preciseness of the procedural description of the dialogue, and

5.   the admixtures of other types of dialogue.

Every persuasion dialogue is based on an initial conflict of opinions, but these conflicts can be of various types. In a simple conflict, only the one party has a positive thesis to defend, the other party being merely a critical doubter or questioner, with no expressed positive viewpoint of his own. In a conflict of contrary opinions, both parties have a thesis to defend, and these theses are contraries.

In all types of dialogue, both parties ideally have a recorded log of their individual commitments to any given point to which the dialogue has progressed, called the participant's "commitment store." This, of course, is a normative ideal which is often not met in ordinary conversation in "real life," where arguers often forget their commitments, or even deny they ever made them, and no record of what really happened may be available for scrutiny. Nevertheless, commitment is a vital innovative ideal in judging argumentation as fallacious or nonfallacious in a given case. Unfortunately, in many cases, not enough context of dialogue is given to yield a sufficient basis of textual evidence to determine whether something is a commitment of some arguer or not.

The persuasion dialogue, as an instrument of conflict resolution, is a kind of balance-of-considerations framework of argumentation where the participant who has the strongest argument—that is, meets the burden of proof successfully—is the one who succeeds in meeting her goal. This is to decide the outcome of the dialogue. Inquiry, by contrast, does not start from a conflict of opinions, but from a problem situation in which neither participant has taken up a particular position. It has the goal of using premises that can be solidly established, so that, hopefully, there will be no need for subsequent retractions, to prove a proposition that would provide a solution to the problem, or alternatively, to show definitely that such a proposition cannot be found or cannot be proved, from what is known. Thus the inquiry has the very important cumulative property of moving forward without ideally there being any retraction at all.

Unlike the inquiry, the deliberation is not based on premises that can be known to be true or firmly established. Deliberation is concerned with how to act most prudently by trying to visualize the future and the plausible consequences of future actions. Deliberation always involves speculation and plausible guesswork, based on assumptions that are subject to change as time passes and new information comes into consideration.

Information-seeking dialogue arises from a situation where one party has some knowledge or information and the other party wants or needs to acquire it, and possibly also to make it available to others. Expert consultation dialogue is one very important subtype of information-seeking dialogue. The interview and the interrogation are still other subtypes.

The quarrel is a subtype of eristic dialogue where both sides, as a result of a hidden grievance, suddenly attack each other in a hostile manner. As a normative model for argumentation, the quarrel is not very positive. But the quarrel is not wholly worthless as a type of dialogue, for it allows for the expression of feelings that would not be polite to give voice to normally in everyday conversation. This process can, in some cases, lead to solidifying human relationships by making the participants more sensitive to each others' deeper feelings. In other cases, however, the quarrel can be highly destructive, and a shift from another type of dialogue to a quarrel is in fact the underlying basis of some of the most serious, major fallacies.

Three mixed types of dialogue are the debate, the committee meeting, and the Socratic dialogue. Each is a mixture of two or more of the normatively more fundamental types of dialogue previously analyzed.

The discussion on medical ethics is a realistic kind of example of an argument that exemplifies many of the features of persuasion dialogue. Although it is a fairly simple example, in many respects, it has a number of features that turn out to be nontrivial to analyze. By and large the participants are reasonable and cooperative, but at some points, they commit some interesting errors and try to attack each other in a negative way. This discussion is the central case for our analysis of commitment in dialogue, and we shall continue to refer to it in chapter 4.

A dialectical shift is a change in the context (type, subject matter, or setting) of dialogue during a conversation, from one type of dialogue to another. Some shifts take place quickly, by means of a *déplacement* in a dialogue, while in the other cases the shift is gradual, a *glissement*.

In some cases the shift is constructive and agreed to by all parties, and it is a licit shift. The second dialogue may even be functionally related to the goal of the original dialogue, in which case we speak of an "embedded dialogue." In other cases, the shift is concealed or otherwise inappropriate, and is an illicit type of shift. Illicit shifts in the context of dialogue in argumentation are frequently associated with fallacies. The fallacy of bargaining, for instance, occurs in a kind of case where the participants were originally supposed to be engaged in a persuasion dialogue, but then the dialogue illicitly shifted to negotiation during the course of the same exchange.

A cascading effect is said to occur when there is a series of shifts from one type of dialogue to another, and then to yet another, and so forth. For example, a critical discussion may shift to a negotiation, and then the negotiation shifts to a quarrel.

In some cases, the shift is from one type of dialogue to another, but in other cases it is internal, in that the type of dialogue remains the same but there is a shift in its subject matter or setting. One sort of shift to another type of dialogue (though not to another *main* type) is a tightening up of a persuasion dialogue, where the argumentation becomes markedly less permissive and more rigorous and exact in the nature and kinds of moves permitted.

Internal shifts in a dialogue can be shifts of attitude, where the attitude of a participant changes, say from merely questioning a thesis to actively opposing it. They can also be shifts of issue, where the subject of discussion changes to a different subject. This has to do with the dialectical relevance of argumentation. Shifts of participation occur where the actual participants in the dialogue change during the course of an ongoing conversation.

Yet another type of shift is a flavor shift where the type of dialogue remains basically the same, but elements from another type of dialogue begin to intrude to some noticeable extent.

Various traditional fallacies can be viewed from the perspective of dialectical shifts, as follows. The *argumentum ad populum,* or playing on popular sentiments (sometimes called "mob appeal"), is associated with a shift from persuasion to epidictic dialogue, a type of inspirational speech used to heighten the adhesion of an audience to common values or ideals they share with the speaker. The *argumentation ad baculum,* or appeal to force, is associated with shifts from persuasion dialogue to negotiation dialogue, or in some cases, even to quarreling.

The *argumentum ad hominem* or personal attack argument, is associated with the quarrel generally, and when this type of argument is used fallaciously, there is an underlying dialectical shift from some other type of dialogue, for example, a critical discussion to a quarrel.

The bias type of *ad hominem* attack is based on the allegation that a participant in a critical discussion has covertly shifted the context to that of a negotiation dialogue.

The *argumentum ad ignorantiam,* or argument from ignorance, is associated with an internal shift of attitude where one party tries to (illicitly, if the argument is fallacious) shift the burden of proof to the other side.

The fallacy of many questions is sensitive to the context of dialogue. A question like "Have you stopped cheating on your income taxes?" could be nonfallacious if the respondent had previously conceded cheating on his tax returns. But otherwise, it could be a quarrelsome tactic to try to browbeat a respondent of committing himself to some incriminating proposition, forcing him to make the effort of challenging the legitimacy of asking such a question within the type of dialogue in which the arguers are engaged. This fallacy involves a flavor shift toward an interrogation.

Use of expert opinion to support one's argument in a dialogue can be perfectly legitimate and constructive, but it characteristically becomes fallacious when a participant in a persuasion dialogue illicitly shifts to an information-seeking dialogue, treating the other party as a docile or passive receiver of information who should not be so bold as to raise critical questions *(argumentum ad verecundiam)*.

In general, a key element in judging argumentation as fallacious or nonfallacious, in a given case, is the context of dialogue surrounding the argument, especially if a dialectical shift has occurred during the course of the argument.

4 Systems of Dialogue Rules

Hamblin and others[1] have used the commitment store as a technical device to keep track of arguers' commitments in dialogue, as part of a method of evaluating argumentation. But how commitment should be incurred or retracted is a function of several factors:

1. the kind of move (speech act) made, for example, a question, a challenge, an assertion or an argument,

2. the type of dialogue in which the move was made,

3. the goal of the dialogue,

4. the speaker's role in the dialogue, and

5. the rules appropriate for this type of dialogue.

Clearly, in order to analyze the concept of commitment further, enough to make it useful as the key component in a practical theory of argumentation, a framework of dialogue rules needs to be set out. The aim of this chapter is to fulfill this objective. In it, we turn to a more systematic approach to the study of commitment in dialogue by conceiving of a structure of dialogue as an explicitly formulated set of rules which provides a normative model for a particular context of discussion. Rules for two types of persuasion dialogue are presented, and it is shown how the case study dialogue on medical ethics contains a shift from the one type of persuasion dialogue to the other.

In section 4.1 we avail ourselves of this case study for a preliminary discussion of the need for two distinct dialogue types. Section 4.2 presents some technical preliminaries in order to prepare for the formulation of formal examples in later sections. Sections 4.3 and 4.4 are each concerned with one type of persuasion dialogue, its general characteristics, and its approach to commitment. Rules for specific systems of these types will be formulated as well. In section 4.5 the two types are integrated into one complex type of persuasion dialogue.

4.1 Tightening Up and Dark-Side Commitment

In the case study dialogue on medical ethics (chapter 3), there was an internal dialectical shift, a tightening up from one phase of the complex dialogue to another. This tightening up needs to be reflected in the rules of dialogue appropriate for each phase.

The first phase of the dialogue was a persuasion dialogue between Bruce and Wilma on the specific issue of whether the decision of Karl and Ethel to go ahead with the birth of their baby was a good decision or not. In Wilma's long argument at lines 33 through 42, we begin to see her deeper fundamental commitments on the issue emerge. She considers the issue from the point of view of the professional obligations of the physician. Bruce appears to feel threatened by this direction that the argument has taken, and, in defence, he adopts a kind of Socratic style of attacking Wilma's commitments. As a result, the dialogue begins to tighten up.

When this tightening-up phase begins, the arguments of both participants turn away from a probing into the underlying, deeper position of the other party. Around line 72 and subsequently, the arguments of both participants center much more around the exact wording and implications of each other's explicit and specific speech acts. Wilma puts forward counterexamples to Bruce's enunciated statements, and Bruce becomes much more defensive about trying to state what he means with some care and precision.

This shift represents a significant change in the underlying structure of the rules of dialogue. Before the shift, both Bruce and Wilma were trying to probe and discover each other's underlying general position—trying to bring out what the other party felt to be the important principles at stake in the case.

But after the shift, this goal of probing toward the other party's deeper position on the issue recedes into the background. What now becomes important is what propositions one's past speech acts explicitly commits one to, either directly or by logical implication, and how these explicit commitments and their implications are open to undermining or refutation by the other party, through finding counterexamples, inconsistencies, and other evidence of weakness or incorrectness in them.

Later (around line 100), the discussion relaxes again, once the tightening up phase is over, and the dialogue goes back to a looser form of discussion where, once again, the underlying, deeper position of each party begins to emerge. After that point, the dialogue is focused less on attacking explicit assertions than on relating an arguer's surface commitments to his or her deeper but less explicit commitments on the issue.

Thus there are two very distinctive types of dialogue involved in the case study dialogue on medical ethics. In the tighter type of dialogue, each party questions or attacks the arguments of the other side by focusing on the exact wording of the frank or overtly given commitments of that person. In the looser type of dialogue, the overt commitments are brought into relation to deeper and darker commitments that are presumed to lie at the basis of the other party's overt commitments.

We could make this distinction by saying that the commitment store of each participant is divided into two sets—a light side of overt, expressed commitments in the dialogue, and a dark side of commitments that are "veiled" or only partly apparent to a participant in the discussion. These dark-side commitments exist as propositions in a participant's commitment store, but they are often not explicitly known, on the basis of the speech acts advanced by that participant in the course of a dialogue.

How a dark-side commitment is used to question an argument is also illustrated by case 2.4, where Bob criticizes George's argument that the post office should be taken over by private enterprise by questioning the consistency of this commitment with George's presumed commitment to socialism. The precise implications of George's underlying, more general political commitment in relation to the issue of post office management are not clear. It is a dark-side commitment. But there is a presumption of inconsistency between it and George's explicit argument. This is enough of a tension to throw a burden of proof onto George's side of the argument and throw it open to critical questioning.

Generally, in persuasion dialogue in everyday conversations, much depends on what the dark-side commitments of a player really are. This of course, is, to some extent, unknown to both participants before moves to draw inferences from ostensible dark-side commitments of a player are made. Hence, to some extent, the outcome of a dialogue is determined by factors external to the explicit knowledge that the players have at the time they are asking questions or advancing other speech acts in a sequence of dialogue.

The best way of resolving clashes of commitments, in the case of George, as well as the previous cases of Antigone and Professor G., is to allow the person in the quandary to resolve the clash in accord with how he sees the relationship between his light- and dark-side commitments at that point in a dialogue, in relation to critical questioning by another person with whom he is engaged in a persuasion dialogue. What is needed is a set of rules for a permissive type of dialogue that allows a certain degree of freedom to reconsider one's commitments and possibly even retract some of them.

The main problem with the management of a persuasion dialogue like the case-study discussion on medical ethics is to provide fair rules and mechanisms for dealing with the fallacies, blunders, clashes, and other problematic situations which arise through one side's critical questioning of the position of the other, as the dark-side commitments begin to be transformed into light-side commitments from which the other participant in the dialogue can draw conclusions by logical inferences. Here retraction looms large as the key problem. Rules governing retraction should be reasonably tolerant and flexible, yet at the same time they must have enough bite to allow for a reasonable fixing of a participant's commitment in relation to what is fundamental to his position on an issue.

This, of course, is the question of the binding nature of commitments discussed in chapter 2. Just how binding a commitment should fairly be judged to be is a matter of interpretation in each particular case. But the question should rightly be judged, in a particular case, in relation to the rules of dialogue that are appropriate for that case.

In persuasion dialogue, commitments are binding in the sense that not living up to one, or inappropriately retracting it, would cause the subject either to lose the game of dialogue or to suffer some loss of credibility, meaning that he would not be doing well in the dialogue. Bindingness here is a matter of degree and is best determined in a particular case by specifying the sanctions and the rules of dialogue involved. This matter of degree must be judged by the degree of strictness and the nature of the commitment rules appropriate for a particular context of dialogue.

To solve this problem, we introduce two distinct types of persuasion dialogue, each of which has its distinctive rules. The permissive type of persuasion dialogue (**PPD**) admits of a reasonable degree of freedom in allowing for moves and retractions. The rigorous type of persuasion dialogue (**RPD**) is much more restrictive in both respects. **PPD** is a Hamblin-type game, and **RPD** is a Lorenzen-type game (see note 1).

4.2 Technical Preliminaries

Before we can proceed to present definitions of the dialectical systems (dialogue games) **PPD** and **RPD**, we must introduce some more or less technical concepts that are needed for a concise formulation of the rules of these systems. We shall introduce a formal language, L, and explain what we mean by a basic argument and by a basic inference. The choice of this particular language L (which happens to be a language "for" propositional logic) is purely conventional and intended to serve illustrative purposes. The same holds for our choice of rules of inference. Together these rules constitute an incomplete deductive system for propositional logic. The incompleteness is intended to reflect the (very likely) situation that the discussants, though they avail themselves of a logically rich and complex language (here, for illustrative purposes replaced by the simple language L) and of a number of rules of inference pertaining to that language, are unacquainted with any complete system of rules of inference for that language.

The basic building blocks of L are the following:

1. An infinite set of proposition letters: $P_0, P_1, P_2, \ldots$

2. Five logical constants: $\bot$ (a constant for absurdity, which shall be used to express the claim that one's opponent's position is absurd or inconsistent), $\neg$ (negation), $\wedge$ (conjunction), $\vee$ (disjunction), and $\rightarrow$ (conditional).

3. Two auxiliary symbols: (,) (left and right parentheses).

The set of atomic sentences comprises the proposition letters and '$\bot$'. The set of *sentences* of L is defined (by induction) in the usual way:

1. Each atomic sentence is a sentence.

2. If A, B are sentences so are $\neg A$, $(A \wedge B)$, $(A \vee B)$, $(A \rightarrow B)$. (Notice that "A" and "B" are not proposition letters. They are not even sentences of L but linguistic variables used to make general statements about syntactic objects.)

3. Nothing is a sentence, unless it can be constructed on the strength of (1) and (2).

The standard logician's definition of an argument would stipulate that arguments are syntactic objects consisting of a (possibly empty) set of sentences of L, called its "premises," and a sentence of L called its "conclusion." This truncated conception of argument is certainly insufficient for the aspirations of informal logic and theory of argumentation.[2] Yet we need something very similar to the standard concept of argument, under one name or another, for our present purpose of describing certain types of argumentative dialectics. In order to indicate our agreement with critics of the standard conception, we prefer to use the term *elementary argument*. Thus the term *argument* is reserved for a richer and more pragmatic conception.[3] Elementary arguments, then, will be our basic building blocks. With them an arguer may construct more complex syntactical objects which we shall call *basic arguments*. The concept of an elementary argument is not intended by us as a substitute for the richer conception of argument hinted at above. Nor are basic arguments supposed to fill this bill. For one thing, basic arguments, too, are purely syntactical objects.

Elementary arguments are configurations of the form:

$$\underbrace{R_1 \ \& \ldots \& \ R_n}_{C} \quad (n \geq 1)$$

where all of $R_1, \ldots, R_n$ and C are sentences of L. C is called the *conclusion* of such an elementary argument, and $R_1, \ldots, R_n$ are called its *premises (reasons)*. All of $R_1, \ldots, R_n$, C, as well as the implicit premise or warrant $(R_1 \wedge \ldots \wedge R_n) \rightarrow C$, will be called *elements* of the elementary argument. Notice that the symbols "R_1," "R_n" and "C" are not themselves sentences of L. They are linguistic variables used by us to refer to sentences of L. Examples of elementary arguments are found in figure 4.1.

This is all very familiar to readers of logic textbooks. Matters of validity are always completely left aside at this stage. So are matters of relevance. There are, however, three points in which we deviate from the standard conception. First, we do not allow an empty set of premises. Second, we use the ampersand to join the premises. Consequently, we have two types of conjunction: one within the language L ($\wedge$) and one used to join the premises ($\&$). Notice that "$\&$" is not itself a symbol of L and that one cannot have an "$\&$" within the scope of another occurrence of "$\&$." The ampersand serves as a reminder that the premises in an elementary argument will, whenever the argument is actually used, express joint (and not independent) reasons for the conclusion. Finally, there is a geometrical aspect to our definition (and this is nonstandard): the conclusion is *below* the premises and linked to the premises by a brace and arrow. The premises are *over* the conclusion. In a word: elementary arguments are configurations.

1. $$\underbrace{P_0 \mathbin{\&} (P_0 \to (P_1 \vee P_2))}_{\downarrow}$$
$$(P_1 \vee P_2)$$

2. $$\underbrace{P_0 \mathbin{\&} (P_1 \to P_0)}_{\downarrow}$$
$$(P_0 \wedge P_1)$$

3. $$\underbrace{(P_1 \vee P_2) \mathbin{\&} (P_1 \to P_0) \mathbin{\&} (P_2 \to P_0)}_{\downarrow}$$
$$P_0$$

4. $$\underbrace{(P_1 \vee P_2)}_{\downarrow}$$
$$(P_2 \vee P_1)$$

Figure 4.1 Examples of Elementary Arguments.

Basic arguments are tree-shaped structures built up from elementary arguments in the following way:

1. Elementary arguments are basic arguments.

2. If Δ is a basic argument with premises $R_1, \ldots, R_i, \ldots, R_n$ and conclusion C, $1 \le i \le n$, and if $Q_1, \ldots, Q_m$ are any sentences of L, then the configuration Δ', which one gets by writing the following configuration of linked premises and a brace and arrow:

$$\underbrace{Q_1 \mathbin{\&} \ldots \mathbin{\&} Q_m}_{\downarrow}$$

over R_i, is again a basic argument. Δ' has the same conclusion, C, as Δ. The premises of Δ' are: $R_1, \ldots, R_{i-1}, Q_1, \ldots, Q_m, R_{i+1}, \ldots, R_n$.

3. Nothing else is a basic argument.

The purport of this (inductive) definition is that basic arguments are precisely those configurations that are either themselves elementary arguments or can be constructed from an elementary argument, in one or more steps, by writing new premises over an old one. The *elements* of a

$$(P_5 \wedge P_6)$$
$$\downarrow$$

$$\neg\, P_3 \qquad (P_1 \to P_4) \,\&\, (P_4 \to P_0)$$
$$\downarrow \qquad\qquad\qquad \downarrow$$
$$(P_1 \vee P_2) \qquad \& \qquad (P_1 \to P_0) \qquad \& \qquad (P_2 \to P_0)$$
$$\downarrow$$
$$P_0$$

Figure 4.2   Basic Argument Constructed in Three Steps

basic argument are the elements of the elementary arguments it contains. The premises of a basic argument are its ultimate premises, that is, the sentences of L that occur in positions where they do not have any sentence written over them. Figure 4.2 shows a basic argument constructed in three steps from the third example of figure 4.1.

In figure 4.2 the premises are $\neg\, P_3$, $(P_5 \wedge P_6)$, $(P_4 \to P_0)$ and $(P_2 \to P_0)$, whereas the conclusion is P_0. Such tree diagrams (or similar ones) are familiar to students of informal logic or theory of argumentation as a means to depict the structure of an argument expressed in some natural language. At present we use the language L instead of a natural language. Also, we have not incorporated a possibility to express independent reasons (convergent argumentation) into our definition of basic argument. A student of formal logic will rather compare our basic arguments with deduction diagrams (for instance, in a Gentzen-type system of natural deduction). The striking difference is, of course, that we did not stipulate any rules of deduction or inference and can therefore not distinguish between correct and incorrect diagrams. In formal (inferential) logic, a structure that violates the rules (of a certain system) is not said to be an "incorrect deduction," it is not a deduction at all in that system! Basic arguments, on the contrary, can be presented by a discussant in order to defend a claim, whether or not they conform to some rules of inference. It's up to the other party in the discussion to accept or criticize the various premises and links in the argument.

Yet it is entirely plausible to assume that the discussants share some rules of logic, that is to say that some formal steps in basic arguments are, by common agreement, unassailable. There is no reason to assume that the system constituted by these common rules is complete. There is no such thing as a complete logic for natural language, and no prospect that one will be developed. This situation is reflected by the incorporation into our dialectic system of an incomplete system for propositional logic consisting of the following rules of inference:

$$\underbrace{A \;\&\; (A \to B)}_{\downarrow}$$
$$B$$

(MP, *Modus Ponens*)

$$\underbrace{\neg B \;\&\; (A \to B)}_{\downarrow}$$
$$\neg A$$

(MT, *Modus Tollens*)

$$\underbrace{(A \to B) \;\&\; (B \to C)}_{\downarrow}$$
$$(A \to C)$$

(HS, *Hypothetical Syllogism*)

$$\underbrace{A \;\&\; B}_{\downarrow}$$
$$(A \wedge B)$$

(CON, *Conjunction Rule*)

$$\underbrace{(A \wedge B)}_{\downarrow}$$
$$A$$

(SEPL, *Separation Left*)

$$\underbrace{(A \wedge B)}_{\downarrow}$$
$$B$$

(SEPR, *Separation Right*)

$$\underbrace{\neg A \;\&\; (A \vee B)}_{\downarrow}$$
$$B$$

(DS$_1$, *Disjunctive Syllogism$_1$*)

$$\underbrace{\neg B \;\&\; (A \vee B)}_{\downarrow}$$
$$A$$

(DS$_2$, *Disjunctive Syllogism$_2$*)

$$\underbrace{(A \vee B) \;\&\; (A \to C) \;\&\; (B \to C)}_{\downarrow}$$
$$C$$

(CD, *Constructive Dilemma*)

$$\underbrace{(A \to B)\ \&\ (A \to \neg\ B)}$$
$$\downarrow$$
$$\neg A$$

(RA, *Reductio ad Absurdum*)

$$\underbrace{A\ \&\ \neg A}$$
$$\downarrow$$
$$\bot$$

(ABS, *Absurdum Rule*)

An *elementary inference* is an elementary argument that conforms in its pattern to one of these rules of inference. For instance, in figure 4.1, elementary argument 1 is an elementary inference according to MP, whereas 3 is an elementary inference according to CD, 2 and 4 are not elementary inferences (even though 4 is valid by classical standards).

A *basic inference* is a basic argument such that each of the elementary arguments it comprises is an elementary inference. So basic inferences correspond to what in formal logic are called "deductions" or "derivations." Both elementary and basic inferences are purely syntactical objects. The simple term *inference* is kept aside for more pragmatic notions, for example, for the action of presenting a basic inference in dialogue in order to refute one's opponent. An example of a basic inference that is not elementary is shown in figure 4.3. Remember that "$\bot$" expresses the claim that one's opponent's position is absurd or inconsistent. Clearly this inference could serve to refute one's opponent if the premises are among his commitments.

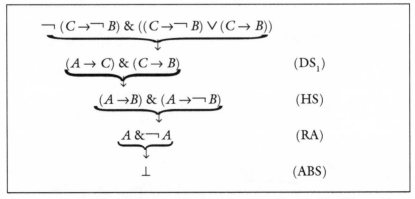

Figure 4.3   An Example of a Basic Inference That is Not Elementary

4.3 Permissive Persuasion Dialogue (PPD)

Below are given eighteen general characteristics or "rules" that define the **PPD** type of dialogue. We call these "rules," in quotation marks, because, strictly speaking, they are not a set of rules of a game of dialogue that define any specific game as such. More accurately speaking, they are characteristics of **PPD** as a general type or format of dialogue. There are a multiplicity of games of dialogue (with specific rules) that fit this general type. In subsection 4.3.4 below, for example, one game of dialogue of the **PPD** type, called $\mathbf{PPD}_0$, is defined by the specific set of rules given for it there. By adding or modifying particular rules of $\mathbf{PPD}_0$, additional games of the **PPD** type, $\mathbf{PPD}_1$, $\mathbf{PPD}_2$, and so on, can be defined.

It is important to begin with a simple and basic structure that meets the general requirements needed to address the basic problems of modeling commitment in dialogue set out in the first three chapters. More specific problems, features of dialogue, fallacies, and so on, are handled by developing carefully regulated games of dialogue that conform to the general description.

4.3.1 General Description of Permissive Persuasion Dialogue

In the general description below, each characteristic is given a number, from 1 to 18. Under the statement of each characteristic, a comment is given, in order to clarify the characteristic or the way it has been expressed.

1.   There are two parties: White (W) and Black (B).
      Comment: There are two participants in a **PPD** type of dialogue, called "White" and "Black," who make moves of various kinds. At each move, the type of move made and the content of the move determine what the commitments of the participant are, as the dialogue proceeds.

2.   There is an *initial conflict description* giving us:
      AW_0: the set of W's initial assertions.
      AB_0: the set of B's initial assertions. $AB_0 \neq \emptyset$.
      CW_0: the set of W's initial concessions. $CW_0 \cap AB_0 = \emptyset$.
      CB_0: the set of B's initial concessions. $CB_0 \cap AW_0 = \emptyset$.
      DW: the set of W's dark-side commitments.
      DB: the set of B's dark-side commitments.
      An assertion or concession is a declarative sentence. All assertions are concessions as well. A dark-side commitment is a proposition,

not necessarily expressed by any statement. The initial assertions (concessions) are the ones the player starts out with, at the opening of the game. Each of these initial assertions is a thesis (designated assertion) that the player is supposed to prove by means of arguments in the dialogue.

Comment: Each player has a set of sentences or propositions called his *commitment store* (or "commitment set"), divided into two subsets or sides called the *light side* and the *dark side*. The light-side set is a set of declarative sentences that are known to both players and are "in full view" to both players. The dark-side set is a definite set of propositions (not necessarily expressed in language), but these propositions are (in general) not known to the players. The player himself does not always know for sure which propositions are in his dark-side commitment store, and the other player is also ignorant of the contents of his partner's dark-side store of commitments. However, the players may have hunches or plausible guesses, in some cases, on whether a proposition is included in a dark-side commitment store. A player is committed to his assertions in a different way from his concessions. If an assertion is challenged, he is obliged to furnish an appropriate proof or justification. Commitment to concessions, by contrast, does not have a burden of proof attached. Commitment to a mere concession may be for the sake of argument, which does not bring with it an obligation to respond to a why question by furnishing an argument defending that commitment.

There can be no persuasion dialogue without there being at least one initial assertion. Therefore, it is stipulated that the set of B's initial assertions is nonempty. It is also stipulated that none of the assertions of one player is conceded by the other player right at the beginning of the dialogue.

3.   Starting with W the parties move alternately according to the rules of the game. Someone has to start, but for the rest the game is symmetric.

Comment: Players take turns making moves in the game, and, by convention, White moves first.

4.   The commitment rules of the game determine the commitments of each party after each move. The dark-side commitment stores are fixed, but the sets of assertions and concessions are variable. After the nth move we have AW_n, AB_n, and so on. Always $AW_n \subseteq CW_n$ and $AB_n \subseteq CB_n$.

Comment: It will become clearer how commitments are inserted into a player's commitment set once you get to some of the characteristics below, but the simplest sort of rule generally is that a participant who asserts any statement, A, immediately becomes committed to that statement (as an assertion). A is immediately inserted into his or her light-side commitment store.

5.   Each move contains any or all of the following components.
     a. retractions
     b. concessions
     c. requests for retractions
     d. requests for concessions
     e. arguments
     f. challenges

Comment: In general, a move is a six-tuple, and a participant can choose to put forward any or all of the six types of components as part of his or her move. For example, a move could be of the form $\langle \emptyset$, concession, $\emptyset$, $\emptyset$, argument, challenge$\rangle$ or $\langle$retraction, $\emptyset$, $\emptyset$, request for a concession, argument, $\emptyset \rangle$. A player can retract one proposition and optionally make a request for concession of another proposition, at the same move. **PPD** is meant to be highly flexible in allowing a participant to make moves that contain a variety of different types of speech acts, all during the same move.

6.   Each party tries to get each of its initial assertions conceded by its adversary and tries to get the other party to retract its initial assertions, or at least some of them.

Comment: It needs to be said that **PPD** is a type of persuasion dialogue, and the aim of the first party is to persuade the second party that the first party's thesis is right. How this is done is by getting the other party committed to propositions that can be used to construct a chain of arguments leading from the other party's concessions or commitments to a conclusion which is the first party's thesis. This chain of arguments is the basis for a player's strategy of persuasion. The player uses such a strategy (if he or she has one) through the question-reply moves made in the sequence of dialogue. Although the rules of **PPD** are permissive, the goal of the game and the aims of the players are clear. This represents a change from Hamblin, who only roughly indicated goals and participant's aims for the games of dialogue he constructed.[4] By contrast, the aims of the players in a **PPD** are clear

in the sense that, in principle, you can tell whether a given sequence of moves in a dialogue constitutes a successful outcome or
win for the player.

7.   It is supposed that initial assertions/concessions have been stated
      and identified in some preparatory moves. Each party in its first
      actual move challenges or concedes each initial assertion presented
      by the other party.

      Comment: Typically, the dialogue begins in earnest when
      the one participant challenges an initial assertion of the other
      participant. To respond to the challenge successfully, the second
      participant must give an argument in support of the assertion
      challenged, see (8a) below. In section 4.2 a distinction was made
      between basic inferences and basic arguments. An argument is
      an inference if it is logically tight according to a system of logic
      incorporated in the system. (This system of logic comprises only
      rules that are agreed upon by all concerned.) The ultimate aim
      of each party is to get his or her own thesis (or theses) conceded
      by the other party. This can be done by constructing an argu-
      ment leading from the other party's concessions to one's thesis.
      It is not required that this argument be an inference. In order to
      be successful, however, every proposition that (explicitly or im-
      plicitly) contributes to the argument must be conceded. Notice
      that the implicit propositions of an inference have to be con-
      ceded (cannot be challenged) by virtue of the logic of the sys-
      tem. But a participant in **PPD** may concede a lot more than
      that.

8.   a. If one party challenges some assertion of the other party, the
         second party is to present, in the next move, at least one argu-
         ment for that assertion.
      b. An assertion may be defended by argument, but only if the asser-
         tion was challenged, and provided that the assertion is not among
         the other party's concessions. There are no other occasions to
         present arguments.

         Comment: PPD, though permissive in the sense that each
         participant should have the opportunity to argue for his or her
         thesis in a number of ways (irrespective of the particular form of a
         given challenge), should still have some features that, perhaps not
         guarantee, but at least enhance the production of relevant and
         interesting arguments.

         In this light some ruling to prevent the ad lib production
         of arguments seems appropriate. In **PPD** every assertion counts as

conceded by the other party as long as it has not been challenged by that party. Since there is no point in a defense of what has already been conceded, there is, in **PPD,** no point in putting forward an argument for an unchallenged assertion. In actual dialogue, argument is often used to forestall a challenge rather than answer one. This practice is often useful to speed up the interchange, but it can also lead to serious digressions, unless there are some rules in force that keep an ad lib arguer in check. In **PPD** we stick, for the time being, to the simplest rule to this effect: no challenge, no argument. But one can easily imagine other rulings that yield more realistic variants.

It is not our intention to have, in **PPD,** any restrictions on the content or the number of arguments that may be produced to defend a particular challenged assertion (except for general limitations of space and time). There remains the subtle point that one may wish the other party to co-assert one's assertion and not merely to concede it, but this surpasses the bounds of **PPD.**

9.   If a party makes an assertion, the other party, in the very next move, is to make clear its position with respect to that assertion (unless this assertion is already among the latter party's concessions or has already been challenged); that is, it should either challenge or concede the new assertion. If a party presents an elementary argument, the same holds for all the elements of the argument. It holds for all the assertions in the argument, of course, but it also holds for the implicit assertion connecting premises and conclusions of the argument. No other challenges are allowed, with the exception of those pertaining to the initial assertions in the first two moves of the game.

Comment: Item (9) stipulates that in **PPD** unchallenged assertions count as conceded. We do not see any reason to admit a middle position. If you do not want to concede something, just challenge it. That would only mean that you are prepared to hear your opponent's reasons. A challenge does not commit you to the opposite view! This can be implemented by a commitment rule that puts each proposition that was asserted by one's opponent, but remained unchallenged at the next move, in one's commitment store. Hence many concessions can remain implicit. But it is important, in **PPD,** that the attitudes toward uttered propositions are clearly and unambiguously assigned. Positions must be as clear as possible. Otherwise, it would be very unclear how one should act (argue) in order to have a chance to persuade the other.

10.   Each assertion, including the implicit assertion connecting premises
        and conclusion of an argument, counts as a concession as well.
        Comment: Assertion is more binding than mere conces-
        sion, as a type of commitment. The types of commitment mod-
        eled by **PPD** are summarized in section 5.4 below.

11.   If a party's concessions include all the premises of the opponent's
        argument, as well as the implicit assertion connecting premises
        and conclusion, this party must—as soon as possible—concede
        the opponent's conclusion.
        Comment: This requirement once again reflects the gen-
        eral point behind **PPD** dialogue. One party is trying to use argu-
        mentation to persuade the other party to concede a particular
        proposition by proving it to that other party, that is, constructing
        an argument with that proposition as conclusion and with pre-
        mises that are commitments of the other party. Generally speaking
        then, if an argument is a good one in these respects, the respon-
        dent should recognize it by conceding the conclusion. However,
        if the respondent doesn't wish to concede the conclusion, there
        are some possibilities for retraction in **PPD,** as we will see.

12.   Each party may try to get more concessions on the other side by
        questioning. After a question, the next speaker must either grant
        the concession or refuse to grant it.
        Comment: In the present context, a question is a request
        for a concession which may then be used as a premise in argument.

13.   One is not allowed to challenge an assertion of one's opponent
        if the content of that assertion is present among one's conces-
        sions. However, one may concede an assertion of one's oppo-
        nent, even if one challenged it. In that case the challenge counts
        as withdrawn.
        Comment: A somewhat similar rule is discussed by
        Hamblin, to the effect that a challenge concerning a statement A
        may not be used unless A is a commitment of the hearer and not
        of the speaker. Hamblin discusses this rule as an option but does
        offer an argument in its favor: "Otherwise the 'Why' is 'aca-
        demic'."[5]

14.   Assertions and concessions can be retracted, in principle. A retrac-
        tion of an assertion does not exclude one's conceding the same
        matter in the same move in which the retraction took place.
        Comment: Retraction should be possible, in principle, in a
        permissive type of dialogue like **PPD.** However, as we will see

below, there must be some penalties on retraction, in some instances. Otherwise—and this is a problem in the Hamblin-type dialogues—the respondent can always keep on replying "No commitment" to a question, thereby successfully thwarting the questioner's attempts to pin her down to specific commitments on an issue.

If one retracts an assertion, but reaffirms its propositional content as a concession, this means that one has changed the type of commitment with respect to that content, without retracting commitment altogether.

15. Each party may demand the resolution of an explicit inconsistency among the other party's concessions (including his assertions). The next move must contain a retraction of either of the two contradictory statements.

    Comment: There is no penalty for having an inconsistency in one's commitment set, but one's opponent has a right to question the inconsistency and also a right to insist that it be removed. This rule already puts some conditions on the possibility of retraction (not banning but requiring it, in this case).

16. If a party challenges an assertion or refuses a particular concession, the other party may ask its opponent to reassess its commitment on the issue. In that case, if the request pertains to a declarative sentence S that expresses a proposition $P(S)$ and if $P(S)$ is in fact a dark-side commitment of the first party, it is assumed that this party will, in its next move, concede S.

    Comment: This requirement is a very important characteristic of **PPD**-type dialogue. It deals with the "No commitment" problem by, in effect, gently forcing a respondent to take on a commitment in certain instances. Because of this rule, the participants' ability to avoid commitment unrestrictedly is impeded by circumstances outside of their control (once the dialogue has begun). If a participant really is committed to a proposition A (on her dark side), and she denies or tries to retract commitment to A by some move in the dialogue, she can be asked to reassess her commitment. If she really is committed to A, then she must concede A at the next move.

    We might add parenthetically here that it is not possible for a participant to retract a dark-side commitment, within this type of dialogue. If a participant in argumentation in a speech event in real conversation were to retract a dark-side commitment, we would regard this as quite a serious change which would be tantamount to a change in one's basic character, and hence as a shift to another specimen of dialogue. For example, if someone who has long been a devoted Communist at some point switches to an equally fervent right-wing position, quite consistently, then we would regard this as a kind of participant shift to a different dialogue framework. But within one and the same **PPD** dialogue it is not possible to retract dark-side commitments.

17.   One is not allowed to concede anything, unless prompted by one's own (10) and one's opponent's assertions (9), or questions (12) including special requests to reassess commitment (16).

Comment: This requirement is meant to ensure some kind of minimal relevance in concessions, in order to promote a connected and purposeful sequence of exchanges. The rule prevents gratuitous or unnecessary commitments from being made, during the dialogue.

18.   At the start of the game there are limits set to the number of symbol tokens the parties may use in their locutions, both per move and *in toto*. Moreover, the number of retractions of mere concessions allowed to each party is limited.

Comment: This rule provides a practical limit on the dialogue. In principle, **PPD** is permissive, but there may need to be practical constraints in the length of time available.

The purpose of **PPD** characteristics as a set of requirements is to have a simple but precise structure which can be used by either participant in a dialogue to elicit commitments from the other participant and use them to prove conclusions in arguments. This purpose is primarily achieved through the specification of the clearly specified and manageable set of rules which govern the incurring and retraction of commitments.

4.3.2 Examples of Permissive Persuasion Dialogues

In figure 4.4, an example is given of a typical case of a few initial moves in a **PPD** dialogue. This will give the reader an idea of how such a dialogue generally goes and how it can be modeled by a matrix that enables one to keep track of the commitments of each participant and the argumentation as it evolves through the sequence of moves in the dialogue. As you can see from figure 4.4, each piece of argumentation is modeled by an argument diagram (only linked arguments are taken account of in our simplified model), and there is a chain or connected sequence of arguments represented in the matrix.

	W			B		
	dark-side commitments	mere concessions	assertions, arguments, challenges	assertions, arguments, challenges	mere concessions	dark-side commitments
move 1 (W) (W challenges B)	$A_1 A_2$	$B_1 B_2$ T_B??	T_W	T_B	$C_1 C_2$	$D_1 D_2$
move 2 (B)				T_W?? $F_1 \& F_2 \underbrace{\rightarrow}$ $A_1 \& E \underbrace{\rightarrow} T_B$		
move 3 (W)		$F_1 F_2$ $(A_1 \wedge E) \rightarrow T_B$	$(F_1 \wedge F_2) \rightarrow E$?? E?? A_1?? $R \underset{\rightarrow}{} T_W$			
move 4 (B)				$Serious\,(A_1)$? $B_1 \& B_2 \underbrace{\rightarrow}$ $(F_1 \wedge F_2) \rightarrow E$ R??	$R \rightarrow T_W$	

Figure 4.4 A Few Initial Moves in a PPD Dialogue

In this case, White starts out by challenging Black to prove his thesis T_B. Black responds by giving an argument for T_B, based on the two premises A_1 and E. A_1 is a dark-side commitment of White. Black also supports E by providing two premises to back it up: F_1 and F_2. At move 3, White concedes F_1 and F_2 and also concedes Black's implicit connecting premise $(A_1 \wedge E) \rightarrow T_B$. At the same move, White questions both the explicit premises A_1 and E as well as the implicit premise $(F_1 \wedge F_2) \rightarrow E$, and moreover gives an argument that supports her thesis T_W.

Finally, at the fourth move, Black responds by asking White, "Are you serious about A_1?" This move arose because A_1 was a dark-side commitment of White, but then at move 3, White questioned A_1. Hence White was open to an "Are you serious?" challenge. At the same time Black also presents a new argument for the connecting premise $(F_1 \wedge F_2) \rightarrow E$, questioned by White at the previous move. Finally, Black challenges White's explicit premise R, while conceding the implicit premise of White's argument.

This brief example gives the reader an idea how a game of dialogue of the **PPD** type generally goes. Each side tries to prove its own thesis by arguments and to question and challenge the arguments of the other side.

As another example, we take lines 16 through 30 of the discussion on medical ethics from chapter 3. Figure 4.5 gives a schematic survey of this segment of the dialogue. Figure 4.6 then shows how the sequence of moves is modeled by a **PPD** dialogue type of matrix.

Unlike figure 4.4, figure 4.6 does not have a separate column for acts of mere concession. All acts by one party are shown in one column. Challenges are identifiable by double question marks, mere concessions by a prefix *"c."* Furthermore, there are columns added that show not the acts, but the contents of each commitment store as a consequence of these acts. There is for each party a column for the set of assertions (AW, AB) and a column for the set of mere concessions (CW, CB). The topmost row, numbered 0, displays the initial situation. This is followed by a row for each move.

Wilma begins by challenging B (Bruce's thesis), and Bruce responds by producing an argument for B. During the same move, Bruce challenges W (Wilma's thesis). The argument diagram at move three shows Wilma's response. She presents an argument for W, the statement that Bruce has challenged. The fourth move in the Bruce and Wilma dialogue contains a rejection, a type of move we cannot yet render fully in a **PPD** setting.

One important thing about these examples is that they show how sets of argument diagrams are associated with every dialogue sequence,

line(s)	Wilma	Bruce
16		*Thesis.* (B) I think it's a good idea [=Ethel and Karl's decision is right.]
21,22	*Thesis.* (W) I think the decision to put that baby on mechanical life-support systems, solely for purposes of salvaging its organs, is wrong. [=Ethel and Karl's decision is wrong.] {*Why* (B)?}	
23–25		*Reason for* (B): (1) The purpose is to save the lives of other babies. *So* (2) the purpose is worthwhile in itself & (3) the purpose is helpful to Karl and Ethel. *So* (4) the purpose here is a good one. {*So* (B)}
23		*Why* (W)?
26	*Concessions.* (1), (2), (3), (4), (1) → (2), ((2) ∧ (3)) → (4). {*Why* (4 → B)?}	
26–29	*Reason for* (W): (H) That baby, when it is born, will be a living human being. *So* (M) putting it on a mechanical life support system may not be justifiable as an act of medical treatment [Ambiguous: (M_1): . . . may not be a *justifiable* act of medical treatment; (M_2): . . . may not be an act of medical treatment and hence not justifiable.] {*So W*}	
30		*Rejection of* (M_2): (rM_2) It is an act of medical treatment {*Why* (H)?, *Why* (H → M_2)?}

Figure 4.5   Discussion on Medical Ethics, Schematic Survey
{ } = implicit, [ ] = comment

	CW	AW	ActsW	ActsB	AB	CB
0.		W			B	
1.			B??			
2.				(1) ↓ (2)&(3) ↓ (4) ↓ B W??	(1) (2) (1)→(2) (3) ((2)∧(3))→(4) (4) (4)→B	
3.	(1) (2) (1)→(2) (3) ((2)∧(3))→(4) (4)	H H→M M M→W	c(1) c(2) c((1)→(2)) c(3) c(((2)∧(3))→(4)) c(4) H ↓ M ↓ W (4)→B ??			
4.				M?? H?? (H→M)??		

Figure 4.6   Discussion on Medical Ethics, PPD Matrix

as revealed by the matrix of the dialogue. You see not only the chain of arguments but also how it is contained in a surrounding context of dialogue.

4.3.3 Problems of Commitment Management in Permissive Persuasion Dialogue

Having set out a general description of the **PPD** type of dialogue, it is now important to give a set of rules for the basic game of dialogue PPD_0. Before this can be done, however, we need to discuss the form rules for the incurring and retraction of commitment will take in certain key situations.

First, let us deal with the problem of incurring commitments. The problem here, as noted previously, is for a questioner to be able to gently induce a respondent to stick to her underlying, important commitments in a dialogue. In the general description of **PPD,** we saw that the way to accomplish this goal is to allow the questioner to make "Are you serious?" challenges to the respondent. But in what circumstances does a respondent have to follow up the challenge by making a concession? And what scope for retraction of commitments should the respondent have? To resolve these problems by having a precise rule in PPD_0, we turn to a prominent case in point in the dialogue on medical ethics from chapter 3.

Toward the end of the case study dialogue on medical ethics, at line 135, Wilma challenges the consistency of Bruce's commitments by pointing out that Bruce's previous "no commitment" move has landed him in some trouble.

At lines 135 through 140, Wilma draws a conclusion from some of Bruce's previous light-side commitments. She reminds Bruce that previously in the discussion, at lines 31 and 32, Bruce explicitly stated that we must have respect for all life and that Ethel's baby is one life to be considered. Wilma infers the conclusion, from these premises, that we must respect Ethel's baby's life, according to Bruce's own concessions.

Now, in fact, Bruce did not contest this conclusion as being a commitment of his, either then or later. But according to another possible rule for **PPD** that would make commitments binding, he could not contest or retract his commitment to this conclusion, once Wilma drew it out. This rule would reflect the requirement that a participant in a serious persuasion dialogue cannot retract commitments freely in every sort of situation. If a conclusion follows from a participant's light-side commitments by the rules of inference of the dialogue—and let us suppose this condition is met in this instance, although it need not be, depending on what the specified rules of inference are—then that participant cannot subsequently retract the conclusion. This type of rule is perhaps too strong to cover all kinds of dialogue. In some instances, it could be weakened to a rule that allows retraction of the conclusion after retraction of at least one of the premises. But let us suppose, for purposes of the discussion, that the stronger rule is operative in this case. Then Bruce would be nonretractably committed to the proposition that we must respect Ethel's baby's life once Wilma has drawn this conclusion from his explicit premises.

But at lines 133 and 134, Bruce appears to contradict his previously secured nonretractable commitment when he claims that he does not see how a "major degree of importance" could be assigned to Ethel's baby's life.

This is definitely a point in the dialogue where questioning or criticism of Bruce's position is appropriate, and Wilma makes the right kind of move at lines 135 through 140 by pointing up the clash. A good version of **PPD** should have rules to handle clashes and demands to resolve them. Bruce then replies to the criticism by claiming that he is not committed to a policy of respect for human life *per se*. Once again, however, Wilma (lines 143 through 145) makes a right move in reply, by pointing to the clash with Bruce's dark-side commitment of respect for human life, supported by the textual and contextual evidence prior to this point, and even much more strongly toward the end of the discussion.

According to one type of rule which might be considered for **PPD**—it could be called the *commitment-extractor rule*—if a player states "No commitment A," and A is in his dark-side commitment set, then A is transferred to the light side. This rule would not be normative, but descriptive. It would reflect the fact that we sometimes become aware of our deeper commitments as we catch ourselves in the act of denying them. Such a rule, if applicable here, would bring restraint to bear on Bruce's freedom to move next. In fact, the previous dialogue evidence would justify the contention that Bruce's arguments are based on an underlying, if not explicitly expressed, commitment to respect for life. Hence, following the commitment-extractor rule, this commitment would be placed in Bruce's light-side commitment store, as soon as he explicitly denies it in the dialogue. A further normative rule of **PPD** could stipulate that commitments incurred in this way are nonretractable in the rest of the dialogue.

These phases of the dialogue give an illustration of how some possible commitment rules of **PPD** could function as a normative model that can aid the fixing of commitment strongly enough to support making some appropriate kinds of criticisms in the dialogue. Such a model would not be the only possible approach to giving structure to the dialogue. But it might provide a kind of regulated structure that is rigorous enough to fix commitments to some extent, while at the same time allowing enough flexibility to deal with an open kind of discussion where implicit and emerging, yet partially unarticulated, commitments are important.

In a **PPD** type of game, winning is not everything. The side benefit of maieutic insight gain is, in some respects, more important for the value of a dialogue. This maieutic function does bring in Hamblin's idea of a gain in information, but does so in a more special way than Hamblin may have had in mind. Hamblin's treatment of games of dialogue is eclectic and pluralistic. He allows various different kinds of games, but he does emphasize the type of game where the purpose is, loosely speaking, information oriented. In this respect, the **PPD** type of game is somewhat different in orientation. The primary goal is persuasion for each player, but successful persuasion brings with it, and also requires, a maieutic aspect of having empathy for the other party's commitments. Internal information is brought to the surface in the successful playing of a **PPD** game.

Another problem of management of commitment concerns retractions of parts of arguments. Suppose a participant in a **PPD** dialogue, say Black, puts forward an argument with a collection of premises $(P_0, P_1, \ldots P_n)$ all of which are commitments of White. Say also that all these premises are connected in one basic argument by a set of implicit connecting premises (warrants) that are also commitments of White. White, then, must concede the conclusion P (rule 11, section 4.3.1). But now suppose that White wants to retract her commitment to the conclusion P by making a move which we will denote by $nc(P)$. Can this be allowed? Or must there be some sanction that prevents White from retracting commitment, in such a case, in too free and easy a way?

For example, suppose in figure 4.7, that White retracts P, but that P follows, according to Black's argument, from some premises that White has conceded at prior moves in the dialogue. What can be done to manage this kind of problem in **PPD**?

The answer that will be reflected in the rules of **PPD**$_0$ is to require White to retract at least one of the premises (prior commitments) on which the argument for P was based. By such a process of selective retraction, White may have to go back up the sequence of premises and retract several, for some of the intervening premises may be based on other premises that are also commitments of White. Thus, in any instance, if there are linked premises that lead by a warrant to a commitment retracted by White, she will have to retract commitment to at least one of these premises, or to the warrant. (In other words, if White concedes all the premises and the warrant, she will have to concede the conclusion.) This general type of situation is pictured in figure 4.7, where commitment to the encircled premises is retracted.

In short, **PPD**$_0$ will require *stability* in the retraction of commitments in the sense that a commitment cannot be retracted in isolation from related commitments in an argument: some premises and/or warrants leading into that commitment (as a conclusion in argument) will also have to be retracted. This is *external stability adjustment*. Hence retraction in **PPD**$_0$ is "sticky," and it may take a number of retractions to restore stability.

A second type of problem of retraction is illustrated by figure 4.8. Suppose White retracts some proposition P that occurred as a premise or conclusion at some point in one of her own arguments that she has advanced in the dialogue? Similarly, here the participant in question will have to restore stability by retracting some of the other premises that led to this key proposition in her argument. This is an *internal stability adjustment*. But the internal stability adjustment of figure 4.8 is more involved. As soon as White retracts P, the premises $R_1, \ldots R_8$ become

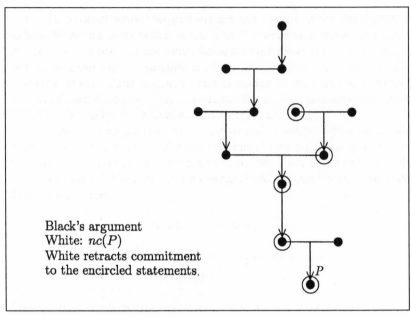

Black's argument
White: $nc(P)$
White retracts commitment
to the encircled statements.

Figure 4.7 External Stability Adjustment

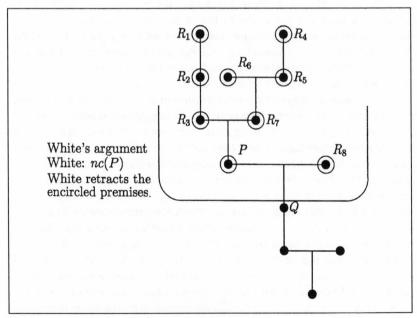

White's argument
White: $nc(P)$
White retracts the
encircled premises.

Figure 4.8 Internal Stability Adjustment

pointless. These assertions, together with P, constituted a basic argument for Q. But once P has been retracted, this argument has to go as well. According to a possible **PPD** rule which we will adopt for $\mathbf{PPD}_0$, White has in principle to retract those of her assertions that appear above the line drawn in figure 4.8.

These features of retraction are built into the rules of $\mathbf{PPD}_0$ presented below.

4.3.4 Rules of PPD₀

There are four types of rule. *Locution rules* indicate the types of permissible moves. *Commitment rules* govern which propositions go in or out of commitment stores in each type of move. *Structural rules* define turn taking and which types of move are permitted or required after each move. *Win-and-loss rules* define the participants' aims in the dialogue— what counts as a "winning" or "losing" sequence of moves. In the rules below, "P," "Q," and so on, stand for sentences of L.

Locution Rules

1. Permitted locutions are of the following types:

Statements:	*Assertions:*	$a(P)$
	Concessions:	$c(P)$
Elementary Arguments:		ΔsoP
Questions:	*Requests:*	$con(P)?$
	Extractors:	$serious(P)?$
	Confronters:	$resolve(P,Q)$
	Challenges:	$P??$
Retractions:	of *commitment:*	$nc(P)$
	of *strong commitment:*	$na(P)$

2. Moves have the following structure:

$$< nc(P)/na(P),\ c(P),\ resolve(P,Q),\ con(P)?/serious\,(P)?,\ \Delta soP,\ P?? >$$

At each slot in the six-tuple more than one element of the indicated type is allowed. Not every slot needs to be filled.

Besides moves of this structure, there are preparatory moves that precede the actual dialogue. In these preparatory moves, the locutions $a(P)$ and $c(P)$ are used. See commitment rule 2 below.

Commitment Rules

1. Each participant (B,W) has three commitment stores. For participant X these are indicated as DX, AX_n, CX_n. (The index n refers

to the stage of the discussion just completed.) DX, the set of X's *dark-side commitments*, remains fixed throughout the dialogue. Its elements are propositions.[6] AX_n and CX_n contain formulas of L. These formulas are called *light-side commitments*. The elements of AX_n are called *assertions* of X and those of CX_n *concessions* of X. The formulas in CX_n that are not in AX_n are called *mere concessions* of X.

2. Preceding the actual dialogue there are some preparatory moves in which the contents of AW_0, CW_0, AB_0, and CB_0 are determined. To put a formula into both AX_0 and CX_0, X uses the expression $a(P)$. To put a formula merely into CX_0, X uses the expression $c(P)$. The locutions $a(P)$ are permitted in preparatory moves only.

3. The preparatory moves (which shall not be formalized in detail) are such that at least $AB_0 \neq \emptyset$ that $CW_0 \cap AB_0 = \emptyset$ and that $CB_0 \cap AW_0 = \emptyset$. (Moreover, clearly $AB_0 \subseteq CB_0$ and $AW_0 \subseteq CA_0$.)

4. a. A *retraction* $nc(P)$ removes P from both the set of the speaker's assertions and the set of the speaker's concessions (if it is there in the first place). That is to say if X utters $nc(P)$ at the nth stage then $P \notin AX_n$ and $P \notin CX_n$.
    b. A *retraction* $na(P)$ removes P from the set of the speaker's assertions, but not from the set of the speaker's concessions.

5. $c(P)$ enters P into the speaker's set of concessions, but not into the speaker's set of assertions.

6. ΔsoP enters all the elements (explicit premises and warrant) of the argument ΔsoP into the set of assertions and into the set of concessions of the speaker.

Structural Rules

1. The parties move alternately. W makes the first move in the actual dialogue.

2. Each party in its first move challenges or concedes each initial assertion presented by the other party.

3. For each move
    a. if the preceding move contained $resolve(P,Q)$, the speaker must use either $nc(P)$ or $nc(Q)$;
    b. if the preceding move contained $con(P)?$, the speaker must either use $c(P)$ or $nc(P)$;

c. if the preceding move contained *serious*(P)?, the speaker utters either *c*(P) or *nc*(P), but if the proposition expressed by P is in the dark-side commitment store of the speaker, the speaker must utter *c*(P);

d. if the preceding move contained Δ*soP* the speaker must, for each element Q in the elementary argument Δ*soP* that is not a concession of the speaker, and has not been challenged by the speaker thus far, either utter *c*(Q) or Q??;

e. if the preceding move contained P??, the speaker must utter an argument Δ*soP*, or utter *nc*(P) or *na*(P).

4. a. If the proposition expressed by P is in the dark-side commitment store of X and X has been confronted with an extractor *serious*(P)?, then the locution *nc*(P) is not available to X for the rest of the dialogue;

   b. *nc*(P) can be used only if either
      1. the preceding move contained *con*(P)? or *serious*(P)?, or
      2. P is a concession of the speaker;

   c. *na*(P) can be used only if P is an assertion of the speaker.

5. A statement *c*(P) is allowed only if P is not a concession of the speaker and either P is an assertion of the other party or the preceding move contained *con*(P)? or *serious*(P)?

6. A request *resolve*(P,Q) may be used only if
   1. P and Q are explicit contradictories, and
   2. P and Q are both concessions of the listener.

7. A request *con*(P)? may be used only if
   1. one of the speaker's assertions is not among the concessions of the listener and
   2. P is not a concession of the listener.

8. The question *serious*(P)? may be used only if the preceding move contained *nc*(P) or P??

9. Δ*soP* may be used only if P is not among the concessions of the listener and some earlier move contained P??

10. P?? can be used only if P is an unchallenged assertion of the listener and not a concession of the speaker (after completion of the move).

11.   In each move the use of locutions of the forms $nc(P)$, $na(P)$, $c(P)$, P?? is to be such that after completion of the move the following are true:

1. For each elementary argument $\{P_1 \ldots, P_n\}soC$ of the listener if $P_1, \ldots, P_n$ and $(P_1 \wedge \ldots \wedge P_n) \to C$ are concessions of the speaker, then the conclusion is also a concession of the speaker.

2. Each unchallenged assertion of the listener is a concession of the speaker.

3. For each basic argument Δ of the speaker and for each Q that is an element of Δ, if Q is retracted by the speaker, then all the elements of Δ that are implicit or explicit immediate premises for Q must be retracted (as assertions, at least); moreover, if Q itself functions in Δ as an immediate premise for P, all Q's copremises for P must be retracted. This procedure is recursive. (However, retraction of an element need not be put through if this element functions as a premise in some elementary argument of the speaker that is no part of a basic argument for Q or for a copremise of Q in Δ.)

12.   A retracted initial thesis (assertion) cannot be reinstated as such.

13.   Each move and each dialogue is limited with respect to the number of its symbol tokens. (We shall not here formulate the precise rules to this effect.)

Win-and-Loss Rules

1.   At the end of the dialogue, if X has retracted its initial thesis P, X is the loser and the other party the winner with respect to P; however, if the other party has got P in its set of concessions by the end of the dialogue, X is the winner and the other party the loser with respect to P. In all other cases the dialogue is a draw with respect to P.

This system of rules, **PPD$_0$**, illustrates a number of features of **PPD** dialogue. For instance, there is a clear distinction between concessions and assertions, related to burden of proof. Dark-side commitments can have their impact on the course of a dialogue when a participant uses the extractor: *serious* (P)? (structural rules 3c and 4a). Elementary arguments build up to form basic arguments on each side. Retraction is sticky: structural rules 11.1 and 11.3 take care of external and internal stability adjustment.

In the following example of a **PPD$_0$** dialogue fragment we first list the moves in chronological order and then discuss the additions to and the deletions from commitment stores that result from each move. The

White's basic arguments   Black's basic arguments

$$P_3$$
$$\downarrow$$
$$\underbrace{P_4 \ \& \ P_5}_{} \qquad P_6$$
$$\downarrow \qquad\qquad \downarrow$$
$$P_2 \qquad\qquad P_2$$

$$\underbrace{\neg P_4 \ \& \ P_5}_{} \quad \neg P_4$$
$$\downarrow \qquad\qquad \downarrow$$
$$\underbrace{P_3 \ \& \ (P_3 \to P_1)}_{}$$
$$\downarrow$$
$$P_1$$

Figure 4.9   Basic Arguments of the Dialogue Fragment

basic arguments that are built up in the dialogue are shown in figure 4.9. White's dark-side commitment store, DW, contains just one proposition: *that P_3*.

Preparatory Moves:

W: $a(P_2)$
B: $a(P_1)$

Dialogue Fragment:

1. W: $con(P_3)?, P_1??$
2. B: $c(P_3), serious(P_1)?, P_3 so P_1, P_2??$
3. W: $nc(P_1), c(P_3 \to P_1), \{P_4, P_5\}so P_2, P_3??$
4. B: $c(P_5), c((P_4 \wedge P_5) \to P_2), serious(P_3)?, \{\neg P_4, P_5\}so P_3, P_4??$
5. W: $nc(P_3 \to P_1), c(P_3), c(\neg P_4), c((\neg P_4 \wedge P_5) \to P_3), P_3 so P_4, (P_3 \to P_1)??$
6. B: $resolve(P_4, \neg P_4), \neg P_4 so P_3 \to P_1, (P_3 \to P_4)??$
7. W: $nc(P_4), nc(P_3 \to P_4), na(P_5), na(P_3), nc((P_4 \wedge P_5) \to P_2),$
         $c(\neg P_4 \to (P_3 \to P_1)), c(P_3 \to P_1), c(P_1), P_6 so P_2$

In this dialogue White comes to accept Black's argument, Black's thesis, and most of Black's criticism, but White does not retract her own thesis. If this were the end of the dialogue (if time were up), the win-and-loss rule would stipulate that Black is the winner with respect to P_1, but that there is a draw with respect to P_2.

The set of White's assertions initially comprises just P_2, $AW_0 = \{P_2\}$. At move 3 White presents an elementary argument, so the elements of the argument are to be added to the set of White's assertions (commitment rule 6). $AW_3 = \{P_2, P_4, P_5, (P_4 \wedge P_5) \to P_2\}$. Similarly, at move 5 the sentences P_3 and $P_3 \to P_4$ are added. $AW_5 = \{P_2, P_4, P_5, (P_4 \wedge P_5) \to P_2, P_3, P_3 \to P_4\}$. In move 7 there are a number of retractions but also some additions, $AW_7 = \{P_2, P_6, P_6 \to P_2\}$. Note that White's dark-side commitment to P_3 makes it impossible to retract P_3 altogether but that $na(P_3)$ is allowed in move 7 (structural rule 4a).

Similarly, for Black's set of assertions we have: $AB_0 = \{P_1\}$, $AB_2 = \{P_1, P_3, P_3 \to P_1\}$, $AB_4 = \{P_1, P_3, P_3 \to P_1, \neg P_4, P_5, (\neg P_4 \wedge P_5) \to P_3\}$, $AB_7 = AB_6 = \{P_1, P_3, P_3 \to P_1, \neg P_4, P_5, (\neg P_4 \wedge P_5) \to P_3, \neg P_4 \to (P_3 \to P_1)\}$.

The set of White's concessions contains at least all of White's assertions at a particular time. Moreover, this set contains White's "mere concessions." At move 3 $P_3 \to P_1$ is added to White's commitment stores as a mere concession: $CW_3 = AW_3 \cup \{P_3 \to P_1\}$. But at move 5 $P_3 \to P_1$ is retracted. At the same move $\neg P_4$ and $(\neg P_4 \wedge P_5) \to P_3$ are added as mere concessions. $CW_5 = AW_5 \cup \{\neg P_4, (\neg P_4 \wedge P_5) \to P_3\}$. Move 5 contains an act $c(P_3)$, but since P_3 also occurs in the argument $P_3 so P_4$, P_3 is not added as a mere concession. When White, in move 7, retracts P_4, she has to effect a number of other retractions in order to maintain internal stability (structural rule 11.3). But note that she is allowed to retain a retracted sentence as a mere concession. As we saw, she is even required to maintain P_3 in this manner. The concession $\neg P_4 \to (P_3 \to P_1)$ induces a number of other concessions in order to maintain external stability (structural rule 11.1). $CW_7 = AW_7 \cup \{\neg P_4, (\neg P_4 \wedge P_5) \to P_3, P_3, P_5, \neg P_4 \to (P_3 \to P_1), P_3 \to P_1, P_1\}$. It is a straightforward, but tedious, exercise to check that the dialogue fragment here presented observes all the rules of $\mathbf{PPD}_0$.

4.4 Rigorous Persuasion Dialogue [RPD]

Whereas **PPD** was symmetric in that both players made the same kinds of moves **RPD** is asymmetric. One player players a positive role of proponent, while the other plays a negative or questioning role of opponent. Each has different kinds of moves outlined in figure 4.10. These are all the possible moves in **RPD**. There is no room for irrelevance in **RPD**, because the kind of response each player can make is tightly regulated.

Opponent:	Proponent:
concession	assertion
challenge	question
concession & challenge	assertion & question
final remark	final remark

Figure 4.10   RPD Moves

Whereas in **PPD** dialogue relevance was Gricean (dependent on cooperativeness), in **RPD** relevance is forced by the rules.

4.4.1 General Description of Rigorous Persuasion Dialogue

1.   There are two *parties* or *roles:* a Proponent (*P*) and an Opponent (*O*).

2.   There is an *initial conflict description* consisting of a set of (*O*'s) *initial concessions* and *P*'s *initial thesis*. Concessions and thesis are sentences of *L*.

3.   Starting with *O*, the parties move alternately, according to the rules of the game.

4.   Each move consists of either a *challenge*, a *question*, a *statement*, a challenge or a question accompanied by a statement, or a *final remark*.

5.   The game is highly asymmetrical: all *P*'s statements are assertions and are (if challenged) called *theses*, all *O*'s statements are called *concessions*. *P* is doing all the questioning, *O* all the challenging.

6.   The initial move, by *O*, challenges *P*'s initial thesis. This is the start of the *first local discussion*. It is *P*'s goal to make *O* concede the thesis. The purpose of *P*'s questioning is to get concessions from *O* and thus bridge the gap between the initial concessions and the thesis. But questioning is optional. Unless the thesis was atomic, there is (according to a *logical rule*) an assertion available for *P* that, if acceptable, would clinch the argument. Such an assertion constitutes a *direct* (or *protective*) *defense move*, whereas the questioning constitutes an *indirect* (or *counter-active*) defense.

7.   Each move by *O* (except for the initial challenge or a *final remark*) is to pertain to *P*'s preceding move. If this move was a question accompanied by an assertion, *O* must either answer the question or challenge the assertion. If *P*'s last move was just a question, *O* is required to answer the question. If it was just an assertion, *O* is required to challenge the assertion.

   Consequence: Each assertion constituting a direct defense move is immediately challenged by *O*.

   Comment: Clearly, this rule greatly restricts *O*'s freedom of choice. Thus, a rigorous persuasion dialogue is "kept on track." There is no similar restriction on *P*'s range of choices, since it is *P*'s task to try to force *O* to accept the thesis by bringing various concessions of O's together. Therefore, P can, for instance, not be limited to questioning O's last made concession. A fuller justification of this and other rules can be found elsewhere.[7]

8.   Each challenge by O of an assertion by P starts a new *local discussion* with this assertion as its *local thesis* and the totality of O's concessions as its *local concessions.*

    Comment: Thus a rigorous persuasion dialogue is segmented into local discussions that each focus upon one local thesis. A new local thesis replaces its predecessor, in the sense that whoever wins the new local discussion may also be declared to be the winner of the preceding local discussion, and so on. Together the local discussions chain up to what E. M. Barth called a "chain of arguments." The winner of the last, and therefore, of the first, local discussion in the chain is the winner of the chain. We shall not here give a theory for dialogues that consist of more than one chain.[8]

9.   Each party may give up, using the final remark "I give up." It then loses, and the adversary wins the dialogue.

10.   A party whose turn it is to move and for whom no legitimate move is available has lost the dialogue, and its adversary has won.

11. a.   If and only if the sentence figuring as local thesis is also found among O's concessions can P conclude the dialogue using the final remark "You said so yourself!"

    b.   If and only if one of O's concessions is a conventional absurdity can P conclude the dialogue using the final remark "Your position is absurd!"

    In these cases P wins and O loses the dialogue. These ways of winning the dialogue are not available to O.

    Comment: These ways of winning are not available to O, because O does not have a thesis to defend in the dialogue. Therefore, O is never in a position to establish that her thesis has been conceded. Nor is there any reason to let O win if P's thesis happens to be conventionally absurd. This would mean that it is P's claim that he can show O's position to be absurd. Such a claim is, in itself, not absurd.

12.   Challenges and direct defenses are required to follow the logical rule. Atomic assertions can be challenged, but there is no direct defense available for them.

Comment: Atomic sentences, being logically simple, are not appropriate objects for questioning by *P.* There are no new concessions to be got from such questioning.

13. Questions are of two kinds. Those that pertain to some particular concession *(bound questions)* are required to follow the logical rule, as are the direct answers to these questions. The other questions are *free.* They are always accompanied by an assertion (a so-called *creative reason*). "Answering" the question consists of conceding the content of the assertion. Otherwise, if *O* does not grant the assertion, *O* is required to challenge the assertion.

Comment: A free question is of the type, "Do you wish to concede or to challenge this assertion?" If *O* does not want to concede it, she should challenge it. There is no reason to have a middle way.

14. There must be rules to ensure that dialogues do not go on indefinitely. For instance, the number of free questions has to be limited.

Examples of **RPD**-styled dialogue can be found in the discussion on medical ethics, even though it would be hard to tell what rules are followed precisely. Lines 68 through 84 show how Bruce, as a Proponent of his thesis that Karl and Ethel made the right decision, tries to force Wilma, as an Opponent, to concede this thesis. The technique used is that of free questioning. Wilma grants a number of concessions, but then at line 85 she refuses to grant the principle that if something is all for the good and hurts no one it would be a good thing to do. Instead of just challenging the principle, as would be required by the rules of an **RPD** system, she starts another **RPD** dialogue as a Proponent of the contradictory of Bruce's principle. So there is a role-shift at line 85. Henceforth, Wilma is the Proponent, and Bruce the Opponent. Wilma tries to make her point by using a counterexample. But the first counterexample is rejected by Bruce (for the wrong reason, as we said before). Wilma, then, has another try. In terms of **RPD,** Wilma tries out another chain of arguments to resolve the same initial conflict. This second attempt of Wilma also fails to be fully convincing. Yet Bruce, at line 95, seems to give up and proposes to return to the first **RPD** dialogue. So now there is another role shift: Bruce is the Proponent again, and Wilma becomes the Opponent. Bruce replaces his principle by a weaker version. (In this respect, Wilma's last argument was a success.) This means that another chain of arguments in the first **RPD** dialogue has been opened up. But Bruce soon abandons it, returning to a **PPD** style of arguing on line 97, and therefore loses this part of the dialogue.

The next section presents a precisely elaborated example of a system of **RPD** rules.

4.4.2 Rules of RPD₀

In this section we present the rules of one specific system for **RPD** dialogue. The system is called "**RPD₀**," and its language is the language *L* introduced in section 4.2. Again we have locution rules, commitment rules, structural rules, and win-and-loss rules. The logical rules are described along with the commitment rules. (See the tables in commitment rules 4 and 6.) Italic capital letters, *"A," "B,"* and so on, refer to sentences of *L*.

Locution Rules

1.   Permitted Locutions are of the following types:
    1. *Statements:* *A* (Statements are just sentences of *L*.)
    2. *Challenges:*

           A??   Sometimes abbreviated: *??*
           $(A \wedge B)??A?$ Usually abbreviated: *L??*
           $(A \wedge B)?? B?$ Usually abbreviated: *R??*

    2.1 *A challenge accompanied by a concession:*
           $(A \rightarrow B)?? A$ Usually abbreviated: *(??)A.*
           $(\neg A)??A$ Usually abbreivated: *(?)A.*

    3. *Questions:*
    3.1 *Bound Questions:*
           $(A \wedge B)? A?$ Usually abbreviated: *L?*
           $(A \wedge B)? B?$ Usually abbreviated: *R?*
           $(A \vee B)?$ Usually abbreviated: *?*

    3.2 *Bound Questions accompanied by an assertion:*
           $(A \rightarrow B)? A$ Usually abbreviated: *(?)A*
           $(\neg A)? A$ Usually abbreviated: *(?)A*

    3.3 *Free questions (always accompanied by an assertion): A(?)*
    4. *Final Remarks:*
           I give up!
           You said so yourself! Usually abbreviated: *!*
           Your position is absurd! Usually abbreviated: *!!*

2.   Each move consists of a locution (simple or complex) of a type listed above, put forward either by *P* or by *O*, together with a label to indicate the statement or move by the other party to which it refers. (Labels referring to the immediately preceding move may be omitted.)

Element of C_p challenged	Form of Challenge	Associated structural protective defense move(s)
$A \to B$	$(??)\ A$	B
$\neg A$	$(??)\ A$	$\perp$
$A \vee B$	$??$	A, B
$A \wedge B$	$L??$	A
$A \wedge B$	$R??$	B
A_0 (an atomic sentence)	$??$	(none)

Figure 4.11   Logical Rule for Challenge and Defense

Commitment Rules

1. Each participant has a commitment store. The elements of a commitment store are sentences of L. P's commitment store is denoted as C_p, O's is denoted as C_0. C_p contains at most one sentence.

2. Each participant has a set of potential defenses or answers. The elements of a set of potential defenses or answers are sentences of L. P's set is denoted as D_p, O's is denoted as D_0.

3. At the outset of the dialogue, C_0 consists of O's initial concessions, and C_p has P's initial thesis as its only element, whereas D_0 and D_p are empty.

4. Each challenge refers to a sentence of C_p. This sentence is then removed from C_p. The structural protective defenses associated with this challenge are entered into D_p. Structural protective defenses are determined by the logical rule. See figure 4.11.

5. Each sentence asserted or conceded, whether or not it accompanies a challenge or a question, is placed in the speaker's commitment store.

6. A bound question refers to an element of C_0 (This sentence is *not* removed from C_0 as the question is asked). The direct answers associated with the question are entered into D_0. Direct answers are determined by the logical rule. See figure 4.12.
   (There is no questioning referring atomic sentences.)

7. A free question $P(?)$, except for adding its asserted sentence P to C_p, adds this same sentence to D_0. (Since its direct answer is P as well.)

Element of C_O questioned	Form of Question	Direct answer(s)
$A \rightarrow B$	$(?) A$	B
$\neg A$	$(?) A$	$\perp$
$A \vee B$	$?$	A, B
$A \wedge B$	$L?$	A
$A \wedge B$	$R?$	B

Figure 4.12   Logical Rule for Question and Answer

8.   An assertion or concession that does not accompany a challenge or a question must be a defense move or a direct answer according to one of the surveys given above. Not only is the asserted or conceded sentence added to the speaker's commitment store, but it is also removed from the set $(D_P$ or $D_O)$ of the speaker's potential defenses. In fact this set of potential defenses is emptied as soon as the speaker makes use of one of them.

Structural Rules

1.   The first move is a challenge of P's initial thesis, executed by O.

2.   The parties move alternately.

3.   In each of its moves P either defends a challenged assertion, using an element of D_P (structural protective defense move), questions an element of C_O (in a way prescribed by commitment rule 6), poses a free question, or makes a final remark.

4.   In each of its moves O either answers a questioned assertion, using an element of D_O, challenges an element (*the* element) of C_P (in a way prescribed by commitment rule 4), or makes the final remark: *I give up!*

5.   Each challenge by O initiates a new *local discussion* focusing on the challenged assertion as its *local thesis*. If and only if the same sentence figures as a local thesis and occurs in C_O, can P make the final remark *You said so yourself!* If and only if $\perp$ is an element of C_O can P make the final remark *Your position is absurd!*

6.   Each of O's moves that is not a final remark and different from the initial challenge must pertain to P's immediate preceding move. That is, if this move was a question, O must answer the

question directly or challenge its accompanying statement (if any); if this move was an assertion without a question, O must challenge this assertion. In all these cases, C_P will be empty after the move.

7.1   A question such that one of its direct answers is already in C_O is not permitted (whether or not the question is accompanied by a statement).

7.2   A sentence that has already functioned as a local thesis in some earlier local discussion may not be put forward by P as an assertion, unless some element was added to C_O after completion of that earlier local discussion.

7.3   The number of occurrences of symbols used by P to formulate free questions may, all such questions taken together, not exceed the number of occurrences of symbols used to describe the initial conflict.

Win-and-Loss Rules

1.   Whosoever states *I give up!* loses the dialogue, and the other party wins.
(Note that if no other move is available, a party may be forced to give up.)

2.   If P makes an (appropriate) statement of *You said so yourself!* or *Your position is absurd!* P wins the dialogue, and O loses it.

In figure 4.13 we present an example of an RPD_0 dialogue. For further examples and explanations the reader is referred to the literature on this type of dialogue.[9] The dialogue in figure 4.13 starts with O's challenging the thesis $\neg P_1$, after which P has the following options: (1) protective defense, (2) a question bound to one of the concessions, (3) a free question. P chooses the first alternative and asserts $\bot$, which actually is a claim that the set of O's concessions is inconsistent. O challenges this claim in move 3. P then (move 4) opts for a free question: are you willing to concede P_2, or are you going to challenge P_2? O challenges P_2 in move 5. P then takes advantage of the concession $P_1 \rightarrow P_2$. To do so P has to assert P_1 and ask whether O wishes to challenge P_1 or to concede P_2 (move 6). O concedes P_2 in move 7. (P could now go on to make a final remark, *You said so yourself!*, since P_2 is the local thesis, but P seems not to be aware of this opportunity.) P then wants to take advantage of the concession $\neg P_2$, and, therefore, has to state P_2 while asking for a concession $\bot$ (move 8). O challenges P_2 in move 9. After this P can make a final remark: *You said so yourself!*, since P_2 was conceded in move 7.

Initial Situation	Commitment Sets:	Defense Sets:
Concessions: (1) $P_1 \to P_2$	$C_O\{P_1 \to P_2, \neg P_2\}$	$D_O = \emptyset$
(2) $\neg P_2$	$C_P\{\neg P_1\}$	$D_P = \emptyset$
Thesis: $\neg P_1$		

Dialogue	Contents of Commitment Sets and Defense Sets After Each Move	
1. $O: (??) P_1$	$C_{O1} = C_O \cup \{P_1\}$	$C_{P1} = \emptyset$
	$D_{O1} = \emptyset$	$D_{P1} = \{\perp\}$
2. $P: \perp$	$C_{O2} = C_{O1}$	$C_{P2} = \{\perp\}$
	$D_{O2} = \emptyset$	$D_{P2} = \emptyset$
3. $O: ??$	$C_{O3} = C_{O1}$	$C_{P3} = \emptyset$
	$D_{O3} = \emptyset$	$D_{P3} = \emptyset$
4. $P: P_2(?)$	$C_{O4} = C_{O1}$	$C_{P4} = \{P_2\}$
	$D_{O4} = \{P_2\}$	$D_{P4} = \emptyset$
5. $O: ??$	$C_{O5} = C_{O1}$	$C_{P5} = \emptyset$
	$D_{O5} = \emptyset$	$D_{P5} = \emptyset$
6. $P: (?) P_1$ (concess. (1))	$C_{O6} = C_{O1}$	$C_{P6} = \{P_1\}$
	$D_{O6} = \{P_2\}$	$D_{P6} = \emptyset$
7. $O: P_2$	$C_{O7} = C_{O1} \cup \{P_2\}$	$C_{P7} = \emptyset$
	$D_{O7} = \emptyset$	$D_{P7} = \emptyset$
8. $P: (?) P_2$ (concess. (2))	$C_{O8} = C_{O7}$	$C_{P8} = \{P_2\}$
	$D_{O8} = \{\perp\}$	$D_{P8} = \emptyset$
9. $O: ??$	$C_{O9} = C_{O7}$	$C_{P9} = \emptyset$
	$D_{O9} = \emptyset$	$D_{P9} = \emptyset$
10. $P: !$	$C_{O10} = C_{O7}$	$C_{P10} = \emptyset$
	$D_{O10} = \emptyset$	$D_{P10} = \emptyset$

Figure 4.13　An Example of an RPD_0 Dialogue

RPD_0 dialogues are conveniently described in a two-column notation. One column shows the acts of O, the other the acts of P. Figure 4.14 gives the same dialogue as figure 4.13, but this time in a two-column notation. Nonempty defense sets (but not commitment sets) are shown as well.

This RPD_0 dialogue is won by P. As we said, P could have won sooner (at move 8, he could have made a winning remark). Also, it may be observed, there is a winning strategy in RPD_0 for P in this case. But in other cases there may be an O winning strategy. In fact RPD_0 is a *zero-sum* game, in which there will always be a winning strategy for precisely one of the parties.

	RPD_0	
	O	P
(1)	$P_1 \rightarrow P_2$	
(2)	$\neg P_2$	$\neg P_1$
1.	$(??) P_1$	$\{\bot\}$
2.		$\bot$
3.	$??$	
4.	$\{P_2\}$	$P_2 (?)$
5.	$??$	
6.	$\{P_2\}$	$(?) P_1$
7.	P_2	
8.	$\{\bot\}$	$(?) P_2$
9.	$??$	
10.		$!$

Figure 4.14   An Example of an RPD_0 Dialogue

4.5 Complex Persuasion Dialogue

The final set of rules needed is for the embedding of **RPD** into **PPD**. These are the rules for the kind of dialectical shift seen in the dialogue on medical ethics where there is a tightening up from a permissive type of persuasion dialogue into a rigorous type of persuasion dialogue, or a loosening up the other way around. Five rules are given in the general description below.

General Description of the Embedding of RPD into PPD

1.   Whenever T is not a concession of a party X, and either there was an utterance $nc(T)$ or $T??$ by this party, the other party, Y, may demand (provided it is Y's move) an **RPD** dialogue on the issue of T, using the locution *Your position implies T*. The **PPD** dialogue is then interrupted to have this **RPD** dialogue.

2.   The initial conflict description for the **RPD** dialogue is made by collecting the concessions granted by X in the **PPD** dialogue: these make up the initial concessions. T is to be the initial thesis. X takes the role of O, Y the role of P.

3.   After the **RPD** dialogue has been won by one of the parties, the **PPD** dialogue is resumed. If X won the **RPD** dialogue, Y has now to make a **PPD** move. If Y won the **RPD** dialogue, X must first utter $c(T)$ before Y is to make a move.

      Comment: The **RPD** dialogue is functionally related to the embedding **PPD** dialogue: the term *embedding* is used in the sense of section 3.3.

4.   Suppose Y won the dialogue as in (3) above; so X had to concede T. In the rest of the **PPD** dialogue, X may utter $nc(T)$ only if X also retracts commitment (by an utterance of an nc-statement) to at least one of the initial concessions of the **RPD** dialogue that was actually used by Y in this dialogue (or to at least one concession induced by free questioning in this dialogue that was actually used by Y).

      Comment: If Y wins the dialogue, then X concedes T. This payoff for Y is nugatory, however, if X can straightforwardly retract T. Rule 4 sees to it that retraction of T may lead to a number of other retractions, perhaps of favored assertions of X, assertions X needs in her own arguments. Thus **RPD** ties a concession to other commitments.

5.   After completion of the **RPD** dialogue, every concession made by X in the course of the dialogue is transferred as such to the **PPD** dialogue.

      Comment: One could object that some of these concessions were only made for the sake of argument. But those concessions are not likely to be assertions or dark-side commitments of X and can easily be retracted if X wishes to do so.

The typical kind of situation in which shift from **PPD** to **RPD** and vice versa would occur is sketched out in figure 4.15 below.

The Bruce and Wilma dialogue fragment discussed in section 4.1 illustrates the embedding of **RPD** dialogue in **PPD** dialogue. To give a formal example of the embedding one could embed the system $\mathbf{RPD}_0$ in $\mathbf{PPD}_0$. To carry this through, one has to formulate rules 1 through 5 in an $\mathbf{RPD}_0$ and $\mathbf{PPD}_0$ idiom (something we steered clear of). We shall not go through this exercise, however, since we trust that the general description given here suffices to show how it can be done. But we shall present an example of a dialogue that follows the rules of the system that would result from the embedding. Let us call this system $\mathbf{PPD}_1$. $\mathbf{PPD}_1$, then, is a system of permissive persuasion dialogue (Hamblin-type dialogue) in which each participant may resort to a system of rigorous

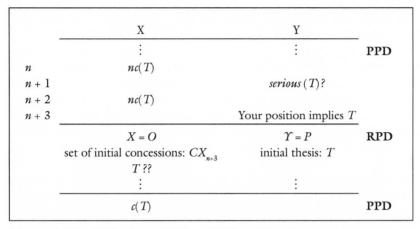

Figure 4.15   Shifts from PPD to RPD and Back

persuasion dialogue (Lorenzen-type dialogue). Structural rule 13 of PPD_0, when specified and translated to PPD_1, is to effectuate a limitation of the number of appeals to RPD_0 open to each participant. In the following PPD_1 dialogue W's dark-side commitment set contains a proposition to the effect that $P_1 \to P_2$.

Preparatory Moves

> W: $a(P_3)$
> B: $a(\neg P_1)$

Dialogue Fragment

1. W: $\neg P_1$??
2. B: $(P_1 \to P_2)so\neg P_1, P_3$??
3. W: $\neg P_2 so P_3, (P_1 \to P_2)$??, $((P_1 \to P_2) \to \neg P_1)$??
4. B: $na((P_1 \to P_2) \to \neg P_1), na(P_1 \to P_2), c(\neg P_2), serious(P_1 \to P_2)?,$
          $(\neg P_2 \to P_3)$??
5. W: $c(P_1 \to P_2), P_4 so(\neg P_2 \to P_3)$
6. B: *Your position implies* $\neg P_1$

> Start of RPD_0 dialogue ($O = W, P = B$). Initial situation similar to that in figure 4.13. Lines 7 through 16 as in figure 4.13 line 1 through 10. End of RPD_0 dialogue.

17. W: $c(\neg P_1)$
18. B: $c(P_4 \to (\neg P_2 \to P_3)), P_4$??

In this example B, in move 4, retracts his argument put forward in move 2. This does not mean that B no longer believes his own argument but rather that he does not know how to argue further for its premises, which are all challenged by W. However, B is convinced that W is actually deeply committed to $P_1 \rightarrow P_2$, and so he attempts to extract this concession. In this he succeeds: W concedes $P_1 \rightarrow P_2$ in move 5, but in move 3 she also asserted $\neg P_2$ as part of an argument. Now B resorts to rigorous dialogue to make W concede his thesis $\neg P_1$. The dialogue is the same as in figure 4.13. B wins this dialogue (in fact, as we know, he has a winning strategy). Now W has to concede $\neg P_1$ (at move 17). Note that it is not easy for W to retract this concession. For, if she did, she would have to retract either $P_1 \rightarrow P_2$ or $\neg P_2$ as well (there are no concessions induced by free questioning). This retraction has to be made by an nc-statement, na doesn't suffice. But $P_1 \rightarrow P_2$, being a dark-side commitment that was brought to light, cannot be retracted in this way ($\mathbf{PPD}_0$ structural rule 4a), and retraction of $\neg P_2$ would result in a surrender as far as W's own argument for her thesis P_3 goes (see move 3).

The type of embedding we have been describing is not recursive: an $\mathbf{RPD}$ dialogue can be embedded in a $\mathbf{PPD}$ dialogue, but then it stops. More complex types of dialogue, however, will surely exhibit recursive embeddings. For instance, as we remarked in section 3.1, inquiries can be embedded in a persuasion dialogue, and persuasion dialogues can be embedded in an inquiry, and so on.

Another important species that can be embedded in persuasion dialogue to yield a more complex type of dialogue is the information-seeking dialogue. In section 3.3 it was pointed out that expert consultation dialogues, for instance, could be useful parts of persuasion dialogues. The discussion on medical ethics, lines 160 through 167, displays an embedded information-seeking dialogue. (The embedding was discussed in the analysis following the dialogue.)

4.6 Problems to Be Solved

In general, the problem with such types of dialogues as $\mathbf{PPD}$ is how to strike a good balance between such leniency as will give each participant sufficient opportunities to express his or her views on an issue and such strenuousness as is necessary for keeping the discussion to the point and avoiding digressions. For instance, could characteristic (8) of $\mathbf{PPD}$ (section 4.3.1) be amended so as to allow more freedom in presenting arguments (even for unchallenged statements) without opening all doors to senseless digression?

The aim of some arguers is more ambitious than that of merely convincing the adversary of their point of view. They try to turn their adversary into a co-assertor, that is, someone who does not merely concede the thesis but is willing to defend it herself vis-à-vis a third party. Can we construct rules of dialogue that allow for a distinction between strong and weak persuasion? Can we define a dialogical concept of proof for strongly persuasive argument?[10]

How could one improve the theory of commitment extraction? Is there anything more for a dialectician to say, or is this a matter of psychology? What other mechanisms (like inferences) can be introduced to speed up dialogues?

A number of possible extensions of PPD_1 will be discussed in section 5.2 below: rules to avoid question begging and many questions, inferences, rejections, objections, hypotheses, defaults, clarifications and definitions, rules that determine the rights and duties of each party in these respects, and rules against hedging (use of weasel words). They all provide subjects for further research.

More study of the specific commitments that go with a concession, such as the obligation to answer questions, or to clarify one's position, would be useful.

It would also be useful to study types of concessions that cannot be refused unless certain conditions are met, such as global presumptions that act as a constraint on the dialogue. (In a presumption, the burden of proof is on the side of the party that refuses to concede, to show why the presumption would not hold in a particular case.) One way to go about this is to analyze presumption as a speech act in dialogue that is different from the speech act of assertion. In assertion, the proponent incurs a burden of proof to defend the proposition if it is challenged by the respondent. In presumption, once the proponent and the respondent agree to accept the proposition in question (as a presumption), then if the respondent wants to reject it, he must disprove it.[11] How this conception of presumption would be exactly modeled in **PPD** and **RPD** is a good question. Also, it would be instructive to find and study some uses of presumption in the discussion on medical ethics.

4.7 Summary

The tightening up of the dialogue around line 70 of the case study dialogue on medical ethics signaled a shift from a permissive (**PPD**) type of dialogue to a rigorous (**RPD**) type of dialogue. Later, around line 100, the discussion shifted back to the permissive type of dialogue. In the permissive dialogue, the commitment store of each party is divided into a light side and a dark side. The light-side commitments are overt, expressed commitments, known to both parties. The dark-side commitments are not explicitly known, but can only be conjectured on the basis of how a participant has performed in the dialogue. The goal of probing into the other party's deeper position (its dark-side commitments) was very important in the permissive type of dialogue, but this goal receded into the background in the rigorous type of dialogue.

Retraction is the key problem posed in this chapter. Hence, the question of the binding nature of commitments, discussed in chapter 2, resurfaces: commitments in dialogue are binding in the sense that not living up to them or inappropriately retracting them leads to sanctions, like loss of the dialogue or part of it. Bindingness, however, is a matter of degree. Rules for retraction need to be somewhat flexible yet have enough bite to fix a participant's commitment on an issue.

In section 4.2, a formal language for arguments is introduced, as a preliminary to **RPD** and **PPD**.

An elementary argument consists of a number of sentences conjoined as premises that stand in relationship to a single sentence that is a conclusion. The premises are shown above the conclusion in the examples of elementary arguments given in figure 4.1. Basic arguments are tree-shaped structures made up of elementary arguments, as shown in the example in figure 4.2. An incomplete set comprising eleven rules of inference (such as *modus ponens*) is formulated for illustrative purposes. This is to reflect the idea that in ordinary circumstances discussants share some logic. Any elementary argument that conforms in its pattern to one of these rules is said to be an elementary inference. A basic inference is said to be a basic argument where each elementary argument in it is an elementary inference.

According to the general description of permissive persuasion dialogue given in section 4.3.1, **PPD** has the following characteristics (sometimes called "rules"). There are two parties, and each has a set of sentences or propositions called a "commitment store" ("commitment set"), which has a light side (of propositions on view) split into a compartment of concessions and a compartment of assertions, and a dark side of propositions not on view. Commitment to assertions, unlike commitment to concessions, has a burden of proof attached. To begin a **PPD** dialogue, the set of initial assertions of one player must contain at least one member. The players take turns making moves, and each move must contain any or all of six components: (1) retractions, (2) concessions, (3) requests for retractions, (4) requests for concessions, (5) arguments, and (6) challenges. The basic objectives for each party are (1) to get the other party to become committed to her (the first party's) initial assertions, that is, to get the other party to concede her theses as right, and

(2) to get the other party to retract commitment to its initial assertions. These two objectives are what makes **PPD** a species of persuasion dialogue. Other rules of **PPD** include the following. If one party challenges an assertion of the other, then the other must give an argument for the assertion challenged, and an assertion may be defended only if challenged. Furthermore, if one party makes an assertion, the other must make clear its position on that assertion. These rules (8 and 9) give the sequences of argumentation relevance by making them responsive to preceding moves and by eliminating superfluous arguments that are not called for by a preceding move. Another rule (12) means that a reply to a question should grant the concession requested by the question or refuse to do so. This assures a kind of question-reply relevance.

Other rules restrict the scope of challenges, allow for retractions, or allow for demands for the resolution of explicit inconsistencies requiring retraction as part of the response. One particularly important rule (16) makes it impossible for a participant to deny or challenge a proposition that she is really committed to in her dark-side set. This rule is an important part of how **PPD** deals with the problem of retraction. It means that retraction is generally possible, but that it is not straightforward if the participant really is deeply committed to a proposition as a part of her underlying, deeper position on an issue. In short, a **PPD** dialogue is a precise structure with clear and definite rules, but it is flexible and open-ended enough to deal with the covert nature of many important commitments that play a key role in persuasion dialogue in everyday conversational exchanges of argumentation on significant issues. In a word, **PPD** is meant to be more realistic, in respect to the management of commitments and retractions, than many simpler types of rigorous persuasion dialogue could hope to be. A case in point is the use of **PPD** to manage the problems of the incurring and retraction of commitments posed by the dialogue on medical ethics. Although Bruce tries to retract a commitment, Wilma is able to show him that he cannot do this in a straightforward manner without running into some trouble that he must straighten out first. This way of structuring **PPD** to make such retractions nonstraightforward reflects, and at the same time promotes, the idea that the so-called maieutic aspect of eliciting a participant's deeper commitments is an important benefit of persuasion dialogue.

A related problem concerns the parts of arguments. What happens if a participant is committed to a set of premises but tries to retract commitment to a proposition that is a conclusion of these premises by a basic argument? Should she be allowed to do this or not? In a specific system for permissive persuasion dialogue called PPD_0, such a participant will have to retract some of the premises that are the basis for the conclusion. This is called a "stability adjustment," and it means that a commitment cannot be retracted in isolation from other commitments that are closely related to it in a structure of argumentation of which it is part. An external stability adjustment is one where the argument structure is in the arguments of the other party (here at least one of the premises will have to be retracted), while an internal stability adjustment is one where the structure occurs among the would-be retractor's own arguments. This latter situation calls (roughly) for a retraction of all premises supporting the retracted conclusion, as well as a retraction of those premises that together with the retracted conclusion form the premise set of a further argument.

PPD as a normative model of permissive persuasion dialogue is very general. It is possible to have all kinds of more specific subtypes of permissive persuasion dialogue that can be categorized as **PPD**-type dialogues. In order to give the reader at least one specific instance of **PPD** dialogue of an elementary kind, in section 4.3.4, the game of dialogue **PPD**$_0$ is outlined. Permitted locutions in **PPD**$_0$ consist of nine types of statements, arguments, questions, and retractions. Each move is made up of six parts, each one of which is to contain specified types of locutions. Each participant in a **PPD**$_0$ dialogue has three commitment stores, one for dark-side commitments, one for assertions, and one for concessions. Assertions and concessions are light-side commitments. Those commitments that are concessions but are not assertions are called "mere concessions." According to the win-loss rule, a party wins (on an issue) if she gets her thesis in the set of concessions of the other side, or if the other side retracts his thesis. The structural rules assure a high degree of relevance between the pairs of moves between the two parties by allowing only certain types of responses, ones that contribute to the progress of the dialogue toward a win or loss by one party. The rules stipulate the following notable requirements (among others). One player may ask the other to resolve a pair of explicit inconsistencies that are concessions of the other. And when she does so, the other must immediately retract his commitment from the one proposition of the pair or the other. A request $con(P)$? (a request to concede P) may be posed by a speaker only if P is not a concession of the listener, and when it is posed, the listener must either concede P or explicitly refuse to concede P as a commitment. A statement $c(P)$ (I concede P) can be made only if P is not already a concession of the speaker and if P is either an assertion of the other party or if the preceding move contained a request to concede P (or an extractor to the same effect).

One rule that is especially characteristic of **PPD**$_0$ is the retraction rule 11.3, which says essentially that if a participant retracts a proposition Q, she must also retract all the premises in her arguments for Q as well as all premises that function, together with Q, in an argument for some other conclusion Q'. This is a form of internal stability adjustment that helps to make commitment "sticky" in PPD_0 dialogues, or difficult to retract.

The example of a sequence of play in PPD_0 dialogue given at the end of section 4.3.4 illustrates generally how such a dialogue might go, in a given case. In this sequence of dialogue, Black is the winner in that he successfully gets White to accept his thesis. But White does not retract her own thesis, so in that respect, the game is declared a draw in PPD_0. Figure 4.9 displays the basic arguments used by both sides.

Now we can see how PPD_0 could be used as a normative model to represent a context of conversation in which two parties are reasoning with each other in a persuasion dialogue and using arguments for this purpose. The structure of the basic arguments on each side can be used to represent the arguments used by each side to persuade the other side. PPD_0 dialogue indicates, as a normative model, how the argumentation should be ideally reconstructed in a type of case where the context of dialogue is appropriate for this type of model to apply.

Section 4.4 outlines a contrasting type of dialogue that is quite strikingly different from PPD in many respects. RPD is much more rigorous, simpler, and asymmetric, meaning that only one party has a positive burden of proof, the other having the role of questioner or critic. Whereas in PPD dialogue relevance depended to a good extent on the cooperativeness (honesty, seriousness, etc.) of the players, RPD forces the players to be relevant at each move. PPD dialogue is more complex than RPD dialogue, partly because much more freedom to choose different kinds of moves, and to respond to previous moves, is allowed in PPD. Moreover, RPD does not have dark-side commitments at all, only light-side commitments. We could say that RPD dialogue is more austere, more exact, and more in the spirit of the traditional formal logic as a model of reasoned argument. PPD is more flexible and dependent on both the cooperativeness of the participants and the nature of the deeper (nonexplicitly expressed) commitments. In these ways, PPD is a much more natural model of typical argumentation exchanges in everyday conversations.

RPD_0 is one specific instance of RPD dialogue, a simple and basic type, presented so the reader can get an idea of how a precise set of rules for a dialogue of this general type is formulated. Figures 4.13 and 4.14 give a working example of this type of dialogue.

In order to model the kind of shift that took place in the discussion on medical ethics, from the more permissive to the more rigorous type of dialogue (the so-called "tightening up" that occurred), section

4.5 gives a set of rules for embedding **RPD** into **PPD** dialogue. The shift from a **PPD** to an **RPD** dialogue occurs in a situation where one participant in an ongoing **PPD** dialogue challenges or retracts (or at least refuses explicitly to concede) a proposition that the other participant suspects she should be committed to in virtue of other overt commitments. In such a case, the other participant has the right to demand an **RPD** dialogue, in order to resolve the conflict. The **PPD** dialogue then shifts to an **RPD** dialogue. Once this **RPD** dialogue has been brought to a conclusion, one way or the other, the dialogue then shifts back to the **PPD** sequence. If the party who demanded the **RPD** dialogue wins it, then the other party has to make the appropriate concession. Moreover, this concession will be sticky, for its retraction would require the retraction of at least one of the concessions used as such in the **RPD** dialogue. And because of the internal stability requirement, such a retraction could be very damaging for the would-be retractor's own arguments. This type of shift is precisely regulated by the five embedding rules given at the beginning of section 4.5. The Bruce and Wilma dialogue fragment studied in section 4.1 is an actual example of the shift from a **PPD** to an **RPD** dialogue. The system $\mathbf{PPD}_1$ (based on $\mathbf{PPD}_0$ and $\mathbf{RPD}_0$) is an instance of a system for permissive persuasion dialogue in which a shift to rigorous persuasion dialogue is possible, a limited number of times, by either participant. We did not construct $\mathbf{PPD}_1$ in detail, but the example illustrates generally how such a system would function.

5 Conclusions and Prospects

One who approaches the study of formal dialogue systems, such as those in chapter 4, from the angle of informal logic and argument evaluation, may well wonder how these systems are to be applied. Typically, there are two reactions. One side would say that, since everyday conversation has an enormous complexity and just doesn't seem to be bound by any definite set of rules, logical or other, you cannot say anything useful about everyday conversation in terms of artificially constrained abstract systems. Any theory in this field would have to be informal and open-ended, in order to be sensitive to the complexities of conversation. Others would say that there is no need to delineate these complexities, or to account for them in any systematic way, and that the attempt in chapter 4 to be a little bit more "true to life" than a system based exclusively on formal logic is ill-conceived.

In section 5.1 we shall discuss the methodological problems of applying systems of dialogue to actual conversations or discussions. We hope to show that systems such as those in chapter 4 can be useful to throw light on argumentation in everyday conversation. But it is to be understood that these systems stand in need of extension and further refinement. In section 5.2, we propose some possible ways to enrich them.

What seems to be particularly troublesome to some people, as they are trying to see how our kind of system could be useful, is the

173

concept of a dark-side commitment. We review the issue in section 5.3. In section 5.4, finally, we summarize our position on the issue of commitment in dialogue.

5.1 How Can Systems of Dialogue Be Used to Evaluate Conversational Argumentation?

A major problem for the logical evaluation of argumentation in natural language conversation has been the rigor and precision of a system of logic, on the one hand, and the permissive, free flow of ordinary conversation on the other. How can a rigorous, well-defined system of, say, first-order predicate logic be brought to bear on an argument about birth control or a televised debate about the North American Free Trade Agreement? The problem is not new, and there are several ways to approach it.

The traditional way is, first, to try to select the crucial passages, interpret and rephrase the arguments in a way that makes them more articulate than they may have been before, add the missing premises or hidden assumptions, translate the argument into a formal language, and finally check for validity by means of some formal or semiformal method. This may work in some cases, but in general the procedure is neither practically feasible nor theoretically well-founded. One direction to take from here would be to add more and more to the formal apparatus and to mechanize the process of interpretation. Some have even claimed that ordinary language *is* a formal language.[1] This may lead to a situation that is theoretically more satisfying, but up till now there has been little in it for those who want straightforward practical advice on how to evaluate a politician's speech or a philosophical argument. It is this inability to be of direct practical use for those who, nevertheless, feel a need for *some* logical guidance, that has led to the development of informal logic.[2] Thus another response to the problem of how to apply logic is to give up interest in formal deductive logic and to try to formulate criteria in an ordinary language that may be directly applied to actual contexts of argument.

Courses on informal logic and critical thinking have expanded enormously in the past few years. These courses are meant to have clear, practical applications, of a kind that is not emphasized, or perhaps not realistically possible, in courses oriented to formal logic of the traditional kind. But the problem is that, while informal logic has proved already to have practical value, it lacks a satisfactory theoretical foundation. As we see it, dialogue theory can provide such a foundation, but only if its concepts are defined with a degree of precision comparable to that of formal logic.

A system of logic may be called a "model of reasoning."[3] It gives us a kind of stylized picture of how people reason or should reason. But this leads immediately to two points of view: is the system meant to render the way people actually reason? Or is it meant to give us norms for reasoning? It would be nice if the answer were clear-cut and if each logic system had a tag on it, saying whether it is to be taken descriptively or normatively. But that is not the way things have worked out. All serious logic systems seem to have descriptive and normative uses, but to different extents. The point is that descriptive accuracy and normative content are both important and, moreover, interdependent. Purely descriptive systems cannot be used as instruments of evaluative criticism. A purely normative system that is too far removed from what actually goes on cannot be applied to what actually goes on.[4]

One way to make logic systems more realistic (i.e., descriptively accurate) and ready for application to real life discussions is to give them a dialogical formulation.[5] This was done by Lorenzen and Hintikka, and it was a good course to take, but their systems are still very far removed from ordinary conversation. What we want, in order to give a viable theoretical foundation to informal logic, is a series of dialogue systems that are at once (1) realistic and (2) have a normative bite. Moreover, we want them to be (3) rigorously formulated and (4) easy to apply to ordinary contexts of argument.

Of these four desirable features, two have a pull toward the ordinary language situation (1 and 4), and two have a pull away from it (2 and 3). Thus 1 and 4 seem to be on the same side, but whereas feature 1 calls for the introduction of additional complexities into a system in order to match the complexities of conversation, feature 4 calls for simplification. Note also that in 2 and 3 we deal with two different kinds of rigor. According to 2, we need rigorous rules of dialogue so that transgressions can be spotted dead right. Generally, this would call for dialogue systems such as **RPD** that leave few options for the participants at each move. But the rigor meant in 3 pertains to the preciseness of formulation of the system (mathematical rigor). The two may, but need not, go together: it is possible to give a precise and rigorous formulation of a relaxed system such as **PPD**. Also, one may limit a person's options rigorously by a command in natural language that is still more or less vague (e.g., "stay close to this tree!").

It seems that if we are trying to use dialogue theory to provide theoretical underpinnings for informal logic, we have to face the problem to what extent we can satisfy the requirements 1 through 4. Trying to satisfy one may be at cross-purposes with trying to satisfy another. Indeed, different theories of dialogue and of argumentation have laid different stresses.

Systems of formal dialogue theory, such as those of Lorenzen and Barth and Krabbe go for rigor, both in formulation and in normative content. They are not very realistic and not easy to apply. Hamblin has shown that systems of dialogue are needed to give a realistic account of traditional fallacies. His systems are rigorously formulated, but not normatively rigorous. They are still very far removed from ordinary conversation and not easy to apply. Some of Mackenzie's systems are normatively more rigorous.

On the other side, there are dialogue rules formulated without a context of a mathematically rigorously defined system, such as Grice's conversational maxims. Grice tried to patch the gap between logic and conversation by the introduction of rules (maxims) for cooperative behavior. These are not normatively rigorous or absolute rules but depend upon the sincerity and cooperativeness of the participants. They may be realistic, but as the development of speech act theory has shown, are not easy to apply.

Van Eemeren and Grootendorst, like Grice, approach the problem from the everyday conversation in natural language side and give rules expressed in ordinary language terms, enjoining participants not to "prevent each other from advancing or casting doubt on standpoints," to defend a standpoint of one's own "if asked to do so," and do so "by advancing argumentation relating to that standpoint," and so on.[6] This is useful, but only up to a point, and although Van Eemeren and Grootendorst are not unfriendly to the use of formal methods in logic, and give a detailed model of dialogue in terms of speech act theory,[7] they nowhere get near a mathematically precise definition of the structure of critical discussion. However, if we abstract from goals of dialogue other than that of conflict resolution, their model is fairly realistic, and it has some normative bite. Moreover, it is often easy to apply the model to a given argument. But then, often when a dialectical move is condemned by their model as a fallacy, we have the feeling that there is more to it than the theory provides.

Thus we seem to have a large gap here, with on the one hand theories of dialogue that are mathematically precise but not very realistic, and on the other hand theories that have no pretence at mathematical precision but fare better when assessed for descriptive accuracy and applicability.

We do not think that a choice should be made. A good theoretical foundation of informal logic needs both mathematically precise models and readily applicable models that are formulated in ordinary language. The precise or rigorous models are to elucidate the concepts used by the theory that formulates the second type of models, which can be looked upon as a kind of interface between the mathematical models of dialogue and actual dialogues.

All the same, we think that it is worthwhile to provide for more realistic mathematical models of dialogue. Therefore, we had to logically regiment, or make logical sense of, the permissive kind of dialogue typically found in ordinary conversational argumentation. However, logic needs to get a "bite" on everyday argumentation that enables us, as critics, to firmly evaluate as fallacious moves we feel to be incorrect or sophistical.

Our solution to this problem lies in the concept of a dialectical shift between two types of dialogue, the permissive and the rigorous. So in one sense, the logic of everyday conversation is reflected in the rules of a permissive dialogue system (**PPD**), but in a more traditional sense of logic, it is the rigorous (**RPD**) type of system that reflects the true logic of conversation. This logic, though not obviously and evidently present in the conversation itself, is still in the background, for there is always a possibility for the dialogue partners to take up an issue in a rigorous way. This again is reflected by the embedding of **RPD** in **PPD** which yielded a new and more complex (**PPD$_1$**) type of dialogue.

Thus we hope to have achieved a real advance in the theory by providing a formally well-defined, clear dialogue structure where two parties reason together, which is at the same time useful as a foundation for informal logic. But, of course, this is not the last word on the theory nor on theory application. For one thing, to make the theory still more realistic we must incorporate many other features. This issue is taken up in the next section.

5.2 Extensions of PPD$_1$

PPD$_1$ is still a very limited model of persuasion dialogue. Not only is **PPD$_1$** restricted to the simple language of propositional logic, but also there are important features of dialogue (such as inferences, rejections, objections, hypotheses, clarifications, and definitions) that are not reflected at all in **PPD$_1$** dialogues. Also, a need may be felt for rules that obviate some of the traditional fallacies. A full **PPD** system should treat

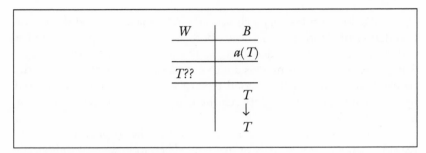

Figure 5.1   Petitio Principii

all of these, and though we cannot complete such a project within the scope of this book, we shall in this section at least discuss some possible extensions of **PPD**$_1$.

One way **PPD**$_1$ could be enriched would be to add additional requirements on the kinds of arguments that can be used to respond to challenges. For example, to ban *petitio principii*, we need to disallow the kind of sequence of dialogue outlined in figure 5.1.

The way to do this generally would be to introduce a rule that requires using only premises other than those identical to the conclusion to be proved. However, it remains an open problem just what "identical to" means in this context. Thus we pose as a problem for further study just what form such a rule should take in devising extensions to **PPD**$_1$. Such a rule should give better guidance to a participant in **PPD** on how to fulfill a proper burden of proof in order to give a useful reply to a challenge. "Useful" means, in this context, a reply that contributes to the goal of the dialogue.[8]

Another type of rule that could be added would deal with *complex questions*. In **RPD** this is not a problem, but in **PPD** the complex nature of a move could allow for complex questioning in forms that could be an interesting problem in connection with the traditional fallacies of questioning.[9]

Inference may at first seem to belong to another branch of logic than dialogue theory. In section 4.2 we presented a number of rules of inference that could have been taken from some textbook on formal deductive logic. However, we pointed out in the same section that it is plausible to assume that discussants share some incomplete system of inference rules. So we must envisage extensions of **PPD**$_1$ that incorporate such rules. How do these rules function in the context of a dialectic system?

One may look upon this matter from a "genetic" point of view. If there were no inference rules, they would have to be invented! Suppose a company of discussants has been using a **PPD** system S for some time. Suppose that an **RPD** system was incorporated in S long ago. On the basis of its experience, the company comes to see that an **RPD** discussion with initial concessions $A \lor B$, $A \rightarrow C$, and $B \rightarrow C$, and a thesis C, can always be won by the Proponent. There is a winning strategy for the Proponent in such a situation. The company may then decide to have recourse to a time-saving device: let there be an inference rule CD (constructive dilemma) attached to the list of rules of S. Thus S is extended to a system S'. The new rule makes elementary arguments of the form of the constructive dilemma unassailable as far as its warrant is concerned. That is, if the argument is of the form $\{A \lor B, A \rightarrow C, B \rightarrow C\}$ *so* C, then a challenge $((((A \lor B) \land (A \rightarrow C)) \land (B \rightarrow C)) \rightarrow C)??$ is ruled out. Whoever concedes $A \lor B$, $A \rightarrow C$ and $B \rightarrow C$ must (in S') concede C. In this way the company may skip a number of **RPD** dialogues that have lost interest.

Other inference rules may be thought of as having been introduced in a similar manner. Thus inference rules are fossilized rigorous persuasion dialogues, one might say. Inferences are not just deductions, but acts in a context of dialogue that take advantage of a common commitment to a rule of inference.

Elementary inferences can be chained to form basic inferences, in which quite lengthy stretches of argument are set forth in a manner which requires the listener to accept the conclusion if he accepts the ultimate premises. Also, the listener is required to retract commitment to one of the ultimate premises if he retracts commitment (by an *nc*-statement) to the conclusion (cf. **PPD**$_0$ structural rule 11.1).

Rejections could perhaps be handled by allowing an assertion $a(\neg A)$ to accompany a challenge $A??$ and an assertion $a(A)$ to accompany a challenge $\neg A??$. Up till now, no new assertions could be made in a **PPD** dialogue, except as part of an argument. Rejections open a new possibility and allow the discussants to take on additional commitments. Rejections are very common as may be seen from the Bruce and Wilma dialogue (e.g., lines 30, 106, 122, and 171–72).[10]

Objections, in one sense, can be understood as challenges together with a requirement as to how the burden of proof is to be met. We have instances of this in **RPD**$_0$: the challenges $(A \land B)?? A?$ and $(A \land B)?? B?$ are of this type. In a quantificational version of **RPD**$_0$, challenges directed at universally quantified formulas are objections. The user of such a challenge demands that his adversary put forward a specific instantiation of the universally quantified formula for further discussion. So we have some examples of objections, in this sense, within **RPD** dialogue, but it seems that the subject is in need of further exploration.

In another sense, objections are strong criticisms or *charges of fallacy*. Here the term *fallacy* is taken in the sense of a move that is not allowed by the rules of dialogue. In order to handle these, one needs a system of dialogue (metadialogue) in which such changes can be discussed. Ordinary **PPD** is then to be embedded in such an encompassing system of metadialogue. This is a very arduous task, but steps toward it have been taken by Jim Mackenzie in several papers.[11]

Another extension of **PPD** that would be useful to model certain arguments would be to add rules (warrants) and patterns of inference that are nondeductive in nature, especially the kind associated with *default reasoning*. This type of reasoning could be put in the following form of inference.

$$* \quad (1) \quad (\text{Rule n:}) \quad B_x \Rightarrow F_x$$
$$(2) \quad B_t$$

(3)   Rule n applies to the present case

$$\text{Therefore } F_t$$

Here F_t may be detached as a conclusion, because rule n applies to the given case in point. The rule does not apply universally (for all x), but applies generally (for any x, unless), subject to exceptions in particular cases. What the format of inference ($*$) shows is that as we incorporate default rules such as rule n in a rule of inference, the general set-up of PPD_0 and PPD_1 could be maintained, including the internal and external stability adjustments (section 4.3.3). Retraction of F_t would lead to retraction of one of the premises. But, of course, new features may have to be added: for instance, that retraction of (3) goes with a burden of proof to show why rule n does not apply to the present case.

Hypotheses, suppositions or *assumptions* appear, in a sense, in the RPD_0 dialogues, where we have concessions for the sake of argument. For instance, the concession A that goes with a challenge $(A \rightarrow B)??A$ or $(\neg A)??A$ could be called a "hypothesis" on which the dialogue then proceeds. "Fossilized" versions of these concessions for the sake of argument would lead to an incomplete Gentzen-type system of inference rules: a so-called system of natural deduction. Thus viewed, the study of natural deduction would be part of dialectics.

The largest and most difficult task, perhaps, would be to extend or redesign PPD_1 so that problems of *clarification* and *definition* can be dealt with. This requires rethinking the relation between formulations used in dialogue and propositional commitment as found in dark-side commitment stores. It is not just a question of devising (or adopting) a semantic theory. What is needed is a dialectical theory of meaning that shows how meanings are changed, developed, and intensified in the course of a dialogue. This dialectical theory should throw light on equivocation, amphiboly, vagueness, neglect of qualifications, question-begging epithets, verbal (dis)agreement, and so on.[12]

5.3 Dark-Side Commitments Again

The intent of having dark-side commitments is to make the modeling of dialogue more realistic. Having only light-side commitments makes the dialogue more precise and easy to manage, as a logical structure. But, as has often been pointed out, implicit assumptions that are not asserted as light-side commitments frequently play an important role in the practical realities of everyday argumentation. Frequently, it is both possible and necessary to infer what someone's commitment may be taken to be, judging from their underlying position and what they have said, even where they have not explicitly committed themselves to a particular proposition in so many words. To reflect this realism of dialogue, as managed in everyday conversation, we have introduced dark-side commitments.

The most serious task with modeling a case study like the one on medical ethics is to lay down rules that help to bring the commitments of a participant out in the open, as elicited by the other participants, in such a way as to cope with the problem of a retraction. This was done partly by making the possibility of retraction depend on whether something is a revealed dark-side commitment of the participant or not. And further, this was done by making **PPD** permissive and maieutic, while at the same time allowing for the possibility of a shift to a rigorous type of dialogue that deals with commitments and logical connections in a more explicit, literal, and tight way (**RPD**).

The desirable features of **PPD** dialogue are its maieutic capabilities for revealing dark-side commitments and its permissive nature, reflected in its general freedom to retract commitments. The desirable features of **RPD** dialogue are its sticking to clear and explicit (light-side) commitments exclusively and its tight logical rigor. The embedding of the one type of dialogue in the other models the case-study discussion on medical ethics naturally, however, because of the way the dark-side commitments enter into the first (embedding) dialogue, and then have significant effects on the subsequent dialogue, while still leaving room open for freedom of questioning and creativity. In **PPD**, winning is not everything, and the game is not rigid and mechanical. The virtues of both types of dialogue can be summarized as in figure 5.2.

PPD Dialogue	RPD Dialogue
many opportunities to invent arguments	little room for creativity (grammatically tied up)
easy on retraction	tough on retraction
more freedom of questioning and of challenging	questioning and challenging often grammatically bound
pay-offs peripheral	pay-offs central (winning/losing)

Figure 5.2   Comparison of PPD and RPD

The embedding of the two systems shows how, in a case like the dialogue on medical ethics, a logically rigorous dialogue may function in the context of an encompassing maieutic persuasion type of dialogue.

Dark-side commitments cannot be challenged directly. Because of their off-record nature, such a direct challenge would be inappropriate, even if it were possible. For example, it would be inappropriate for Wilma to challenge Bruce by saying, "Prove that one should have respect for life." This type of challenge in a critical discussion would have no function or produce no gain. Bruce would be startled by the challenge, because he is not yet clearly aware that respect for life is one of his fundamental commitments in the discussion. There is not one particular assertion in the dialogue that articulates this commitment of his, and he is in no position to try to prove such a proposition to Wilma by citing some argument to support it. Yet his whole, general line of argumentation throughout the dialogue rests on this commitment to respect for life and supports it or is consistent with it in a general and oblique way.

The rules of the **PPD** type of dialogue do not directly force any participant to state, concede, or let alone prove any of his dark-side commitments. That is not how the rules work in this permissive type of dialogue. Instead, the rules gently push a discussant toward serious and honest participation—it is a matter of a cooperative attitude in a collaborative dialogue.[13]

For example, when Wilma (in effect) asks Bruce, "Are you serious?" (at lines 143 through 145), she is gently getting Bruce to show that he is being serious, instead of frivolously disregarding what was evidently an important commitment for him, as indicated by the previous context of the dialogue. Previously, Bruce had given all kinds of evidence, in the verbal exchanges of the discussion, that he was deeply committed to a principle of respect for life. Now—at lines 141 and 142—he seemed to contravene his commitment to this principle by claiming not to be committed to a policy of life.

This deep conflict was challenged by Wilma, not by claiming that Bruce had broken a rule of the dialogue, but by questioning Bruce's seriousness as a co-operative and sincere participant in the dialogue. Bruce has not committed some error or fallacy which is clearly a breach of some rule of **PPD**. But he has argued in such a way that his line of argumentation has taken a direction which has gone against the spirit of his position in the dialogue.

In this case, Wilma had justification for attacking Bruce, using the circumstantial *ad hominem* argument, accusing him of being pragmatically inconsistent. Clearly he has revealed a principle of respect for life as a dark-side commitment or basic principle behind his argumentation throughout the dialogue. At lines 16 and 17, Bruce approvingly described Ethel and Karl's decision as "life-supporting." At line 25, Bruce said that the purpose of saving the lives of other babies was "highly worthwhile in itself." At line 108, he commended a "life-giving procedure." Each time, the basis of his argument was a principle of respect for life. Yet now, at lines 141 and 142, he appears to be denying the importance of respect for a human life in one of his own statements. It is a classic case of "You do not practice what you preach." So Wilma was certainly justified in accusing Bruce of practical or pragmatic inconsistency, using this *ad hominem* criticism against him.

Wilma, however, is gentle in her criticism, only challenging Bruce by (in effect) asking him, "Are you serious?" when she questions what she rightly supposes to be his underlying position. Clearly, however, the question has force, and demands an adequate reply. And Bruce takes it seriously. For if he did not, his credibility as a sincere and honest participant in the dialogue would be seriously compromised.

Thus in **PPD** dialogue, the moves are not dictated rigorously by the rules. But if your moves in a dialogue are flagrantly at odds with the goals of the type of dialogue you are supposed to be participating in, you can be challenged by a charge of critical failure of co-operativeness. When you are thus challenged (justifiably) by your opponent, your seriousness as a collaborative participant in the dialogue becomes open to questioning.

In Bruce's case, his move at lines 141 and 142 indicated that he was trying to "shrink away" from his commitment to respect for life. This was an action that went against the spirit of the rules of a critical discussion, even though it did not literally violate any rule. Should such a case be called a "fallacy" or not?

Perhaps such a failure could be called a "fallacy" in an enlarged sense of the word *fallacy*, but perhaps it would make more sense to describe it as a critical failure or weakness that is not as serious or extreme as a fallacy.

The charge of fallacy is a strong refutation that is meant to result in the rejection or overthrow of the argument it was directed against. Many charges against an argument are much weaker than this, however, while still having critical force. A weak refutation is a kind of criticism that raises critical questions about any argument. It is a kind of criticism that exposes a weakness in an argument that demands a reply, but the argument is not destroyed beyond redemption if an adequate reply is not given. This weaker type of charge could be called a "charge of critical failure," as opposed to a charge of fallacy, because it is a defeasible type of criticism that does not pretend to strongly refute the argument it was directed against (as contrasted with the charge of fallacy).

The charge of fallacy is a strong and serious charge to make in dialogue. It borders on impoliteness, by suggesting that the arguer charged has committed a serious, underlying systematic error that is bad enough to destroy his whole argument, once exposed. It is very dangerous to come forward with a charge of fallacy in dialogue, because it can always be denied. And if it is denied successfully, the accuser is made to look very bad, very unfair, and aggressive.

In this case, Wilma did not accuse Bruce of committing a fallacy. Instead, she chose a method of gently inducing Bruce to iron out the apparent conflict in his commitments. Had Bruce not given in to this inducement to make corrections, the sanction would have been a loss of trust, a feeling that he was not sincerely collaborating in the discussion in an honest and constructive way. This could suggest, for example, that Bruce might be really quarreling instead of engaging in critical discussion. Any evidence of this sort would cast doubt on Bruce's motives in entering into the spirit of the argument and would reflect on Bruce's credibility as a serious advocate of his point of view.

In such a case, whether or not you have committed a critical failure at a particular move is not dictated by the rules of the dialogue *simpliciter*. Instead, it is a matter of questioning your performance in the dialogue as a whole, in relation to your dark-side commitments as they have emerged during the course of the dialogue.

To substantiate a judgment of critical failure of this type requires a metadialogue evaluation presuming a third-party critical evaluator who is looking at the dialogue as a whole, and who must interpret your seriousness as a collaborative participant in the dialogue. Thus charges of critical failure function as external ways of getting a participant in a **PPD** type of dialogue to be serious in participating in the dialogue.

Wilma's challenge to Bruce, questioning his seriousness as a participant in the dialogue, presumes that Bruce's light-side commitments are permanently recorded in his commitment store as the dialogue proceeds. This is a kind of assumption which may or may not be met in a real case, for people often forget what they said previously in a discussion. There may not be a secretary around to "take minutes," or the discussion may not be recorded on tape. The assumption is a normative ideal of a critical discussion.

Also presumed in a **PPD** type of dialogue is the existence of dark-side commitments, revealed partially and gradually through the course of the discussion. But once there is evidence furnished by the sequence of the dialogue that there is a clash of commitments on the part of one of the participants, the other participant can ask whether the first participant is seriously and sincerely entering into the spirit of the dialogue. In this way, a participant can be admonished and gently induced to keep the spirit of the rules of a **PPD**.

Bruce gives in at lines 146 and 147. He then clarifies his position. At lines 152 through 154, he combines a respect for life principle with a utilitarian principle—it is the value of *other* lives (or of all lives, collectively) that need to be taken into account.

Does this move restore the consistency of Bruce's commitments, enabling him to reply to Wilma's challenge successfully? This could still be questioned further, but at any rate Bruce has done enough to restore *prima facia* consistency among his now better-articulated commitments in order to give reassurance that he is a serious participant in the dialogue.

At lines 188 through 190, at the end of the dialogue, Bruce is led to articulate his dark-side commitments that have emerged from the discussion. He emphasizes his fundamental commitment to his two basic principles by repeating that the "ultimate goal of medicine is saving life" and that saving life sometimes involves sacrifice "for the greater good of all." Through the dialogue, he has been led by Wilma's questioning and critical testing of his arguments to explicitly articulate these underlying principles. At the beginning, they were dark-side commitments, but the dialogue served to bring them to light as Bruce's underlying principles behind his position.

Notice that the dialogue on medical ethics did not resolve the original conflict of opinions on whether Ethel and Karl's decision was right or not. Yet the persuasion dialogue could still be judged at least partially or significantly successful in that it did contribute to the maieutic function of throwing light on the underlying positions of the two opposed sides of the issue. The maieutic function worked, largely because of the way the dark-side commitments of both participants were brought out and handled in the dialogue. The commitments were dealt with and argued out by both parties in a way that was logically reasoned through-out. Yet the logical reasoning was tighter and more rigorous at some stages of the dialogue, permissive and more flexible at other stages of the dialogue. By embedding, these stages were brought into a functional relationship that had a positive effect on the dialogue as a whole.

Although commitment has turned out to be a subtle concept that changes from one context of dialogue to another, we have seen how it can be defined in a clear and useful manner in these different normative contexts of dialogue.

5.4   Summary: Three Types of Commitment

In general, we recognize three types of commitment. A commitment of the first type is incurred by making a *concession,* which is a statement that the participant is committed to in a weak sense which carries with it no burden of proof. In other words, the participant is not obliged to defend his statement if he is challenged to justify it by the other party. What one is committed to, in the case of a concession, is not to object to it. One's positive obligation with respect to a concession is to allow the other party in the dialogue to use it in his attempts to give an acceptable argument for, or to infer his point of view.

A commitment of the second type is called an *assertion,* which is a statement that the participant is obliged to defend if the other party makes a request that she justify it. Commitments of the second type are statements that represent the arguer's overt position, her theses or stand-points in the dialogue.

Commitments of the third type are the participant's *dark-side commitments.* He is not directly obliged to defend these propositions, but, as we say, he can be challenged on whether he is seriously taking part in the dialogue if he refuses to concede or rejects what appears to be one of his commitments of this sort. He can be charged with committing a critical failure or even a fallacy, at the metadialogue level, if he shows that he is not seriously taking part in the dialogue.

Both the second and the third type of commitment represent the arguer's position in the dialogue, or in the case of the dark-side commit-ments, what the analyst takes to be his position. The second type repre-sents the expressed or overt position of the arguer. This type of commitment is the legitimate target of a why question put forward by the other party in the dialogue as a request to justify the proposition in question. The third type represents the off-record position. Commitments of either of these types may be called "substantive."

Not everything in one's commitment set is a suitable target for why questions. Some commitments are concessions that one party asks the other to take on as commitments, provisionally, to advance the discussion. In this case there is no implication that this other party fully accepts this statement as something that reflects her position so that if challenged on it, she would be obliged either to defend her commitment to it or to give it up.

Concessions yield commitments that a party in dialogue freely accepts provided she has no good reason not to accept them at the time. But she is not necessarily making the concession because she actually has any evidence or good arguments to back up her commitment to it. So commitment in the case of mere concession, where there is no burden of proof, is not always brought into one's commitment store because there was a convincing argument to back it up.

To emphasize this key difference, we could say that the concession type of commitment can be contrasted to the other types of commitment by calling it a kind of "nonsubstantive" commitment. Whereas the assertion type of commitment is substantive in the sense that these commitments represent the arguer's position on the issue in a way that concessions do not.[14]

In dialogue, the same sentence can be both asserted and conceded. So we may define a *mere* concession as a kind of commitment that is of the first type only.

We can now reformulate the contrast between an assertion and a concession in dialogue. An assertion carries with it a substantive commitment to the statement asserted, whereas a mere concession does not. Moreover, making an assertion carries with it a burden of proof (if challenged) on the participant who made the assertion, whereas a concession can be made purely for the sake of expediting the dialogue, without implying any substantive commitment to the statement conceded.

In general, in this book, we have recognized three types of commitments: concessions, assertions, and dark-side commitments. Both the second and the third types of commitment represent the arguer's position in a dialogue. Assertions represent the arguer's expressed or overt position. Dark-side commitments represent the arguer's off-record position. Both are substantive, as contrasted with concessions, which are not suitable targets of why questions and do not have a burden of proof attached to them. Thus important qualitative differences mark off the various commitments in dialogue.

Appendix: A Précis of Action-State Semantics

0. **Set-theoretical notations**

We cannot here present an introduction to set theory, but this brief list of notations and definitions may suffice to make this précis accessible to readers interested in a set-theoretical formulation of action-state semantics.

- $a \in A$: a is an **element** of the set A.
- $a \notin A$: a is **not** an element of the set A.
- $\emptyset$: the **empty** set.
- $A \subseteq B$: A is a **subset** of B, i.e., every element of A is an element of B.
- $A \subset B$: $A \subseteq B$ and $A \neq B$: A is a **proper subset** of B.
- $\{a\}$: the **singleton** of a, i.e., the set with a as its only element.
- $\{a, b, \ldots\}$: the set with $a, b, \ldots$ as its (only) elements.
- $< a, b >$: the **ordered** pair of a (first) and b (second).
- $\{x \mid (\cdots x \cdots)\}$: the set of all x such that $(\cdots x \cdots)$. Here "$(\cdots x \cdots)$" stands for a predicate or sentence form (like "x is even"). Thus "$\{x \mid x$ is even$\}$" denotes the set of even numbers.

- $\{(- - - x - - -) \mid (\cdots x \cdots)\} = \{y \mid$ for some $x : y = (- - - x - - -)$ and $(\cdots x \cdots)\}$, in other words: the set of all $(- - - x - - -)$ such that $(\cdots x \cdots)$. Here "$(- - - x - - -)$" stands for a description form (like $3x^2$) and "$(\cdots x \cdots)$" stands for a sentence form. Thus "$\{3x^2 \mid x$ is even$\}$" denotes the set of all numbers $3x^2$ such that x is even. This notation is also used with more than one variable, for instance : $\{< x,y > \mid x \leq y\} = \{z \mid$ there are x and y such that $z = < x,y >$ and $x \leq y\}$.
- $A \cup B = \{x \mid x \in A$ or $x \in B$ (or both)$\}$: the **union** of A and B.
- $A \cap B = \{x \mid x \in A$ and $x \in B\}$: the **intersection** of A and B.
- $A \setminus B = \{x \mid x \in A$ and $x \notin B\}$: the **difference** of A and B.
- $A \times B = \{< x,y > \mid x \in A$ and $y \in B\}$: the **Cartesian product** of A and B.
- A (binary) **relation** is a set whose elements are ordered pairs.
- A **function** is a relation f such that if $< x,y > \in f$ and $< x,z > \in f$ then $y = z$.
- If f is a function and $< x,y > \in f$, we write $f(x) = y$. Here y is the **value** of f for the **argument** x.
- $D(f) = \{x \mid$ for some $y : < x,y > \in f\}$. $D(f)$ is the **domain** (of **definition**) of f.
- $R(f) = \{x \mid$ for some $y : < y,x > \in f\}$. $R(f)$ is the **range** (**of values**) of f.
- $f \restriction A = \{< x,y > \mid x \in A$ and $< x,y > \in f\}$. $f \restriction A$ is the **restriction** of f to A.
- $A^B = \{f \mid f$ is a function and $D(f) = B$ and $R(f) \subseteq A\}$: the set of all functions defined on A with values in B, or the set of all functions **from B into** A.
- $max(m,n)$: the **maximum** of the numbers m and n.

1.   **Basic sets**

- T : the set of natural numbers $(0,1,2,\ldots)$, conceived as **moments of time**. (Hamblin uses integers, but we find natural numbers somewhat easier to handle.)
- P: the set of **doers**.
- D : the set of **possible deeds** of any doer.
- H : the set of **possible happenings**.

It is supposed that these sets are nonempty and mutually disjoint. Unlike Hamblin, we do not introduce a set of states: the state of the world at a particular moment of time may be conceived as the totality of all that happened or was done by any doer up till that moment of time.

2. A world w is a function defined on T with values in $H \times D^P$. So, given a world, there is in this world, for each time t, just one (big) happening and a deed assigned to each doer. $W^+ = (H \times D^P)^T$: the set of all worlds.

3. **Postulate:** $\emptyset \neq W \subseteq W^+$
    W is the set of **possible worlds**. Hamblin distinguishes **logically possible, physically possible, actively possible** (from one doer's perspective), and **choosable** worlds. We shall not pursue these distinctions here. One may think of W as the set of physically possible worlds, or as the set of worlds that are actively possible from the perspective of the doer for whom strategies and commitments are defined. This latter set comprises only those physically possible worlds in which all the *other* doers behave relatively normal. For this application one has to write $W(p)$ instead of W and reformulate what follows accordingly.

4. $t^* = \{t' \mid t' \in T \text{ and } t' < t\}$.
    Let $w \in W$, $t \in T$. The restriction, $w \lceil t^*$, of w to t^* is the **history up till t according to** w. If $w \in W$ and $j = w \lceil t^*$, for some $t \in T$, j is an **initial segment** of w, and w is a **completion** of j. We write $j \prec w$. If $t \in T$ and $j = w \lceil t^*$, for some $w \in W$, j is a **(possible) history up till t**. This time t is uniquely determined, given j, and we write $t(j) = t$.

5. Let $t \in T$. $J_t = \{j \mid j \text{ is a history up till } t\}$. $J = \{j \mid \text{there is a } t \in T \text{ such that } j \text{ is a history up till } t\}$. Then J_t is the **set of (possible) histories up till t**. J is the **set of (possible) histories**. Let $t, t' \in T$, $t \leq t'$, $j \in J_t$, $j' \in J_{t'}$ and $j \subseteq j'$. Then j is the **t-segment of j'**, and j' is a **continuation of j up till t'**. If j is the t-segment of j', for some t, j is an **initial segment** of j' and j' a **continuation** of j. Notation $j \preceq j'$. If, moreover, $j \neq j'$ we may speak of a **proper initial segment** and a **proper continuation**. Notation $j \prec j'$.

6. Let $j \in J$. $W(j) = \{w \mid w \in W \text{ and } j = w \lceil t(j)^*\}$. $W(j)$ is the **set of completions** of j. Let $w \in W$, $t \in T$. $W(w,t) = W(w \lceil t^*)$. $W(w,t)$ is the set of all worlds whose history up till t is equal to that of w. Hamblin distinguishes "**temporally logically possible words** relative to world w at time t," "**temporally physically possible worlds**," "**temporally choosable worlds**," and "**actively possible worlds**," (1987), p. 149. Cf. 3 above. For the set of (temporally) active possible worlds, one has to write $W(p,w,t)$ instead of $W(w,t)$.

7. Let $j \in J$. $H(j) = \{h \mid h \in H$ and for some $f \in D^p$:
    $j \cup \{< t(j), < h,f>>\} \in J_{t(j)+1}\}$. $H(j)$ is the set of **possible happenings** at $t(j)$, given j.
    Fact: $H(j) \neq \emptyset$, if j is a history.

8. Let $j \in J$. $F(j) = \{f \mid f \in D^p$ and for some $h \in H$:
    $j \cup \{< t(j), < h,f>>\} \in J_{t(j)+1}\}$. $F(j)$ is the set of **possible deeds-assignments** at $t(j)$, given j.
    Fact: $F(j) \neq \emptyset$, if j is a history.

9. Let $j \in J$, $p \in P$. $D(p,j) = \{f(p) \mid f \in F(j)\}$, $D(p,j)$ is the set of **deeds that can be done** by doer p at $t(j)$, given j.
    Fact: $D(p,j) \neq \emptyset$, if p is a doer and j is a history.

10. Let x be either a history or a possible world. Let $t \in T$. If x is a history, let $t < t(x)$. If $x(t) = < h,f>$, we write: $h(x,t) = h$ and $f(x,t) = f$. If, moreover, $p \in P$, we write $d(x,p,t) = f(x,t)(p)$. So, $h(x,t)$ is the happening at time t (according to x), $f(x,t)$ is the deed assignment at time t (according to x), whereas $d(x,p,t)$ is the deed done by p at time t (according to x).

11. Let $p \in P$, $t \in T$. A **partial strategy** for p starting at t is a function q such that:

    a. $D(q) = \{j \mid t \leq j(t)\}$, and
    b. if $j \in D(q)$, then $\emptyset \neq q(j) \subseteq D(p,j)$.

    If q is a partial strategy for p starting at t we write $t(q) = t$. The notion of a partial strategy is intensional, in the sense that the strategy prescribes behavior with respect not only to the actual history, but also to other possible histories.

12. A partial strategy q is a **(full) strategy** if, for each $j \in D(q)$, there is a $d \in D$ such that $q(j) = \{d\}$.

13. **Fact**: if q is a partial strategy for p, and $t(q) \leq t$, and if, moreover, $q' = q \lceil \{j \mid t \leq t(j)\}$, then q' is a partial strategy for p, starting at t.

14. Let q be a partial strategy for p. We say that q is **vacuous** at j if for all j' such that $j \preceq j'$: $q(j') = D(p,j')$. So a partial strategy becomes vacuous, given a history of the world j, for which it is defined, as soon as no restrictions on p's behavior are prescribed by the strategy for any of the possible continuations of j.

15. Let q be a partial strategy for p. $Pr(p,q) = \{w \mid w \in W$ and for all t such that $t \geq t(q) : d(w,p,t) \in q(w \lceil t^*)\}$, $Pr(p,q)$ is the set of

prospects for p, if p carries out q. Cf. Hamblin's W_{strat} (p,q_t), (1987), p. 156.

16. Let q be a partial strategy for p, and let $t(q) \leq t$.
$Pr^t(p,q) = \{w \lceil t^* \mid w \in Pr(p,q)\}$. $Pr^t(p,q)$ is the set of **prospects** for p **up till** t, if p carries out q.

17. Let q_1 and q_2 be partial strategies for p, and let $j \in D(q_1) \cap D(q_2)$. q_1 and q_2 **clash**, given j, if and only if $q_1(j) \cap q_2(j) = \emptyset$. (Similarly, for more than two partial strategies.)

18. Let q_1 and q_2 be partial strategies for p, and let $J' \subseteq J$. q_1 and q_2 are **consonant** on J', if and only if, for no $j \in J' \cap (D(q_1) \cap D(q_2))$, q_1 and q_2 clash, given j. Otherwise q_1 and q_2 are **inconsonant** on J'. We define consonance relative to a set J' of possible histories. For $J' = J$ one gets an absolute notion of consonance. Usually, however, what is interesting is not absolute consonance, but consonance within certain bounds. For instance, suppose that p at time t considers partial strategies q_1 and q_2. Suppose p knows that the actual history j up till t falls within a proper subset $J'' \subset J_t$. Then p will be primarily interested, not in absolute consonance, but in consonance of q_1 and q_2 on $J' = \{j \mid j \in J$ and for some $j'' \in J''$: $j'' \leq j\}$. (Consonance for more than two partial strategies is to be defined in a similar way.)

19. Let q_1 and q_2 be partial strategies for p, and let $W' \subseteq W$. q_1 and q_2 are **compatible** on W', if and only if $W' \cap (Pr(p,q_1) \cap Pr(p,q_2)) \neq \emptyset$. Otherwise, q_1 and q_2 are **incompatible** on W'. We define compatibility relative to a set W' of possible worlds for the same reason we define consonance relative to a set of possible histories. (Compatibility for more than two partial strategies is to be defined in a similar way.)

20. Let Q be a nonempty set of partial strategies. We say that Q **starts at** t, if t is the smallest natural number t' such that for some $q \in Q : t(q) = t'$. We write $t(Q) = t$.

21. Let Q be a set of partial strategies. Q is said to be **homogeneous** if, whenever $q \in Q$, $t(q) \leq t$, then $q \lceil \{j \mid t \leq t(j)\} \in Q$.

22. A **(possible) object of commitment** of p (or, p-**commitment**, for short) is a nonempty homogeneous set Q of partial strategies for p. Commitment is not tied to one partial strategy. A doer may shift strategy and yet live up to her commitment. Homogeneity of

the set of eligible partial strategies guarantees that one possible choice will always be to stick to the strategy she has adopted before. We skip the problem of wavering.

23. Let Q be a p-commitment. $Pr(p,Q) = \{w \mid w \in W$ and for all t such that $t \geq t(Q)$ there is a $q \in Q$ such that $t(q) = t$ and such that $d(w,p,t) \in q(w \lceil t^*)\}$. $Pr(p,q)$ is the set of **prospects** for p, if p lives up to her commitment Q (assuming that p is not mistaken about the world or about her commitment).

24. Let Q be a p-commitment, and let $t(Q) \leq t$.
$Pr^t(p,Q) = \{w \lceil t^* \mid w \in Pr(p,Q)\}$. $Pr^t(p,q)$ is the set of **prospects** for p **up till** t, if p lives up to her commitment Q.

25. Let Q_1 and Q_2 be p-commitments, and let $t \geq max(t(Q_1), t(Q_2))$, $j \in J_t$. Q_1 and Q_2 **clash**, given j, if and only if, for every pair $q_1 \in Q_1$, and $q_2 \in Q_2$ such that $j \in D(q_1) \cap D(q_2)$, q_1 and q_2 clash, given j. (Similarly, for more than two commitments.)

26. Let Q_1 and Q_2 be p-commitments, $J' \subseteq J$. Q_1 and Q_2 are **consonant** on J', if and only if for no $j \in J'$: Q_1 and Q_2 clash, given j. Otherwise, Q_1 and Q_2 are **inconsonant** on J'. The motivation for defining consonance between commitments relative to a set J' of possible histories is the same as with consonance between partial strategies. Different choices of J' give us reconstructions of the notions of absolute and legislative quandary freedom defined in section 2.4. (Consonance for more than one p-commitment is to be defined in a similar way.)

27. Let Q_1 and Q_2 be p-commitments, $W' \subseteq W$. Q_1 and Q_2 are **compatible** on W', if and only if $W' \cap (Pr(p,Q_1) \cap Pr(p,Q_2)) \neq \emptyset$. Otherwise, Q_1 and Q_2 are **incompatible** on W'. As with partial strategies, compatibility is defined relative to a set W' of possible worlds. (Compatibility for more than two p-commitments is to be defined in a similar way.)

28. Let Q_1 and Q_2 be p-commitments, $J' \subseteq J$. Q_1 **implies** Q_2 on J', if and only if for each $t \geq max(t(Q_1), t(Q_2))$, and for each $j \in J_t \cap J'$ and $q_1 \in Q_1$ such that $t(q_1) \leq t$: if $d \in q_1(j)$ then there is a $q_2 \in Q_2$ such that $t(q_2) \leq t$ and such that $d \in q_2(j)$.

29. A goal is any set G such that $\emptyset \neq G \subseteq W$. For instance, given a **simple action commitment statement**, with associated imperative i, the set of worlds that extensionally satisfies i (called "W_i" by Hamblin) constitutes a goal.

30. Let $p \in P$, $W' \subseteq W$, G a goal. q is a **safe partial** G-**strategy** for p, within W', if q is a partial strategy for p such that $Pr(p,q) \cap W' \subseteq G$. W' may be thought of as the set of possible worlds that actually need to be taken into account in some context, e.g., considering what is known about past history. Thus if p knows at time t that the actual history j up till t falls within a proper subset $J' \subseteq J_p$, p will be primarily interested, not in absolute safety ($W' = W$), but in safety within $W' = \{w \mid w \in W$ and for some $j \in J' : j \prec w\}$.

31. Let G be a goal, $W' \subseteq W$, $j \in J$, $p \in P$ and $d \in D(p,j)$. We say that d (by p) **guarantees** G within W', given j, if for each $j' \in J$ such that $j' = j \cup \{< t(j), < b, f >>\}$ and $f(p) = d : W(j') \cap W' \subseteq G$. We say that d (by p) **obstructs** G within W', given j, if $G \neq W$ and d (by p) guarantees $W \backslash G$ within W', given j.

32. Let $p \in P$, $W' \subseteq W$. Let G be a goal. q is a **partial** G-**strategy** for p, within W', if q is a partial strategy for p, and for each $j \in D(q)$:

   a. if there is a q' such that q' is a safe partial G-strategy for p, within $W(j) \cap W'$, starting at $t(j)$, then $q \lceil \{j' \mid t(j) \leq t(j')\}$ is also a safe partial G-strategy for p within $W(j) \cap W'$.

   b. if there is a $d \in D(p,j)$ such that d (by p) does not obstruct G within W', given j, then for each $d' \in q(j) : d'$ (by p) does not obstruct G within W', given j.

   This definition explains, within our framework, what is meant by a partial i-strategy, viz., a partial G-strategy, where $G = W_i$.

33. Let G be a goal, $W' \subseteq W$, $p \in P$, $t \in T$. The **object of** p's **commitment** to G, within W', at t is the set $Q(p,G,W',t) = \{q \mid q$ is a partial G-strategy for p, with W', and $q(t) \geq t\}$.

   Fact: $Q(p,G,W',t)$ is a nonempty homogeneous set of partial strategies for p and, therefore, a p-commitment.

34. Let G be a goal, $W' \subseteq W$, $p \in P$. The **object of** p's **commitment** to G, within W', is the set $Q(p,G,W') = Q(p,G,W',0)$.

35. Let G be a goal, $p \in P$. The **absolute object** of p's **commitment** to G is the set $Q(p,G) = Q(p,G,W)$.

Notes

Introduction

1. *Logik und Agon* was first published as Lorenzen (1960) and reprinted in Lorenzen and Lorenz (1978), pp. 1–8. *Agon* is the Greek word for 'contest' or 'struggle.' It can be contrasted with the word *eris*, which means 'strife' but has more negative connotations of struggling with an enemy.

2. *Logik und Agon*, Lorenzen and Lorenz (1978), p. 1.

3. This perspective on Lorenzen games was developed in Barth and Krabbe (1982), esp. ch. 3.

4. The major publications on dialogue logic written in German by Paul Lorenzen and Kuno Lorenz were assembled in Lorenzen and Lorenz (1978). Other major publications in German are Kamlah and Lorenzen (1973), Lorenzen and Schwemmer (1975), Lorenzen (1982), Haas (1984), and Lorenzen (1987). The following materials available in English: Stegmüller (1964), Lorenzen (1969), Van Dun (1972), Lorenz (1973), several papers in Barth and Martens (eds.) (1982), Barth and Krabbe (1982), Felscher (1985a), (1985b), and Krabbe (1985a), (1985b).

5. Starting with Hintikka (1968) we are presented with a game-theoretical approach to logical semantics. Though, actually, this development concerns semantics and not dialectics, the similarities to Lorenzen's dialogue games are obvious. Cf. also Hintikka (1981). Discussion and plausibility are studied in Rescher (1977). Hegselmann (1985) offers an approach to the theory of rational discussion that takes into account both the interaction between disputants and the internal reasoning of each of them. (The book moreover contains a worthwhile survey of contemporary approaches to dialectics.) Hamblin (1970) was the most seminal work of the last decades. It was followed up by many papers on fallacies by John Woods and Douglas Walton (see their 1989) and by a number of interesting studies on dialogue rules by Jim Mackenzie (e.g., Mackenzie 1979a, 1979b, 1981, 1985, 1989).

6. Hamblin (1970), p. 254.

7. *Op. cit.*, p. 256. The term *formal dialectic* was introduced by Hamblin.

8. *Loc. cit.*

9. *Loc. cit.*

10. *Op. cit.*, pp. 256, 257.

11. *Op. cit.*, p. 264.

12. Hamblin (1987).

1. The Anatomy of Commitment

1. Webster (1981), Lemma on *commit*, sense 3d(1).

2. Webster (1981), Lemma on *commitment*, sense 3b(1).

3. *Loc. cit.*, sense 3b(2), marked as philosophical.

4. Cf. Katriel and Dascal (1989).

5. It is left to the reader to imagine a standard context for these examples. Admittedly, "the audience is bound to laugh," might sometimes express a commitment, viz., if (1) the audience forms a collective (Cf. note 6) and (2) this collective has agreed to laugh at set times, e.g., whenever a sign "laughter" is shown. But generally audiences are not collectives (they lack structure).

6. Cf. Spit (1986). Spit mentions the following characteristics of collectives: (1) having structure (e.g., rules that assign tasks, regulate decision taking), (2) durability, (3) allowing for coordinated action by means of communication, (4) definiteness as to membership, (5) representability, (6) being constructed.

7. Hamblin (1987), ch. 4.

8. Hamblin, (1987), p. 58.

9. There is also an unproblematic reading of this sentence; viz., "There is at least one person who is bound to open the door." The problematic case arises when there is no particular person who should open the door rather than someone else.

10. The first problem is, whether the antecedent phrase *if John takes out the garbage* falls within the scope of the "bound to" operator. The second problem is whether this makes much difference, etc.

11. Or, perhaps, "If you see a burglary, report it to the police (addressed to any citizen)!," etc.

12. On conditional imperatives, cf. Hamblin (1987), pp. 83–87.

13. Hamblin (1987), pp. 151, 152.

14. *Op. cit.*, p. 155. Hamblin's italics. We took the second word *imperatives* to be a misprint for *imperative* and corrected it accordingly.

15. We here try to summarize some of the main points of Hamblin's action-state semantics. Unfortunately, Hamblin's exposition of his views is rather sketchy, perhaps due to his untimely death. For instance, there are two definitions of the term *partial i-strategy* in the text, both rich in content but not necessarily equivalent (*op. cit.*, pp. 158 and 159). Therefore, we here propose our own definition, taking elements of both. Partial strategies are similar to Segerberg's *routines* (1984, 1985), see also section 2.3. The term *partial* refers to the fact that these strategies assign on each occasion a set of deeds, rather than one single deed. A précis of action-state semantics has been added as an appendix.

16. We have inserted the phrase *as far as he or she knows* in order not to assume too much knowledge on the part of the addressee (strategic omniscience). Hamblin does not discuss the problem of wavering, i.e., changing strategies all the time so as not to reach the goal, nor shall we. As to the addressee's estimate of the history of the world,

this too, is an element brought in by us; Hamblin speaks of the "true history" (*op. cit.*, p. 160).

17. Hamblin (1987), ch. 1: on The Varieties of Imperative.

18. Cf. Katriel and Dascal (1989).

19. Commitment stores have existed in dialogue theory since Hamblin (1970), or even earlier, for of course the set of concessions in a Lorenzen-type dialogue would fall under this concept. Notice that sanction sets are sets of (objects of) commitments, too, but that they are not commitment sets in the present sense. As to the codification of the history of a game, with an eye to possible strategies, cf. the concept of a 'dialogue sequent' in Barth and Krabbe (1982), p. 117f. The concept of a 'dialogue situation' (*op. cit.*, p. 83), seems to be equivalent to that of the participant's agenda as far as the C_1-commitments are concerned.

20. That there are quite different concepts of fallacy around, will be clear even to a casual reader of the issue of *Argumentation* on fallacies edited by John Woods (1987). Our use of the term concurs with one proposed by Barth and Martens (1977), p. 96, recently explained in Van Eemeren and Grootendorst (1987). Note that the use of the term *fallacy* proposed in Walton (1987b), p. 329, covers breaches of reasonable procedure as well as other weaknesses or deficiencies that would make an argument untenable. Hence the concept of fallacy envisaged there is somewhat wider than the present one, as it includes some blunders (But it might be narrower if not all moves in dialogue are called "arguments"). Cf. also Grootendorst (1987).

21. Segerberg (1984), p. 78.

22. Hamblin (1987), ch. 2.

2. The Dynamics of Commitment

1. Hamblin (1970), p. 265ff.

2. Woods and Walton (1978a).

3. Hamblin (1970), (1971), and Mackenzie (1979a), (1979b), (1981).

4. Hamblin (1970), p. 264.

5. See Hamblin (1987), p. 159.

6. This case is summarized from the account given in P. F. Kluge (1988).

7. Kaufmann (1987), p. 6.

8. In order for this to be a case of implication we must suppose that the set of possible histories of the world is restricted to those in which the neighbourhood shops close up early.

9. Cf. Hamblin's qualms about imperative inference (1987), pp. 87–89.

10. Cf. the dark side of commitment stores in **PPD** dialogue (ch. 4).

11. Cf. the notion of 'immediate consequence' and its impact on propositional commitment in dialogue games (section 2.2). Cf. section 5.2 on 'inference.'

12. Cf. the ways in which dark-side commitments get to the light side of the commitment store in **PPD** (ch. 4).

13. Thus one may incur wrong commitments based on a wrong perception of the world.

14. Cf. Næss (1966), p. 34ff. on depth of intended meaning.

15. Segerberg (1985).

16. *Op. cit.*, p. 188.

17. *Op. cit.*, pp. 187, 188.

18. *Op. cit.*, p. 188.

19. A similar point was made by J. Woods in a lecture (1987). Cf. the Woods-Mackenzie discussion in *Argumentation*, Woods (1988a), (1988b), and Mackenzie (1988). *Horror contradictionis* and our discussion of quandaries and of cases 2.10 through 2.13 derive from Krabbe (1988b), (1990).

20. See Hamblin (1970), pp. 180, 181, and also "Clincher" [3], p. 186. In Hamblin's historical survey, there seems to be no other mention of contradictory reason or inconsistency as a fallacy. The contradictory reason fallacy in the *Nyaya Sutra* is presented in a text on controversies (a dialectical setting, we may say), so it deserves more attention than we can give it here. From Hamblin's report we are unable to decide whether contradictory reason could not as easily be classified as a weakness or blunder.

21. Mackie (1967), pp. 176, 177.

22. Johnson and Blair (1983), pp. 59–63.

23. Rescher (1987).

24. Johnson and Blair, *op. cit.*, are much concerned with substantiating charges of fallacy. But this seems characteristic more of assaults on weaknesses or blunders than of charges of fallacy (in our sense). In the case of a fallacy (in our sense) it would ordinarily suffice to point out the particular dialectical rule one's opponent has violated. Mackie (1967) explicitly admits that it would be a "fallacy to suppose that because your opponent has tried to have it both ways, he cannot have either way—that every part of an inconsistent position must be false" (p. 177). So part of an inconsistent argument may survive in further debate. This again is characteristic of weak arguments.

25. There may be propositional commitments on the dark side of an agenda of which the subject itself is not fully aware: the so-called dark side of the commitment store, cf. Walton (1984), p. 247ff. Cf. also the **PPD** dialogues (ch. 4).

26. Or an infinite but inversely well-ordered one.

27. Cf., Mackenzie (1979b), p. 715ff., and (1981), p. 172. Mackenzie speaks of dialogues that are *legal* versus dialogue that are *legal**, or *legal in an extended sense.*

28. Hamblin (1987), pp. 177–81.

29. See Barth and Krabbe (1982). Minimal dialectics is the dialectical system corresponding to I. Johansson's "Minimalkalkül" (1936).

30. Cf. Krabbe (1982).

31. In this example we are paraphrasing the pictures and quoting the dialogue from a well-known comic strip: Hergé (1989), pp. 22, 23.

32. Technically, other solutions are possible. Cf. classical dialectics in Barth and Krabbe (1982).

33. Barth and Krabbe (1982).

34. Following Makinson (1964).

35. It is argued by Keith Lehrer (1975) that $P, S_1 \ldots S_m$ could all be true, because the book might have contained other statements than it actually does. (Lehrer doesn't frame the paradox in terms of a book, but that does not matter.) Lehrer is right if we assume that the phrase "all assertions that follow" in P refers descriptively to the

assertions that follow (different ones in different possible worlds). Here, we have assumed this phrase to be no more than a shorthand for the list of propositions and hence to refer rigorously to them (in every possible world to the actual ones).

36. Makinson (1964), Lehrer (1975), Rescher and Brandom (1980).

37. Cf. Barth and Krabbe (1982): "*It is not irrational to lose a discussion.* . . . But it is . . . irrational *not to admit* that one has lost (. . .)" (p. 71).

38. Epicure. Letter to Menoeceus, *ap. Diog. X* 125.

39. Manor (1975).

40. Van Eemeren and Grootendorst (1984), pp. 141–49.

41. Cf. Hamblin (1987), p. 196, for some idea of what is involved.

3. Dialogues: Types, Goals, and Shifts

1. As we use the concept of a "persuasion dialogue," it appears to be essentially the same as Barth and Krabbe's concept of a "discussion" (1982), p. 57, and Van Eemeren and Grootendorst's notion of an "argumentative discussion" (1984), p. 2. When they want to stress the critical aspect of such a discussion these authors sometimes use the term *critical discussion.* Systems of norms and rules for critical discussions (called "dialectic(al) systems") are presented and motivated by Barth and Krabbe in chapters 3 and 4 of their 1982 work. Van Eemeren and Grootendorst propounded a code of conduct for rational discussions comprising seventeen rules. Shortened and/or simplified expositions of these systems are available: Barth (1982), Krabbe (1985a), section 2.1, Van Eemeren and Grootendorst (1987). In the sequel, we shall use the terms *persuasion dialogue* and *critical discussion* as equivalent to each other.

2. Van Eemeren and Grootendorst (1984), pp. 5, 79. Cf. the statemental dialogical attitudes defined in Barth and Krabbe (1982), p. 58.

3. The term *thesis* is used by Barth and Krabbe (1982), p. 56. Their term *avowed opinions* seems to cover concessions as well. Van Eemeren and Grootendorst use the term *expressed opinion* for the question at issue ("the subject of the argumentation") (1984), p. 5. In the sequel, we shall use the terms *thesis, assertion,* and *expressed opinion*

equivalently. At present we cannot meticulously handle the different levels of abstraction on which such terms may be used. For instance, we may denote by the term *thesis* (or *assertion* or *expressed opinion*) a certain *propositional content* in abstraction from all use of language. But, more often, we shall refer to a particular formulation of a propositional content, a *sentence type*. Finally, the term *thesis* may also be used to refer to an *utterance* of such a sentence type, or *statement* for short. (Barth and Krabbe, *loc. cit.*). Similar remarks hold for the term *concession (loc. cit.)*. Van Eemeren and Grootendorst do not incorporate initial concessions in their definitions of types of disputes (conflicts) (1984), p. 80.

4. Van Eemeren and Grootendorst (1984), p. 78.

5. *Op. cit.,* p. 75 (italics as quoted).

6. *Op. cit.,* p. 80. In some of their other publications these authors draw a slightly different distinction between simple and compound disputes.

7. Barth and Krabbe (1982), p. 56, and section 3.11 on mixed conflicts.

8. Cf. Hintikka (1981), p. 216.

9. Barth and Krabbe (1982), p. 19, use a subscript 3 and write "formal$_3$" whenever they want to make it clear that the word "formal" refers to procedures and activities that are regulated by a set of rules (and not merely syntactical rules). Thus they speak of "formal$_3$ dialectics."

10. Hamblin (1970), p. 275.

11. The "dialogue rules" in Walton (1984, 1985, 1987a) are here called "structural rules." The "strategic rules" in Walton (1984, 1985) are here, as in Walton (1987a), called "win-loss rules." The present terminology permits us to use the term *dialogue rules* as a general term covering all four types of rule. The term *strategic rules* shall henceforth refer to rules that help a participant find a suitable strategy among the many permitted by the dialogue rules. Thus strategic rules are not dialogue rules, since they are not themselves constitutive of a dialogue system.

12. See Fisher and Ury (1981), Pruitt (1981), and Donohue (1981) for fuller accounts of the characteristics of negotiation.

13. This is not a sufficient condition. It is usually understood that the proofs adduced for the conclusions should be apt to convince a larger company of critics.

14. Cf. Socratic dialogues (end of this section).

15. Cf. the "material procedures" in Barth and Krabbe (1982), section 4.5. "Such a procedure may employ all kinds of *ostensive means*— including *experimentation*—*consultation* of authoritative sources, and *computation* of various kinds" (*op. cit.*, p. 104).

16. Practical reasoning is described and analyzed in detail in Walton (1990a), where it is shown that four kinds of critical questions are appropriate for each use of a practical inference in deliberation, or in contexts of dialogue: (1) Are there alternative means of realizing the goal? (2) Is it in fact possible to carry out the action indicated in the means premise? (3) Does the agent have other goals that may conflict with the one in the goal premise? (4) Are there negative side effects of the action?

17. Hamblin (1970), p. 256.

18. See Woods and Walton (1982), ch. 2.

19. Some analysts have portrayed debate as a complex of persuasion dialogues among each of the primary participants and a third party. A detailed pragma-dialectical analysis of this type has, for forensic debate, been provided by E. T. Feteris (1989). In our view, such an analysis is very useful for highlighting the critical and persuasive aspects of the debate. But, ultimately, the debate has also very important eristic aspects that are hard to subsume under the heading of "conflict resolution." The subtle interplay, moreover, between the several persuasion dialogues involved, makes it that the debate is really a distinctive type of dialogue in its own right.

20. Robinson (1953), ch. 2, esp. p. 14.

21. *Op. cit.*, p. 15.

22. *Loc. cit.*

23. Johnson and Blair (1983), p. 34.

24. In doing so, Bruce presents an argument which is, at least partially, a form of the *argument du gaspillage*. Cf. Perelman and Olbrechts-Tyteca (1969), pp. 279–81, (1976), pp. 375–79.

25. See Gumperz (1972).

26. See Barth and Krabbe (1982) on material procedures and Van Eemeren and Grootendorst (1984) on intersubjective testing procedures.

27. Walton (1985), (1987a), ch. 9, (1989b), ch. 6.

28. Walton (1987a), pp. 33–38, (1989b), pp. 84–93.

29. Perelman and Olbrechts-Tyteca (1976), pp. 62–68.

30. Walton (1987a), pp. 39–42 (1989b), pp. 93–101.

31. Cf. Fearnside and Holther (1959), p. 132.

32. John Schwartz, Erik Calonius, David L. Gonzalez, and Frank Gibney, Jr., "A Boss They Love to Hate," *Newsweek*, March 20, 1989, 20–24.

33. *Ibid.*, p. 24.

34. Woods and Walton (1978b). Walton (1989b), pp. 43–49.

35. Robinson (1971), p. 107.

36. Walton (1989a), ch. 2, esp. p. 61.

37. Walton (1989b), ch. 7.

38. Hamblin (1970), p. 12.

39. Donohue (1981).

40. Van Eemeren and Grootendorst (1984), p. 81.

41. Walton (1991a).

4. Systems of Dialogue Rules

1. Hamblin (1970), ch. 8; cf. the game *CBV* in Walton (1984), p. 252 ff. Lorenzen and Lorenz (1978); cf. the dialectic system $C \wedge D$ in Barth and Krabbe (1982), p. 94.

2. There is no lack of critics of the truncated conception. Toulmin (1958) argues for a more complex layout of arguments, nowadays known as the "Toulmin model." Hamblin (1970), ch. 7, criticizes the traditional concept from the perspective of fallacy theory but deems that there "is little to be gained by making a frontal assault on the question of what an argument *is.*" Instead, we should "approach it indirectly by discussing how arguments are appraised and evaluated" (p. 231). He then goes on to discuss alethic, epistemic, and dialectical sets of criteria. The next chapter (ch. 8 on formal dialectic) clears the ground for richer conceptions of argument. Yet

the truncated conception is still with us. According to Johnson (1987), "informal logic textbooks offer the reader an anemic conception of argument, one which does not differ markedly from that which appears (when it does appear) in other standard introductory logic textbooks . . . " (p. 53). He mentions Scriven (1976) as an exception and Van Eemeren and Grootendorst (1984) as presenting us with a full-bodied conception of argumentation. By now, the terminology has become pretty confusing. We have "argument," "inference," and "implication." Cf. Walton (1990b) for a survey and for proposals on how to use the terms *reasoning* and *argument*.

3. Cf. Walton (1990b), p. 411: "*Argument* is a social and verbal means of trying to resolve, or at least to contend with, a conflict or difference that has arisen or exists between two (or more) parties."

4. In Hamblin (1970), ch. 8, the goal of the "Why-Because system with questions" and its variants is no doubt argumentative (p. 265ff.). Presumably, "certain logical goals [are] part of the general goal" (p. 256). But nowhere are rules for winning and losing formulated that would fix the participant's aims and give us more insight in what "the general goal" is. Notice that these aims are clear for the obligation game (p. 260f.). In Hamblin (1971) the games of dialogue defined in that paper are vaguely described as "information-oriented" (pp. 133, 137), whereas the earlier systems are characterized as "not strictly information-oriented" and as concerned with "argument-development" (p. 148). Hamblin did not try to explain precisely, or quantify, what counts as information.

5. Hamblin (1970), p. 271.

6. For our purpose we may equate propositions with equivalence classes of logically equivalent formulas of L.

7. Barth and Krabbe (1982), ch. 3, esp. 3.15 on FD D7; Barth (1982).

8. Barth and Krabbe (1982), sections 3.6 and 3.13.

9. *Op. cit.* The system $\mathbf{RPD}_0$ roughly equals $C \wedge D$ in that book, but *free questioning* is a new feature (cf. the *creative moves* in Krabbe [1988a]). As we said in section 4.1, $\mathbf{RPD}_0$ is a Lorenzen-type game. Cf. Lorenzen and Lorenz (1978).

10. Some steps in this direction were taken by Krabbe (1991b), (1995?).

11. This analysis is given in Walton (1992), ch. 2.

5. Conclusions and Prospects

1. Montague (1974).

2. Blair and Johnson (1987).

3. The term *model* is here used in a sense different from that of model theory. In our sense, a formal language together with its "models" (from model theory) constitutes a model of reasoning, whereas the language together with a set of deduction rules constitutes another.

4. Basically, these two aspects, the descriptive and the normative, correspond to the two sources of validity pointed out by E. M. Barth (Barth and Krabbe [1982], section 1.4), to which the reader is referred for further elucidation on this issue. For logic systems as models (or representations) see *op. cit.*, section 2.1.

5. Cf. E. M. Barth's concept of pragmatization, Barth (1985), p. 383.

6. Van Eemeren and Grootendorst (1987), (1992).

7. Van Eemeren and Grootendorst (1984), (1992).

8. The theory is put forward in Walton (1991b), p. 293, that a probative function must be fulfilled for an argument to avoid begging the question.

9. The fallacy of complex questions, and related problems of commitment in questioning, are dealt with in Harrah (1984) and Walton (1989a).

10. Ultimately, a full **PPD** system is to incorporate various forms of active argument evaluation. Cf. Finocchiaro (1980), ch. 15, 17.

11. Cf. note 27 to ch. 2. Cf. also Krabbe (1992).

12. Cf. Hamblin (1970), ch. 9, Næss (1966).

13. Taken together the rules spell out what Grice's cooperative principle amounts to for the participants involved in a permissive persuasion dialogue. Cf. Grice (1975).

14. Hamblin (1970), p. 274, made the distinction between the substantive and the purely concessive types of commitment when he suggested two different types of notations to mark two different types of commitments in a participant's commitment store. This approach amounts to regarding "commitments which are the results of concession rather than of personal statement as different in character from the others" and marking the difference in the commitment store entries accordingly. Hamblin himself never followed up this suggestion, however.

Bibliography

Barth, E. M. 1982. "A Normative-Pragmatical Foundation of the Rules of Some Systems of Formal$_3$ Dialectics." In Barth and Martens, eds. (1982), pp. 159–70.

———. 1985. "A New Field: Empirical Logic: Bioprograms, Logemes and Logics as Institutions." *Synthese: An International Journal for Epistemology, Methodology and Philosophy of Science* 63, 375–88.

Barth, E. M., and E. C. W. Krabbe. 1982. *From Axiom to Dialogue: A Philosophical Study of Logics and Argumentation.* Berlin and New York: Walter de Gruyter.

Barth, E. M., and J. L. Martens. 1977. "Argumentum ad Hominem: From Chaos to Formal Dialectic: The Method of Dialogue-Tableaus as a Tool in the Theory of Fallacy." *Logique et analyse,* n.s., 20e Année, 76–96.

Barth, E. M., and J. L. Martens, eds. 1982. *Argumentation: Approaches to Theory Formation: Containing the Contributions to the Groningen Conference on the Theory of Argumentation, October 1978.* Amsterdam: John Benjamins.

Blair, J. A., and R. H. Johnson. 1987. "Argumentation as Dialectical." *Argumentation* 1, 41–56.

Donohue, W. A. 1981. "Development of a Model of Rule Use in Nego-tiation Interaction." *Communication Monographs* 48, 106–20.

Fearnside, W. W., and W. B. Holther. 1959. *Fallacy: The Counterfeit of Argument.* Englewood Cliffs, N.J.: Prentice Hall.

Felscher, W. 1985a. "Dialogues as a Foundation for Intuitionistic Logic." In D. Gabbay and F. Guenthner, eds., *Handbook of Philosophical Logic, III. Alternatives to Classical Logic.* Dordrecht: Reidel, pp. 341–72.

————. 1985b. "Dialogues, Strategies and Intuitionistic Provability." *Annals of Pure and Applied Logic* 28, 217–54.

Feteris, E. T. 1989. *Discussieregels in het recht: Een pragma-dialectische analyse van het burgerlijk proces en het strafproces* (Rules of Discussion in Law: A Pragma-Dialectical Analysis of Proceedings according to Civil and Criminal Law). Dissertation, University of Amsterdam.

Finocchiaro, M. A. 1980. *Galileo and the Art of Reasoning: Rhetorical Foundations of Logic and Scientific Method.* Dordrecht, Boston, and London: Reidel.

Fisher, R., and W. Ury. 1981. *Getting to Yes.* Boston: Houghton Mifflin.

Grice, H. P. 1975. "Logic and Conversation." In P. Cole and J. L. Morgan, eds., *Syntax and Semantics III: Speech Acts.* New York: Academic Press, pp. 41–58.

Grootendorst, R. 1987. "Some Fallacies about Fallacies." In Van Eemeren, Grootendorst, Blair, and Willard, eds. (1987), pp. 331–42.

Gumperz, J. J. 1972. "Introduction." In J. J. Gumperz and D. Hymes, eds., *Directions in Sociolinguistics: The Ethnography of Communication.* New York: Rinehart and Winston, pp. 1–25.

Haas, G. 1984. *Konstruktive Einführung in die formale Logik.* Mannheim: Bibliographisches Institut.

Hamblin, C. L. 1970. *Fallacies.* London: Methuen.

————. 1971. "Mathematical Models of Dialogue." *Theoria* 37, 130–55.

————. 1987. *Imperatives.* Oxford and New York: Blackwell.

Harrah, D. 1984. "The Logic of Questions." In D. Gabbay and F. Guenthner, eds., *Handbook of Philosophical Logic II: Extensions of Classical Logic.* Dordrecht: Reidel, pp. 715–64.

Hegselmann, R. 1985. *Formale Dialektik: Ein Beitrag zu einer Theorie des rationalen Argumentierens.* Hamburg: Felix Meiner.

Hergé. 1989. *The Adventures of Tintin: Red Rackham's Treasure.* Trans. Leslie Lonsdale-Cooper and Michael Turner. London: Methuen Children's Books. (*Les aventures de Tintin: Le trésor de Rackham le Rouge.* Casterman, 1945.)

Hintikka, K. J. J. 1968. "Language-Games for Quantifiers." In N. Rescher, ed., *Studies in Logical Theory,* Oxford: Blackwell. *(American Philosophical Quarterly Monograph Series 2),* pp. 46–72. Reprinted in Hintikka (1973), pp. 53–82.

———. 1973. *Logic, Language-Games and Information. Kantian Themes in the Philosophy of Logic.* Oxford: Oxford University Press/Clarendon.

———. 1981. "The Logic of Information-Seeking Dialogues: A Model." In W. Becker and W. K. Essler, eds., *Konzepte der Dialektik.* Frankfurt a/M: Vittorio Klostermann, pp. 212–31.

Johansson, I. 1936. "Der Minimalkalkül, ein reduzierter intuitionistischer Formalismus." *Compositio Mathematica* 4, 119–136.

Johnson, R. H. 1987. "Logic Naturalized: Recovering a Tradition." In Van Eemeren, Grootendorst, Blair, and Willard, eds. (1987), pp. 47–56.

Johnson, R. H., and J. A. Blair. 1983. *Logical Self-Defense.* 2nd ed. Toronto: McGraw Hill Ryerson. First edition 1977.

Kamlah, W., and P. Lorenzen. 1973. *Logische Propädeutik: Vorschule des vernünftigen Redens.* 2nd ed. Mannheim: Bibliographisches Institut. First edition 1967.

Katriel, T., and M. Dascal. 1989. "Speaker's Commitment and Involvement in Discourse." In Y. Tobin, ed., *From Sign to Text: A Semiotic View of Communication.* Amsterdam and Philadelphia: John Benjamins, pp. 275–95.

Kaufmann, J. 1987. "Towards an Integral Analysis of International Negotiations." Paper contributed to the Conference on Processes of International Negotiations, IIASA, Luxenburg, Austria, May 18–22, 1987.

Kluge, P. F. 1988. "A Diamond as Big as the Ritz—Well, Just About That Big." *Smithsonian,* May, 72–82.

Krabbe, E. C. W. 1982. "Formal Dialectics as Immanent Criticism of Philosophical Systems." In E. M. Barth and J. L. Martens, eds. (1982), pp. 233–43.

———. 1985a. "Noncumulative Dialectical Models and Formal Dialectics." *Journal of Philosophical Logic* 14, 129–68.

———. 1985b. "Formal Systems of Dialogue Rules." *Synthese: An International Journal for Epistemology, Methodology and Philosophy of Science* 63, 295–328.

———. 1988a. "Creative Reasoning in Formal Discussion." *Argumentation* 2, 483–98.

———. 1988b. "Inconsistente verbintenissen: drogreden, blunder, of impasse?" (Inconsistent Commitments: Fallacy, Blunder or Quandary?) In F. H. van Eemeren and R. Grootendorst, eds., *Taalbeheersing in ontwikkeling. Lezingen van het VIOT-taalbeheersingscongres gehouden op 16, 17 en 18 december 1987 aan de Universiteit van Amsterdam* (Speech Communication Moving On: Proceedings of the VIOT-Conference on Speech Communication, December 16–18, 1987, at the University of Amsterdam) Dordrecht and Providence R.I.: Foris, pp. 49–58.

———. 1990. "Inconsistent Commitments and Commitment to Inconsistencies." *Informal Logic: Reasoning and Argumentation in Theory and Practice* 12, 33–42.

———. 1991b. "*Quod erat demonstrandum.* Wat kan en mag een argumentatietheorie zeggen over bewijzen?" (QED. What Can and May a Theory of Argumentation Tell Us about Proofs?) In M. M. H. Bax and W. Vuijk, eds., *Thema's in de taalbeheersing: lezingen van het VIOT-taalbeheersingscongres gehouden op 19, 20 en 21 december 1990 aan de Rijksuniversiteit Groningen* (Themes in Speech Communication: Proceedings of the VIOT-Conference on Speech Communication, December 19–21, 1990, at Groningen University), Dordrecht: ICG, pp. 8–16.

———. 1992. "So What? Profiles for Relevance Criticism in Persuasion Dialogues." *Argumentation* 6, 271–83.

———. 1995? *Arguments, Proofs, and Dialogues.* To be published.

Lehrer, K. 1975. "Reason and Consistency." In K. Lehrer, ed., *Analysis and Metaphysics: Essays in Honor of R. M. Chisholm.* Dordrecht: Reidel, pp. 57–74.

Lorenz, K. 1973. "Rules versus Theorems." *Journal of Philosophical Logic* 2, 352–69.

Lorenzen, P. 1960. "Logik und Agon." In *Atti del XII Congresso Internazionale di Filosofia (Venezia, 12–18 Settembre 1958), IV: Logica, linguaggio e comunicazione*. Florence: Sansoni, pp. 187–94. Reprinted in Lorenzen and Lorenz (1978), pp. 1–8.

———. 1969. *Normative Logic and Ethics*. Mannheim: Bibliographisches Institut.

———. 1982. "Die dialogische Begründung von Logikkalkülen." In Barth and Martens, eds. (1982), pp. 23–54.

———. 1987. *Lehrbuch der konstruktiven Wissenschaftstheorie*, Mannheim: Bibliographisches Institut, Wissenschaftsverlag.

Lorenzen, P., and K. Lorenz. 1978. *Dialogische Logik*. Darmstadt: Wissenschaftliche Buchgesellschaft.

Lorenzen, P., and O. Schwemmer. 1975. *Konstruktive Logik, Ethik und Wissenschaftstheorie*. 2nd ed. Mannheim: Bibliographisches Institut. First edition 1973.

Mackenzie, J. D. 1979a. "Question-Begging in Non-Cumulative Systems." *Journal of Philosophical Logic* 8, 117–33.

———. 1979b. "How to Stop Talking to Tortoises." *Notre Dame Journal of Formal Logic* 20, 705–17.

———. 1981. "The Dialectics of Logic." *Logique et analyse*, n.s., 24e Année, 159–77.

———. 1985. "No Logic Before Friday." *Synthese: An International Journal for Epistemology, Methodology and Philosophy of Science* 63, 329–41.

———. 1988. "Woods on Ideals of Rationality in Dialogue." *Argumentation* 2, 409–17.

———. 1989. "Reasoning and Logic." *Synthese: An International Journal for Epistemology, Methodology and Philosophy of Science* 79, 99–117.

Mackie, J. L. 1967. "Fallacies." In P. Edwards, ed., *Encyclopedia of Philosophy*, vol. 3. New York and London: MacMillan & The Free Press, and Collier-Macmillan, pp. 169–79.

Makinson, D. C. 1964. "The Paradox of the Preface." *Analysis* 25, 205–7.

Manor, R. 1975. "Propositional Commitment and Presuppositions."
American Philosophical Quarterly 12, 141–49.

Montague, R. 1974. *Formal Philosophy: Selected Papers of Richard Montague.* Ed. R. H. Thomason. New Haven, Conn., and London: Yale University Press.

Næss, A. 1966. *Communication and Argument: Elements of Applied Semantics.* Oslo, London, and Totowa, N.J.: Universitetsforlaget, Allen Unwin, and Bedminster. Transl. by A. Hannay of *En del elementære logiske emner* (Some Elementary Logical Topics), Oslo: Universitetsforlaget. First edition 1947.

Perelman, Ch., and L. Olbrechts-Tyteca. 1969. *The New Rhetoric: A Treatise on Argumentation.* Trans. J. Wilkinson and P. Weaver. Notre Dame, Ind.: University of Notre Dame Press. (Translated from *Traité de l'argumentation. La nouvelle rhétorique.* 2 vols. Presses Universitaires de France, 1958.)

———. 1976. *Traité de l'argumentation. La nouvelle rhétorique.* 3rd ed. Brussels: Editions de l'Université de Bruxelles. First edition 1958.

Pruitt, D. G. 1981. *Negotiation Behavior.* New York: Academic Press.

Rescher, N. 1977. *Dialectics.* Albany, N.Y.: State University of New York Press.

———. 1987. "How Serious a Fallacy Is Inconsistency?" *Argumentation* 1, 303–16.

Rescher, N., and R. Brandom. 1980. *The Logic of Inconsistency: A Study in Non-Standard Possible-World Semantics and Ontology.* Oxford: Blackwell.

Robinson, R. 1953. *Plato's Earlier Dialectic.* 2nd ed. Oxford: Clarendon Press.

———. 1971. "Arguing from Ignorance." *Philosophical Quarterly* 21, 97–108.

Scriven, M. 1976. *Reasoning.* New York: McGraw-Hill.

Segerberg, K. 1984. "Towards an Exact Philosophy of Action." *Topoi* 3, 75–83.

———. 1985. "Routines." *Synthese: An International Journal for Epistemology, Methodology and Philosophy of Science* 65, 185–210.

Spit, I. W. M. 1986. *Multisubjectieve activiteit en morele verantwoordelijkheid. Multisubject Activity and Moral Responsibility (With a summary in English)*. Dissertation, Utrecht University.

Stegmüller, W. 1964. "Remarks on the Completeness of Logical Systems Relative to the Validity-Concepts of P. Lorenzen and K. Lorenz." *Notre Dame Journal of Formal Logic* 5, 81–112.

Toulmin, S. 1958. *The Uses of Argument*. Cambridge: Cambridge University Press.

Van Dun, F. 1972. "On the Modes of Opposition in the Formal Dialogues of P. Lorenzen." *Logique et Analyse*, n.s., 15e Année, 103–36.

Van Eemeren, F. H., and R. Grootendorst. 1984. *Speech Acts in Argumentative Discussions: A Theoretical Model for the Analysis of Discussions Directed towards Solving Conflicts of Opinion*. Dordrecht and Cinnaminson: Foris.

———. 1987. "Fallacies in Pragma-Dialectical Perspective." *Argumentation* 1, 283–301.

———. 1992. *Argumentation, Communication, and Fallacies: A Pragma-Dialectical Perspective*. Hillsdale, N.J., Hove, and London: Lawrence Erlbaum.

Van Eemeren, F. H., R. Grootendorst, J. A. Blair and Ch. A. Willard, eds. 1987. *Argumentation: Across the Lines of Discipline: Proceedings of the Conference on Argumentation 1986*. Dordrecht and Providence, R.I.: Foris.

Walton, D. N. 1984. *Logical Dialogue-Games and Fallacies*. Lanham, New York and London: University Press of America.

———. 1985. *Arguer's Position: A Pragmatic Study of Ad Hominem Attack, Criticism, Refutation, and Fallacy*. Westport, Conn., and London: Greenwood Press.

———. 1987a. *Informal Fallacies*. Amsterdam: John Benjamins.

———. 1987b. "What Is a Fallacy?" In Van Eemeren, Grootendorst, Blair, and Willard, eds. (1987), pp. 323–30.

———. 1989a. *Question-Reply Argumentation*. Westport, Conn.: Greenwood Press.

————. 1989b. *Informal Logic: A Handbook for Critical Argumentation.* Cambridge: Cambridge University Press.

————. 1990a. *Practical Reasoning, Goal Driven, Knowledge-Based, Action-Guiding Argumentation.* Savage, Md.: Rowman and Littlefield.

————. 1990b. "What Is Reasoning? What Is an Argument?" *The Journal of Philosophy* 87, 399–419.

————. 1991a. "Bias, Critical Doubt, and Fallacies." *Argumentation and Advocacy* 28, 1–22.

————. 1991b. *Begging the Question: Circular Reasoning as a Tactic of Argumentation.* New York: Greenwood Press.

————. 1992. *The Place of Emotion in Argument.* University Park, Pennsylvania: Pennsylvania State University Press.

Webster. 1981. *Webster's Third New International Dictionary.* Chicago: Enc. Britannica, Inc.

Woods, J. 1987. "What Rationality Is Not." Lecture at the University of Amsterdam, February 22, 1987.

————. 1988a. "Ideals of Rationality in Dialogic." *Argumentation* 2, 395–408.

————. 1988b. "Rationality, Ideals and Mentality." *Argumentation* 2, 419–24.

Woods, J., ed. 1987. "Fallacies." *Argumentation* 1, no. 3.

Woods, J., and D. N. Walton. 1978a. "Arresting Circles in Formal Dialogues." *Journal of Philosophical Logic* 7, 73–90. Reprinted in Woods and Walton (1989), pp. 143–59.

————. 1978b. "The Fallacy of *Ad Ignorantiam.*" *Dialectica* 32, 87–99. Reprinted in Woods and Walton (1989), pp. 161–73.

————. 1982. *Argument: The Logic of the Fallacies.* Toronto, Ont.: McGraw-Hill Ryerson.

————. 1989. *Fallacies: Selected Papers 1972–1982.* Dordrecht and Providence, R.I.: Foris.

Index

217